Practical Theology and Qualitative Research

John Swinton and Harriet Mowat

scm press

British Library Cataloguing in Publication data

A catalogue record for this book is available
from the British Library

978 0 334 02980 9

First published in 2006 by SCM Press
Invicta House, 108-114 Golden Lane,
London EC1Y OTG

Fifth Impression 2013

Typeset by Regent Typesetting, London
Printed and bound by
CPI Group (UK) Ltd, Croydon, CR0 4YY

Contents

Acknowledgements

As with all such projects, this book is indebted to many people: those with whom we have worked and learned from as colleagues and fellow researchers and those who have given us the honour of allowing us to explore their lives as research participants. In particular we are grateful to our friend and colleague Cory Labanow for his contribution to this book in Chapter 5. His careful research and challenging theological perspectives have helped us to see many things differently. Beyond all else we would like to thank our long-suffering spouses, Donald and Alison, for putting up with our often hermit-like existence and encouraging our wild ideas. We thank them for loving us even in the midst of our psychological absences. We hope this book is a contribution and a blessing to the field and that all who read it will be challenged to engage in the fascinating and transformative journey that is practical theology and qualitative research.

Introduction

Practical Theology is an intricate and complex enterprise. Contemporary developments within the field have shown it to be a rigorous theological discipline which, while retaining a unique approach to theology and theological development, continues to offer a significant contribution to the wider field of theology and the practices of the Church and the world. There is of course no question that Practical Theology is theologically diverse. Its works span the breadth of the theological spectrum from liberalism to conservatism and its practitioners inhabit a diversity of methodological and theological positions. In line with the literature produced by the other theological disciplines there is no single, standardized way of doing practical theology and it is not owned by any particular wing of theology.

Nevertheless, while there is a good deal of diversity, there remains a good deal of continuity. Irrespective of the theological and methodological diversity, the common theme that holds Practical Theology together as a discipline is its perspective on, and beginning-point in, human experience and its desire to reflect theologically on that experience. Practical Theology has a particular focus on specific situations. It seeks to explore the complex dynamics of particular situations in order to enable the development of a transformative and illuminating understanding of what is going on within these situations. A key question asked by the Practical Theologian is: is what *appears* to be going on within this situation what is *actually* going on? Practical Theology approaches particular situations with a hermeneutics of suspicion, fully aware that, when the veil is pulled away, we often discover that what we *think* we are doing is quite different from what we are *actually* doing. Thus through a process of critical reflection on situations, the Practical Theologian seeks to ensure faithful practice and authentic human living in the light of scripture and tradition.

Practical theology and the social sciences

A good deal of the diversity within Practical Theology relates to the various methods through which this knowledge of situations is captured, analysed, understood and recorded. Historically, the primary mode of analysis and data collection has emerged from a continuing dialogue with the social sciences. The social sciences have offered practical theologians vital access to the nature of the human mind, human culture, the wider dimensions of church life and the implications of the social and political dimensions of society for the process of theological reflection. It is true that some usages of the social sciences have been uncritical and theologically questionable. Nevertheless, they have offered Practical Theology a useful mode of dialogue that has enabled it to uncover important data for theological reflection. While a variety of social sciences have been utilised by Practical Theology – psychology, sociology, philosophy, anthropology – in this book we will explore the relationship between theology and the social sciences specifically as it relates to the use of qualitative research methods in the process of theological reflection. We will argue that qualitative research is one way in which we can begin to look behind the veil of 'normality' and see what is actually going on within situations.

The relationship between theology and the social sciences has always been tense. Some argue that the social sciences are wholly incompatible with theology and that social science methods are therefore inappropriate tools in the task of doing theology (Milbank 1990). We are fully aware of the dangers of accepting the social sciences as tools for doing theology without engaging in any meaningful theological critique. However, for reasons that will become clear in Chapter 3, at least in regard to qualitative research methods, we do not accept that they are fundamentally incompatible. Like any other source of knowledge the social sciences require to be dealt with critically and carefully. Left to their own devices, such sources of knowledge can easily subsume theology and orient the theological task towards goals and assumptions that are inappropriate and theologically questionable. Nevertheless, the fact that a source of knowledge may be complex and potentially dangerous does not make it unusable. It does, however, mean that we need to approach it with a degree of suspicion and be prepared to take the time and offer the theological and intellectual energy that will enable it to be drawn into the process of theological enquiry in a way that is faithful and illuminating. Integrating qualitative research in this way is not an easy task. It involves a complex process of conversion and sanctification, a process that we outline in some detail in Chapter 3. Here it will suffice to say that when thought through clearly and theologically, there is no necessary contradiction between theology and the use of qualitative research. We would not presume that our argument is necessarily generalizable to all of the social sciences. It is however wholly appropriate as applied to qualitative research methods.

The intention of the book

This book is not intended to be a textbook on qualitative research. The primary purpose of this book is to address the question: How can we faithfully use qualitative research to provide accurate data for theological reflection? The term 'faithfully' is important. As we will see in Chapter 1, Practical Theology as we understand it is a *theological* discipline. This means that it does not simply seek after knowledge for the sake of knowledge. Rather, the knowledge generated by Practical Theological research is intended to increase our knowledge and understanding of God and to enable us to live more

loving and faithful lives. It is in examining how qualitative
research methods can function in the process of enabling such
a goal that this study finds its primary locus. While taking very
seriously issues of rigour, method and credibility, the Practical
Theologian always uses her tools for this specific purpose. This
being so, a book which brings together Practical Theology and
qualitative research methods can never simply be a 'textbook
on qualitative research'. This book is intended to enable Practical Theologians to generate knowledge which is faithful and
transformative. This book revolves around that central Theo-
centric dynamic and this dynamic shapes its direction, method
and purpose.

It is intended that this book should function as a critical
foundation for the process of integrating Practical Theology
and qualitative research in a way which retains the integrity of
both disciplines. The book provides a model of Practical Theology and an approach to qualitative research and examines
the ways in which these two disciplines can be brought together both at a conceptual and at a practical level. We will
make a case that the process of Practical Theological research
is assisted but not defined by the utilization of qualitative
research methods.

The structure of the book

The book falls into two parts. Part 1 (Chapters 1–3) lays down
the methodological foundations for the book. Here we locate
the book within the discipline of Practical Theology and begin
to show the ways in which Practical Theology and qualitative
research can come together in ways which are constructive
and faithful. Chapter 1 presents the understanding of Practical
Theology that underpins the book. It argues that Practical
Theology relates to the critical, theological explorations of
situations. Situations are complex and complexing entities that
are filled with hidden values, meanings and power dynamics.
The task of the Practical Theologian is to excavate particular
situations and to explore the nature and faithfulness of the

practices that take place within them. Such an exploration of situations and practices enables the Practical Theologian to inhabit a unique and vital role within the process of theological reflection and development.

In Chapter 2 we offer a perspective on qualitative research as it relates to the central intentions of Practical Theology. Here we explore the central tenets of qualitative research, and their underlying epistemological bases and how these philosophical presumptions shape and form the various methods that make up the practice of qualitative research.

Chapter 3 examines some of the key tensions between Practical Theology and qualitative research, with a particular focus on the ways in which these two modes of enquiry can be brought together without one collapsing into the other. Drawing specifically on a particular understanding of the doctrine of the Trinity and the theological ideas of conversion and sanctification, this chapter offers an original and thoroughly theological model of integration that will enable Practical Theologians to work effectively and faithfully with qualitative research methods. These three chapters form the bedrock upon which Part 2 is built.

Part 2 moves from these theoretical and methodological issues to focus on a series of qualitative research projects carried out by the authors. Each case study is designed to show a different dimension of the way in which Practical Theology can use qualitative research. Each contains different methods and each is designed to be written for a different audience. In this way we offer a wide perspective on Practical Theology and qualitative research as it relates to different modes and intentions. Here we examine such approaches within qualitative research such as ethnography, hermeneutics, phenomenology and participatory research. Part 2 explores a number of different methods and approaches and provides insights into the process of question development, interviewing, working with focus groups, validation and rigour, the concept of transforming resonance and generalizability and the interpretation of texts. Each study is divided into sections covering: *the*

situation, the method, analysis, and theological reflection.
In this way the reader is enabled to see the various ways in
which the methodological positions highlighted in Chapters
1–3 work themselves out within the complexities of exploring
human experience.

The final chapter offers a model of Practical Theology as a
'theology of action', arguing that the underpinning approach
to qualitative research within the framework of Practical Theology is 'action research'. In qualitative research settings this is
a method of enquiry and practice which encourages controlled
and focused change using the knowledge and expertise of those
involved in the research setting (Hudson and Bennet, 1996).
In Practical Theology it can be understood to be a framework
of enquiry which is driven by the desire to create the circumstances for transfomative action that not only seeks after truth
and knowledge, but also offers the possibility of radical transformation and challenging new modes of faithfulness.

Taken as a whole this book offers a unique and important
insight into the relationship of Practical Theology to qualitative research and presents a way of approaching Practical Theology which is theologically coherent and practically vital. It is
our hope that readers will find this book useful and challenging and that as they work through its implications, they will be
enabled to think more clearly about this important area, and
practise more faithfully in terms both of their research and of
their personal spiritual journey.

Part 1

Theoretical Foundations

I

What is Practical Theology?

The church does not exist fundamentally to meet needs; in its being, the church, like Christ, exists to glorify the Father.

(Kunst 1992, p. 163)

As one reviews the various schools and perspectives on Practical Theology it very quickly becomes clear that it is a rich and diverse discipline. Its range of approaches embraces research which is empirical (Van der Van 1993, 1998), political (Pattison 1994; Ali 1999; Chopp and Parker 1990; Couture and Hunter 1995), ethical (Miles 1999), psychological (Fowler 1981, 1987, 1996; Armistead 1995), sociological (Gill 1975, 1977), pastoral (Patton 1993; Swinton 2000a), gender-oriented (Ackermann and Bons-Storm 1998; Miller-McLemore *et al.* 1999) and narrative-based (Wimberley 1994; Swinton 1999). Practical Theology locates itself within the diversity of human experience, making its home in the complex web of relationships and experiences that form the fabric of all that we know. The wide range of approaches and methodological positions apparent within the discipline reflects a variety of attempts to capture this diversity and complexity. While it may not be possible to capture all of the complex dynamics of Practical Theology within a single definition, for current purposes it is necessary to tie it in to some kind of conceptual framework which will enable us to understand and work within the discipline. The understanding of Practical Theology developed in this chapter reflects the model that these authors have found most helpful in their work with qualitative research methods.

It is not the only way in which Practical Theology can be done, but it is the model that will guide this book.

Performing the faith

Practical Theology, as it will be defined and explored within this book, is dedicated to enabling the faithful performance of the gospel and to exploring and taking seriously the complex dynamics of the human encounter with God. Stanley Hauerwas describes the idea of 'faith as performance' thus:

> One of the things that liberal democratic society has encouraged Christians to believe about what they believe is that what it means to be a Christian is primarily belief! . . . This is a deep misunderstanding about how Christianity works. Of course we believe that God is God and we are not and that God is Father, Son and Holy Spirit . . . but this is not a set of propositions . . . rather [it is] embedded in a community of practices that make those beliefs themselves work and give us a community by which we are shaped. Religious belief is not just some kind of primitive metaphysics . . . in fact it is a performance just like you'd perform *Lear*. What people think Christianity is, is that it's like the text of *Lear*, rather than the actual production of *Lear*. It has to be *performed* for you to understand what *Lear* is – a drama. You can read it, but *unfortunately Christians so often want to make Christianity a text rather than a performance.*
> (*Homiletics Online* 2005) (italics added)

Practical Theology takes seriously the idea of performing the faith and seeks to explore the nature and in particular the faithfulness of that performance. The idea of faithful *performance* is key for the model of Practical Theology that we present in this chapter. Despite the fact that there are many ways in which *Lear* can be interpreted, there remains a fundamental plot, structure, storyline and outcome without which it would be unrecognizable. Lack of adherence to these key aspects of *Lear* indicates that the performer has 'lost the plot'. The performer requires the 'stage whisperer' to remind them of the script and the plot and to challenge and encourage them to return to the text as originally given. Of course, performers have scope for improvization and innovation, and sometimes that improvization brings out new, hidden and 'forgotten' aspects of the original text. Nevertheless, performers always perform within boundaries, scripts and recognizable and accepted narratives which to go beyond, would require the creation of another play. Practical Theology recognises and respects the diversity of interpretation within the various expositions of the performed gospel and seeks to ensure and encourage the Christian community to remain faithful to the narrative of the original God-given plot of the gospel and to practise faithfully as that narrative unfolds. Practical Theology therefore finds itself located within the uneasy but critical tension between the script of revelation given to us in Christ and formulated historically within scripture, doctrine and tradition, and the continuing innovative performance of the gospel as it is embodied and enacted in the life and practices of the Church as they interact with the life and practices of the world.

The significance of experience

Practical Theology takes human experience seriously. One of the things that marks Practical Theology out as distinct from the other theological disciplines is its beginning point within human experience. However, we must be careful what we mean by such a suggestion. Taking human experience seriously does not imply that experience is a source of revelation. Experience and human reason cannot lead us, for example, to an understanding of the cross and the resurrection. Rather, in taking experience seriously, Practical Theology acknowledges and seeks to explore the implications of the proposition that faith is a performative and embodied act; that the gospel is not simply something to be believed, but also something to be lived. Human experience is a 'place' where the gospel is grounded, embodied, interpreted and lived out. It is an interpretive context which raises new questions, offers challenges and demands answers of the gospel which are not always obvious when it is reflected on in abstraction. Human experience is presumed to be an important locus for the work of the Spirit.[1] As such it holds much relevance for the continuing task of interpreting scripture and tradition and the development of our understanding of theology and faithful practising. By beginning its theological reflection within the human experience of life with God, rather than in abstraction from such experience, Practical Theology takes seriously the actions of God in the present and as such offers a necessary contextual voice to the process of theology and theological development.

A provisional definition

It will be helpful to begin with a provisional definition of Practical Theology which will guide us through this chapter:

> Practical Theology is critical, theological reflection
> on the practices of the Church as they interact
> with the practices of the world, with a view to
> ensuring and enabling faithful participation in God's
> redemptive practices in, to and for the world.

There are four key points that should be highlighted within this understanding. First, practical theological enquiry is *critical*. It assumes that the various practices that are performed by the Christian community are deeply meaningful and require honest critical reflection if they are to be and to remain faithful to the 'script' of revelation. In opposition to models which view Practical Theology as applied theology, wherein its task is simply to apply doctrine worked out by the other theological disciplines to practical situations, within this definition Practical Theology is seen to be a critical discipline which is pre-

---

1. 1 Corinthians 6:19: 'Do you not know that your body is a temple of the Holy Spirit, who is in you, whom you have received from God? You are not your own.'

pared to challenge accepted assumptions and practices. As we have mentioned, this is *not* to suggest that human experience is a locus for fresh revelation (a new script), that will counter or contradict the script provided by scripture, doctrine and tradition. It *is* however to recognize that the questions that we ask of scripture and theological traditions *always* emerge from some context. The questions that emerge in the light of the human experience of God are often different from those which emerge from the solitude of the academic's office. In asking different questions the practical theologian begins to understand the script differently and pushes towards modes of theological understanding and practical action which enable faithful living.

Second, Practical Theology is *theological* reflection. One of the criticisms of Practical Theology is that, at times, it has lost sight of its theological roots. It has been the case that the way in which it has utilized other sources of knowledge, such as the social sciences, has tended to push its primary theological task into the background. We will explore the implications of this more fully in Chapter 3. Here it will be enough to note that theology is (or at least should be) the primary source of knowledge which guides and provides the hermeneutical framework within which Practical Theology carries out its task.

Third, the locus of investigation for Practical Theology is not simply the practices of the Church and the experiences of Christians. The theological reflection that *is* Practical Theology also embraces the practices of the world. However, the practical theologian explores the interplay between these two sets of practices in a particular way. Alastair Campbell is helpful on this point:

> The actions of Christians are celebrations of and attestations to God's reconciling work in the world which begins and ends in Jesus Christ. The relationship of these actions to non-Christians is one of both similarity and difference. The similarity is that all human actions both participate in and fall short of the purposes of God. The difference is that

those who profess belief and adhere to membership of the
church have been called to make explicit the celebration of
God's work. (in Forrester 1990, p. 16)

We live in a world created by God within which some notice
this fact and others are oblivious to it. Because we live in God's
creation, <u>all</u> human beings, implicitly or explicitly, participate
in the unfolding historical narrative of God. The practices of
the Church cannot be understood as ontologically separate or
different from the practices of the world. Both occur within
God's creation and both are caught up in God's redemptive
movement towards the world. Within a creation which is profoundly fallen and broken, *all* human beings, including the
Church, fall short of the good purposes of God. In that respect
all human practices are inadequate, including the practices of
the Church. There is therefore significant similarity and continuity between the practices of the Church and the practice
of the world.

However, there is also a radical dissimilarity and dis-
continuity. The Church differs from the world insofar as it
notices and seeks to live out the significance of residing in a
world which we recognize as creation; it recognizes that we
are residents in a place which we do not own, and in recognizing this acknowledges the need for redemption. The difference between the Church and the world lies in the fact that
the Church recognizes who Jesus is and seeks to live its life
in the light of this revelation, and the world does not. However, the Church's noticing and acknowledging of creation
and redemption has radical implications. The practices of the
Church which seek faithfully to embody this mode of noticing
and acknowledgement, have radically different meanings and
a significantly different telos.

So, for example, as one of the authors has written elsewhere,
the relationship of friendship is shared both by Church and
world (Swinton 2000b). At one level it appears to be nothing
but a foundational human relationship. However, when we
reflect theologically on this relationship we discover signifi-

cant differences; differences which emerge because of the Church's recognition and acknowledgement of Jesus. Within our society we tend to develop friendships on the basis of personal satisfaction. As long as a relationship is fulfilling our needs we will sustain it, but if it falls short we will terminate it and move on to another relationship that we hope will fulfil our needs. Friendships tend to be built on the 'principle of likeness', that is that like-minded people will be attracted to one another. However, when we explore the friendships of Jesus we discover something else going on. He befriended tax collectors, prostitutes, lepers, those who in many senses were socially 'not like' him. Indeed the incarnation indicates God's willingness to enter into friendships with human beings who are radically not like Him. So in the friendships of Jesus we discover relationships based on the 'principle of grace'; friendships which are sustained, nurtured and celebrated on a very different basis from the relationships we assume to be normal within contemporary liberal society. On the surface the friendships of the Church and the world *appear* to be the same, but when we reflect on them theologically we see that they are quite different. There is always a temptation for the Church to 'forget' crucial differences such as these. The task of Practical Theology is to 'remind' the Church of the subtle ways in which it differs from the world and to ensure that its practices remain faithful to the script of the gospel.

Fourth, the primary task of Practical Theology is to ensure and enable faithful practices. Ackermann and Bons-Storm define Practical Theology as 'the theological discipline which is essentially involved with living, communicating and practising the life of faith' (1998, p. 1). As such, Practical Theology has a particular goal: to enable faithful living and authentic Christian practice. This is an important point to reflect on. Practical Theology has a telos and a goal that transcends the boundaries of human experience and expectation. While at one level it certainly begins with and takes seriously human experience, that experience is neither the goal nor the end-point of practical theological reflection. Rather, the goal and end-point of Practical Theology is to ensure, encourage and enable faithful participation in the continuing gospel narrative.

Practical Theology takes seriously the givenness of the gospel, but also, as will be explored in more detail in Chapter 3, recognizes the inevitable interpretive-hermeneutical issues surrounding the interpretation and authentic performance of that revelation. By reflecting critically and theologically on the practices of the Church as they interact with the practices of the world, Practical Theology seeks to reveal and reflect on the intricate, diverse but complementary meanings of Christian practices and to enable faithful presence and action.

Seeking truth

This does not, of course, mean that the practical theologian considers herself to be infallible or that she has a complete grasp of the gospel and the nature of faithfulness! Practical Theology takes seriously the reality of sin, the need for redemption and the inevitable uncertainty and fickleness of human knowledge and understanding. Practical Theology approaches its task, including the task of self-reflection, with a hermeneutic of suspicion. Nevertheless, the Practical Theologian assumes the reality of truth and the possibility of moving towards it. Indeed as a discipline, Practical Theology is fundamentally concerned with the discernment of truth. As Duncan Forrester correctly points out:

> The refusal to take the question of truth seriously leads to practice which is ill-considered and dangerously responsive to the pressures of the powerful and of the moment . . . Practical Theology is that branch of theology which is concerned with questions of truth in relation to action. This points to a deep reciprocity between theory and practice, whereby theological understanding not only leads to action, but also arises out of practice, involvement in the life of the world: 'He who does what is true comes to the light.' . . .

Practical Theology is therefore concerned with the doing of the truth, and with the encounter with truth in action. (Forrester 2000: 16)

Practical Theology takes seriously the reality of truth and the importance of normativity, and faithfully seeks to explore the implications and meanings of such a suggestion for the performance of theology.

Reflecting theologically

In the light of the previous discussion it is important to observe one thing which is often overlooked in discussion around the nature of Practical Theology. While we have suggested that the starting point for Practical Theology is human experience, in fact this is not strictly the case. *God* and the revelation that God has given to human beings in Christ is the true starting point for all Practical Theology. The discipline of Practical Theology emerges as a response to and recognition of the redemptive actions of God-in-the-world and the human experience which emerges in response to those actions. It is in taking seriously those responses that Practical Theology finds its vital initial reflective position and carves out an important position within the wider theological enterprise.

In the same way as systematic theology can be understood as the interpreter of doctrine and tradition, and biblical studies as the interpreter of the sacred scriptures of the Christian faith, Practical Theology should be understood as that aspect of the theological enterprise that focuses on the interpretation of the practices of church and world as an ongoing source of theological interpretation and understanding. Practical Theology is thus seen to be a *theoretical* enquiry, in so far as it seeks to understand practice, to evaluate, to criticize; to look at the relationship between what is done and what is said or professed. At the same time it is also a deeply *practical* discipline, which does not only seek to understand the significance of practice for theology, but also recognizes as a primary goal the guiding and transforming of future practices which will inform and shape the life of faith.

In the light of this, the ongoing hermeneutical task of the practical theologian will relate to the effective 'reading' of particular situations in order that the forms of practice carried out within them can be understood and reflected on critically in the light of scripture and tradition with a view to enabling faithful practice. As we shall see, this hermeneutical task necessitates considerably more than simply *applying* theory to the practices of the Church through the development of effective techniques. Rather, it will mean a careful theological exegesis of particular situations within which the practices and experiences that emerge from these situations are explored, understood, evaluated, critiqued and reconsidered. The implications and details of this suggestion will need to be explored more fully as we move on. Here it will be helpful to begin to develop our understanding of Practical Theology by examining two important concepts that have emerged from the discussion thus far but which still require clarification: *situations* and *practices*. Reflection on these two concepts will enable us to develop an aspect of Practical Theology that is particularly important for the purposes of this book.

Interpreting situations

Because of its starting point within experience, Practical Theology tends not to be (sometimes quite self-consciously), a unified, systematic discipline. Instead it offers fragments and themes that emerge from particular situations and contexts. It uses the language of themes and patterns, rather than systems and universal concepts, seeking to draw us into the divine mystery and drama by providing reflective experiences that enable us to re-imagine the world and our place within it. The language and grammar of Practical Theology eases us into new places and opens us up to the possibility that the way the world is is not the way it has to be, or indeed will be.

These fragments of theological truth challenge us to see the world differently and help us make sense of a world which is itself deeply fragmented. It is however important to recognize that these fragments are deeply connected with and crucial to wider systems of theological knowledge. There is therefore a necessary and potentially constructive conversation between Practical Theology and the other theological disciplines. Nevertheless, the fragments and perspectives offered by Practical Theology may well challenge and disturb certain accepted understandings and assumptions. This critical and prophetic role of Practical Theology in relation to the internal conversation between the theological disciplines is a vital dimension of Practical Theology's dialogical focus on enabling faithful practice.

Complexifying situations

We would suggest that one way of understanding the focus of Practical Theology which bears much relevance for this book, is that it seeks critically to *complexify* and explore *situations*. To complexify something is to take that which at first glance appears normal and uncomplicated and through a process of critical reflection at various levels, reveal that it is in fact complex and polyvalent. Take for example a soccer match. For most people the key thing is that 22 players come together to kick a ball around for 90 minutes, the most important thing being that one team gets the ball into the opposition's net more than the other team. At this level it seems quite straightforward; it is just a game. However, when one begins to complexify it, things start to change. What are the rules of the game and how did they come to be the way they are? Why is it that the top two or three teams have the majority of the money and can therefore afford the best players thus assuring that they remain in the top three? Why is it that certain teams change the design of their strips one or two times per season? To make profit presumably, but what does that say about their respect for the fans, particularly those on a low income? What kind of pension scheme, if any, do clubs have to care for young players whose careers may end very quickly due to injury or lack of form? As we begin to complexify the situation, we discover that it is more than 'just a game'. It is a complex commercial business which has important ethical and moral aspects which are rarely reflected on systematically.

The significance of this process of complexifying and interpreting situations is important for Practical Theology, but it is also important for theology in general. One of the most persistent criticisms of academic theology is that, rather than encouraging the activity of faith, it can create a significant distancing from the life of faith. The questions asked of scripture and tradition from within the academy are often quite different from the questions asked by the Christian community. Consequently, theologians who do not take cognisance of the importance of contextual questions often fail in significant ways to address the needs and problematics of particular situations that are of vital significance to the people of God. In this way, the interpretative activity of the Christian community in the world is subsumed to the distantiated presumptions of academic questioning. When this happens it is easy to forget that, faith exists in specific situations within which the gospel is embodied, interpreted, shaped and performed. To omit this situational dynamic is to omit a dynamic of interpretative questioning which is of great importance.

Farley makes a helpful observation:

In the traditional approach, theology is involved in interpretation but the object of interpretation is the past and the texts of the past. And while believers and church leaders do in fact interpret situations (culture, war, marriage, death, etc.), they do so directly out of the tradition without passing through an inquiry which would uncover what is occurring when we interpret a situation theologically. We do thematize interpretation as it is directed to texts, hence, we are at home in problems of historical method, exegesis, and textual hermeneutics. We have not thematized – become methodically self-conscious about – the interpretation of situations. (Poling and Mudge 1987, ch. 1)

If Farley is correct, and we believe that he is, interpreting situations is an important 'missing dimension' of the theological enterprise. As such, 'remembering' this forgotten dimension is one important contribution that Practical Theology can offer to the field of theology. This is *not* of course to suggest that historical texts are unimportant. As has been suggested, dialoguing with historical texts and Christian tradition is an important dimension of Practical Theology. It *is* however to suggest that the text of human experience in general and the experience of the Church in particular holds interpretative significance for theological development.

Understanding situations

Situations are complex, multifaceted entities which need to be examined with care, rigour and discernment if they are to be effectively understood. Farley describes the complex nature of situations in this way:

> Discerning the components of a situation is not simply taking a photograph. It is an act of serious and even theological self-criticism . . . A situation is not like a basket of fruit, so that discerning the situation is merely enumerating what fruits occupy the basket. The components of a situation are always different *kinds* of things, things of very different *genre*; human beings as individuals, world views, groups of various sorts, the pressure of the past, futurity, various strata of language (writing, imagery, metaphors, myths, etc.), events, sedimented social power . . . 'Reading a situation' is the task of identifying these genres of things and discerning how they together constitute the situation. (Poling and Mudge 1987, ch. 1)

Situations have cultures and histories, they occur within particular contexts which often have their own traditions and

expectations and they contain specific forms of practice that
again themselves contain history, tradition, theology and social
experiences and expectations. Most of us tend to live within
situations in ways which are unreflective and uncomplicated.
Many of the aspects of our situation are experienced as nothing more than background noise. It is only when problems
arise through crisis or our engaging in a process of complexification that the complicated nature of our situation emerges.
It is at these points of 'unnatural' self-reflection that 'situations evoke self-conscious interpretative responses.' (Poling
and Mudge 1987, ch. 1). A key aspect of the practical theological task is to evoke such 'unnatural self-reflection' and to
raise people's consciousness to previously hidden dimensions
of everyday situations. As will become clear, it is within this
process of complexifying situations that qualitative research
proves to be most useful.

Autonomy and unity

It is important to emphasize again at this point that the knowledge gained from complexifying situations and reflecting
on them theologically is not independent of the knowledge
gained through theological reflection on scripture and tradition. Theological knowledge gained through the exploration
of situations is gained in constant dialogue with scripture
and tradition and should be put through the same rigorous
processes of discernment and validation as other modes of
theological reflection. As Farley correctly points out: 'similar demands are placed on the believer's interpretation of
situations as on the believer's interpretation of ancient texts,
or of "heresies" and doctrines.' (Poling and Mudge 1987,
ch. 1). Practical Theology is not an enterprise that occurs apart
from critical dialogue with the other theological disciplines.
Its conclusions both challenge and are constrained by the wisdom of tradition and the revelation of scripture. Similarly, the
task of the other theological disciplines can never be complete
without the theological knowledge gained from situational

interpretation. Enabling and facilitating this type of critical dialogue is central to the practical-theological task.

The meaning of our practices

If Practical Theology is critical theological reflection on practices that are carried out within particular situations, then it is important that we are clear as to what is meant by the term *practice*. Thus far we have used this term as if it had a common meaning which was shared by all readers. This, of course, is not the case. The term 'practice', as we are using it in this book, means considerably more than simply 'the things that people do'. The term 'practice' is much more complex.

Because of its focus on the theological significance of forms of practice, the primary task of Practical Theology is often assumed to be the *application* of theology to specific forms of action (primarily the actions of the ordained clergy), through the development of particular techniques which enable better preaching, teaching, pastoral care and so forth. Historically this has meant that Practical Theology has tended to focus on the *technical* actions of the Church (techniques) rather than their *theological* content and intent. Within this limited understanding, the term 'practice' is related first and foremost to particular technical procedures that ministers must learn in order that they can minister effectively. Theology, biblical studies, historical and philosophical studies are taken by the practical theologian and used to develop techniques for ministry. This forms the basis for the *applied theology* model of Practical Theology.

However, such an approach is problematic not least in the way that it assumes the other theological disciplines *not* to be inherently practical. As Dykstra observes,

> When practice means the application of theory to contemporary procedure, then biblical studies, history, systematic theology, philosophy, and ethics all become theoretical disciplines in which practice has no intrinsic place. (in Murphy *et al.* 2003, p. 163)

When this happens an inevitable and harmful split between theory and practice occurs with Practical Theology assumed to be the main practical discipline and the other theological disciplines presumed to be primarily theoretical. Perhaps more importantly, by stripping the other theological disciplines of their practicability, they become 'de-souled'; trapped in an internal conversation which ultimately makes a difference only to a select group, with no necessary relevance for the Christian community or the continuing mission of God in history. Such a split leads to an understanding of practice which is individualistic, technological, ahistorical and abstract.

Techno-theology

By combining this information with insights from other sources of knowledge, chiefly the social sciences, the practical theologian is charged with the responsibility to develop specialized techniques which are then put into the service of God via the practices of ordained ministers. Here the theory–practice relation is assumed to be analogous to the relationship between science and technology (Dykstra, in Murphy *et al.* 2003, p. 166), with theology offering the theoretical content and ministry perceived as the locus for technological application. Within such a framework of understanding, the authenticity of any particular practice is determined not by anything inherent within the practice itself, but rather by the *effect* that it has. The theological content, development and history of the practice are deemed insignificant. What matters is its pragmatic potential to do good, the definition of 'good' assumed to be defined by the positive effect of the practice. When we think of practice in this way, we almost automatically see *someone doing something*.

> the underlying assumption is that 'the person doing something to and for others is the one engaged in the practice. The preacher, the teacher the counsellor is the one who is doing the thing we are interested in. The others are objects

or recipients of the practice.' (Dykstra, in Murphy *et al.* 2003, p. 165)

Within this understanding it is assumed that practice is something that *individuals* do to one another. The individual and the action carried out are assumed not to have any necessary connection with the wider community, or the social and historical context within which the practice emerges and is carried out. Of course, the development of forms of action which have practical outcomes that result in enabling people to do things well is not in itself an unworthy goal. However, when the *effect* of the action is understood to be the goal and end in and of itself, practices becomes separated from their historical and theological roots and begin to lose their true meaning, purpose and goal.

The telos of our practices

The understanding of the term 'practice' which underpins Practical Theology is of a different nature. The technological approach to practice outlined above overlooks the crucial fact that all human practices are historically grounded and inherently value-laden. Practices such as prayer, hospitality and friendship contain their own particular theological meanings, social and theological histories, implicit and explicit norms and moral expectations. The ways in which we practise and the forms of practice in which we participate are therefore filled with deep meaning, purpose and direction. Put slightly differently, the forms of practice that we participate in are *theory-laden*. Browning notes the theory-laden nature of practices and the way in which acknowledgement of this fact rules out the widely held assumption that theory is distinct from practice:

> By using the phrase theory-laden, I mean to rule out in advance the widely held assumption that theory is distinct from practice. All our practices, even our religious practices, have theories behind and within them. We may not notice the

theories in our practices. We are so embedded in our practices, take them so much for granted, and view them as so
natural and self-evident that we never take time to abstract
the theory from the practice and look at it as something in
itself. (Browning 1983, p. 6)

There is no such thing as a value-free form of practice. Whether
acknowledged or otherwise, all of our practices are underpinned with very particular theories and theologies. In a very
real sense belief is within the act itself. This, of course, takes us
back to the metaphor of Gospel-as-performance highlighted
previously and the suggestion that theology and performance
are inseparable. The practice is found to be performative of
particular beliefs and as such is an appropriate subject for critical theological enquiry.[2] We previously illustrated this with
regard to the practice of friendship. Christian friendship when
complexified and reflected on theologically was found to be
a mode of practice which was filled with theological content.
We could easily do the same with other practices such as hospitality, forgiveness and so forth, all of which when complexified and reflected on theologically are found to be deep, rich
and often radically countercultural (Swinton 2006).

Defining practices

Practices, then, contain values, beliefs, theologies and other
assumptions which, for the most part, go unnoticed until they
are complexified and brought to our notice through the process of theological reflection. Importantly, practices are also
the bearers of traditions and histories. They are not therefore
simply individual actions. Rather they are communal activities that have developed within communities over extended
periods of time. Even though they may be manifested in par-

---

2. In this sense practice finds its biblical foundation in the actualization
of John 3:21: 'But whoever lives by the truth comes into the light, so that it
may be seen plainly that what he has done has been done through God.' And
see Swinton 2000c.

ticular instances, Christian practices always relate to particular communities; communities with specific histories and traditions which give meaning, value and direction to the particular forms of practice. Alasdair MacIntyre defines a practice in this way:

> any coherent and complex form of socially established cooperative human activity through which goods internal to that form of activity are realized in the course of trying to achieve those standards of excellence which are appropriate to, and partially definitive of, that form of activity, with the result that human powers to achieve excellence, and human conceptions of the ends and goods involved, are systematically extended. (1981, p. 187)

This definition is helpful in that it indicates the social and communal dimensions of a practice, the significance of its internal values and in-built norms and excellences and the necessity for communal action in order for them to be actualized. A practice then, as Forrester correctly points out, is 'not an isolated matter; it takes place in fellowship, solidarity with others' (Forrester 2000, p. 6). Importantly, as Dykstra and Bass point out, practices which are specifically Christian contain a normative element which is crucial for Christian formation and faithful living:

> The constituent elements in a way of life that becomes incarnate when human beings live in the light of and in response to God's gift of life abundant. Thus, when we refer to Christian practices we have something normative and theological in mind. Each element in our approach presumes that Christian practices are set in a world created and sustained by a just and merciful God, who is now in the midst of reconciling this world through Christ. Christian practices address needs that are basic to human existence as such, and they do so in ways that reflect God's purposes for humankind. When they participate in such Christian practices people are taking part in God's work of creation and

new creation and thereby growing into a deeper knowledge
of God and of creation. This is something that is necessarily done with other people, across generations and cultures.
(Dykstra and Bass 2002)

The key thing in this understanding is not that the practice
brings particular benefits to individuals or communities
(although it may do). The important thing is that the practice bears faithful witness to the God from whom the practice
emerges, and whom it reflects, and that it enables individuals
and communities to participate faithfully in Christ's redemptive mission. Thus the efficacy of the practice (the good to
which it is aimed), is not defined pragmatically by its ability
to fulfil particular human needs (although it will include that),
but by whether or not it participates faithfully in the divine
redemptive mission.

   This understanding of practice is very different from the
technique-oriented approach which has typified some aspects
of the development of Practical Theology. As Meador and
Shuman helpfully put it:

Techniques are forms of action that are expected to produce specific objective results that are external and instru-
mental to the actions themselves, without respect to their
embeddedness in particular ways of life. Practices may also
produce goods external to the action, but that is not their
primary point. The ends at which practices aim explicitly
are always internal to the ways of life in which they are embedded; this cannot be said of techniques, because technique
does not require to be embedded in a way of life. (Shuman
and Meador 2003, p. 91)

Practices occur in situations and are therefore central to the
type of theological reflection on situations that we discussed
earlier in this chapter. Reflection on practices will reveal
deep meanings about the nature, purpose and intentions of
the actions and assumptions of particular individuals or communities, be they religious or otherwise.

The content of our practices

The model of Practical Theology we have outlined thus far is clearly rooted within the Christian tradition. To call something 'Christian' is to make the assumption that the activity or activities described relate to a particular theological framework, a specific historical narrative and a particular set or sets of moral, ethical and metaphysical assumptions. To call a practice Christian assumes that it relates to a similar conceptual and theoretical foundation. All Christian practices emerge from reflection on and interpretations of the nature and purposes of the practices of God in history. We learn how to practise faithfully as we participate in and reflect upon what Duncan Forrester has described as 'the communicative practice of Jesus' (2000, p. 9).

> The Bible speaks of a God who acts, creating, sustaining and redeeming, a God who gives the law to God's people and enjoins them to be perfect as God is perfect – and that involves acting in the style or manner that God acts. This is not the remote, apathetic god of the Stoics or the Deists, who is a detached lawgiver, but a God who is involved. (Forrester 2000, p. 8)

It is in enabling people to learn and participate in 'the communicative practices of Jesus' and the continuing quest to perform them faithfully, that Practical Theology finds its focus and goal. This wider theological context for the enabling of faithful practice is important. All human practices emerge from and seek to participate in the wider practices of God. As Thomas Groome puts it,

> God is not only the ultimate telos but also the primary source from which all historical action, consciousness, and reflection arise . . . Because the world is the arena of God's saving activity, human history must be the primary locus, the point of departure and arrival for all rational discourse about God . . . Theology must arise from and return to the

locus of God's universal activity – the world. (in Mudge and Poling 1987, p. 61)

Groome and Forrester in different ways point to the fact that it is the practice of 'God in history as it is co-constituted through human praxis [that] is our primary text and context for doing theology' (Groome, in Mudge and Poling, p. 61). This is the dynamic which grounds, drives and energizes the reflective, prophetic and critical dimensions of the discipline of Practical Theology. One of the primary tasks of the practical theologian is to ensure that the practices of the Church remain faithful to the practices and mission of God as revealed in the life, death and resurrection of Jesus Christ and his continuing redemptive practices.

Christian practices

In conclusion, Christian practices, as described in this chapter, must always be understood within the context of the Church and the reign of God rather than in narrowly individualistic terms (Forrester 2000, p. 9). Christian practices are a reflection of the Church's attempts to participate faithfully in the continuing practices of the triune God's redemptive mission to the world. In like manner to the way in which John's Gospel emphasizes the interconnectedness of the practices of Jesus with those of the Father and the Holy Spirit,[3] so also the practices of the Christian community should reflect faithful participation in the Trinitarian actions of God in the world. When a practice loses this dynamic and becomes 'merely technique', it ceases to be faithful. Of course in reality, all practices are carried out imperfectly. Indeed practices can easily become distorted and even evil. One of the main critical tasks of Practical Theology is to recognize distorted practice and to call the

---

3. John 17:21 'That they all may be one; as thou, Father, [art] in me, and I in thee, that they also may be one in us: that the world may believe that thou hast sent me' (John 17:21 KJV).

Church back to the theological significance of its practices and to enable it to engage faithfully with the mission of God.

Conclusion

We can now return to our initial definition of Practical Theology. We defined Practical Theology as *critical, theological reflection on the practices of the Church as they interact with the practices of the world with a view to ensuring faithful participation in the continuing mission of the triune God.* We have shown both the complexity and the depth of this definition and the way that it carves out a unique space for Practical Theology within the overall process of theological construction and ensuring faithful and transformative practice. This definition holds in tension the unique, revelatory role of 'the Church as the hermeneutic of the gospel' (Newbigin 1989): that place where the nature and purpose of the gospel is interpreted, lived out and revealed in the character and practices of those who would call themselves the Church, with its role as a messenger and missionary presence in, to and for the world.

In the light of the above, we can see that the task of the practical theologian, *inter alia*, is to work towards the unification of the Church's theological understandings and her practices in the world, and in so doing, ensure that her public performances of the faith are true to the nature and actions of the Triune God. In concluding this chapter it will be helpful to highlight six points relating to the task of Practical Theology, which will help guide the remainder of this book.

1. The focus of the practical theological task is the quest for truth and the development and maintenance of faithful and transformative practice in the world.

The fundamental aim of Practical Theology is to enable the Church to perform faithfully as it participates in God's ongoing mission in, to and for the world. As such it seeks to reflect critically and theologically on situations and to provide insights and strategies which will enable the movement towards faithful change.

2. The task of Practical Theology is to mediate the relation between the Christian tradition and the specific problems and challenges of the contemporary social context.
It therefore moves from practice, to reflection on practice, and back to practice, a dynamic movement that is carried out in the light of the Christian tradition and other sources of knowledge and is aimed at feeding back into the tradition and the practice of the Church.

3. Practical Theology seeks to examine the theories and assumptions which underlie current forms of practice as well as to contribute to the development and reshaping of new theories which are then fed back into the practices of church and world.
Because scripture, tradition and church communities are not ahistorical, they are often profoundly impacted by aspects of society and culture which stand at odds with the essential message of the gospel. Part of the practical theological task is to discern such discrepancies in the practices of the Church and the world and to point towards more authentic alternatives.

4. Practical Theology is an interpretative discipline which offers new and challenging insights into Christian tradition in the light of fresh questions which emerge from particular situations.
In this sense it seeks to bring the practice of the Church into the continuing process of theological formulation, clarification and construction.

5. Practical Theology 'stays close to experience' (Fowler 1995, p. 7).
While concerned with theory as a necessary aspect of practice, it is not focused on the development of comprehensive, theological systems which understand themselves as concerned with the development of forms of knowledge extrapolated from any form of practice. The aim of Practical Theology is to enable personal and communal *phronesis*; a form of practical wisdom which combines theory and practice in the praxis of individuals and communities. This phronesis does not aim for knowledge for its own sake, but for an embodied,

practical knowledge which will enable a particular form of God-oriented lifestyle. This suggestion resonates with Farley's concept of 'habitus': a disposition or orientation devoted to the practical but critical living out of faith.[4] This form of habitus reveals the coming kingdom of God in a tangible form. One does not simply proclaim the gospel with one's mind, but with the whole of one's being. Practical Theology is therefore a holistic discipline which sees theology as pertaining as much to embodied existence as to abstract intellectual propositions which demand particular cognitive dispositions.

6. Practical Theology is a fundamentally missiological discipline which receives its purpose, its motivation and its dynamic from acknowledging and working out what it means to participate faithfully in God's mission. While staying close to experience, Practical Theology understands particular situations within the wider, overarching context of God's ongoing mission of redemption to the world. This mission provides the critical hermeneutic which guides the practical theologian in each dimension of her task. The aim of Practical Theology is therefore not simply to understand the world but also to change it. However, its task is not one of pragmatic regurgitation, but of critical discernment. The dominant question for Practical Theology is not 'What difference will this make in the pulpit and pew?' but rather 'Who is God and how does one know more fully His truth?[5]

---

4. Farley (1983) outlines this concept in considerably more detail.

5. Kunst states this point poignantly when she notes that, 'the church does not exist fundamentally to meet needs; in its being, the church, like Christ, exists to glorify the Father' (1992, p. 163). It is not unreasonable to suggest that this should in fact be *the* leading motif in all of the Church's practical-theological endeavours.

What is Qualitative Research?

In Chapter 1 we laid down a foundational understanding of Practical Theology. This has allowed us to orient ourselves within the field and to begin to see some of the potential ways in which a constructive, critical dialogue between Practical Theology and qualitative research methods has the potential to be fruitful and illuminating. We previously noted that the intention of this book is to explore the interface between Practical Theology and qualitative research methods with a view to offering insights, perspectives and schemas that will allow researchers to work effectively and faithfully with both disciplines. In this chapter we will look in some detail at the nature and purpose of qualitative research and provide an overview of what qualitative research is and what it can provide the practical theologian with. The chapter is not intended to offer a comprehensive exploration of the entire field of qualitative research. Such a task would obviously be impossible within the confines of a single chapter. There are a number of excellent texts which do this well. These are listed in the references and include Morse *et al.* 2001, Mason 1996, Ritchie and Lewis 2003, Denzin and Lincoln 2000, Denzin 2002 and a practical quide to real world research by Robson 2002. Our intention here is to introduce the reader specifically to those aspects of qualitative research that we consider to be of particular relevance for practical-theological research, and to lay down a framework within which the mutuality and complementarity of the two disciplines becomes apparent.

Defining qualitative research?

In like manner to what we discovered in our initial exploration of Practical Theology, one of the difficulties that confronts the newcomer to qualitative research methods is the wide range of approaches and the rather vague definitions that make up the field. Like Practical Theology, the field of qualitative research is open-ended and has a wide range of perspectives: empirical, political, sociological, pastoral, gender-oriented, and narrative-based. This makes it difficult to tie down and define. As Denzin and Lincoln correctly point out:

> the open ended nature of the qualitative research project leads to a perpetual resistance against attempts to impose a single umbrella-like paradigm over the entire project. (2000, p. xv)

Qualitative research is therefore slippery and difficult to contain within a single definition. Nevertheless, we need to find a way of orienting ourselves within the field.

Denzin and Lincoln define qualitative research thus:

> Qualitative research is multi-method in focus, involving an interpretative, naturalistic approach to its subject matter. This means that qualitative researchers study things in their natural settings, attempting to make sense of, or interpret, phenomena in terms of the meanings people bring to them. (1998, p. 3)

Qualitative research involves the utilization of a variety of methods and approaches which enable the researcher to explore the social world in an attempt to access and understand the unique ways that individuals and communities inhabit it. It assumes that human beings are by definition 'interpretive creatures'; that the ways in which we make sense of the world and our experiences within it involve a constant process of interpretation and meaning-seeking. Qualitative research assumes that the world is not simply 'out there' waiting to be discovered. Rather, it recognizes 'the world' as the locus of complex interpretive processes within which human beings struggle to make sense of their experiences including their experiences of God. Identifying and developing understandings of these meanings is the primary task of qualitative research.

A simple way to conceptualize good qualitative research is by using the analogy of a detective story. A good piece of qualitative research is like a detective story without a fixed ending. It involves the painstaking and complex process of unpicking the detail of who did what, when, and why within particular situations and formulating this into evidence which will enable a fair judgement to be made. Occasionally an unexpected piece of information throws new light on the situation and allows intellectual jumps to be made that enable the researcher's thinking to move on in unexpected and challenging ways.

However, unlike the detective the qualitative researcher does not seek to *solve* the problem or 'crack the case'. She is very much aware that neither is possible. The evidence can tell many stories, and all of them contain varying degrees of truth. Her story is just part of a wide variety of evidence that will be offered to the 'court' as it seeks to discern what is truthful and what is not. The researcher's task is to tell her story about the situation as well and as accurately as she can; to create her evidence convincingly and to bring that evidence before the 'judge' who will read her report and pronounce the final verdict. Thus, contrary to what is often assumed, good qualitative research, like good detective work, is rigorous, painstaking, exacting, complex and difficult, requiring a wide range of technical skills including the ability to collect and analyse data using informed and multidisciplinary frameworks, the ability to interview, and to transcribe and accurately interpret data, and a deep and thorough knowledge of the theory and practice of hermeneutics and interpretation. Subsequent chapters will demonstrate the complexity of the qualitative research approach in more detail.

Seeing and discovering

It may be helpful to think of qualitative methods as offering a particular way of *seeing* and *discovering*. John McLeod defines qualitative research in a way that draws out and illuminates this suggestion:

> Qualitative research is a process of careful, rigorous inquiry into aspects of the social world. It produces formal statements or conceptual frameworks that provide new ways of understanding the world, and therefore comprises knowledge that is practically useful for those who work with issues around learning and adjustment to the pressures and demands of the social world. (McLeod 2001, p. 3)

This definition is helpful in a number of ways.

1 It suggests that qualitative research relates to the careful exploration of the ways in which human beings encounter their world, an exposition that offers new ways of understanding and interpreting the world. It takes human experience seriously and seeks to understand and interpret that experience in a variety of ways.

2 Qualitative research is careful and rigorous. As a mode of research, qualitative research is often caricatured as anecdotal, lacking in rigour; 'merely storytelling'. In fact qualitative research, when done well, is a thorough and rigorous discipline. Certainly it is narrative-based, but that fact does not make it any less rigorous. Indeed, as we will argue later in this chapter, the narrative base of qualitative research is crucial in terms of the significance of its contribution to human knowledge. Bearing in mind that theology and religious experience are communicated primarily within stories, this narrative emphasis within qualitative research should not be problematic for the practical theologian.

3 McLeod's definition emphasizes the importance of knowledge that has practical utility, that is, knowledge that has the potential not simply to comment on the world, but to change the world. In the light of what we have suggested in Chapter 1

concerning the nature and purpose of Practical Theology, this action-oriented aspect of qualitative research knowledge-production immediately resonates.

4 Finally, this definition emphasizes the important role that qualitative research plays in complexifying the world. Qualitative research locates the researcher in the world in a very specific way. It offers her a position that enables her to render the familiar strange (Dowie 2002). The 'way of seeing' provided by qualitative research presupposes certain assumptions about the nature of reality and suggests that things are going to be much more complicated than they appear at the outset. By placing common-sense understandings of the world under scrutiny, the world is complexified, challenged and transformed as the envisioned eye of the qualitative researcher encounters it.

These provisional reflections on qualitative research point us towards an understanding of what it is, and begin to tease out some of the ways in which it may be allied to the task of Practical Theology.

Epistemological foundations and assumptions

Because qualitative research has a distinctive perspective on the world, it will be helpful to begin by looking at the *epistemology* that underlies qualitative approaches to research. The term 'epistemology' relates to the branch of philosophy that is concerned with the theory of knowledge. In essence it seeks to ask and to answer the question 'How do we know what we know?' indeed, 'How can we know at all?' The epistemology of qualitative research relates to the particular theory of knowledge that underpins this approach. In looking at the epistemological underpinnings of qualitative research we will be focusing on this central question: 'How do we know what we know?' How we answer that question will determine how we look and what we see within the research process. It is therefore a question of vital importance.

The question of knowledge: How do we know what we know?

Let us begin by examining the types of knowledge that qualitative research makes available to us. McLeod (2001, p. 3) suggests that there are three types of knowledge that one can get through involvement in qualitative research:

1 Knowledge of the other
2 Knowledge of phenomena
3 Reflexive knowing.

All three types of knowing bear relevance for practical-theological research.

Knowledge of the other occurs when the researcher focuses on a particular individual or group and explores in-depth the ways in which they view and interact with the world. This 'knowledge of the other' feeds into practice and enables people to develop in-depth understandings of those whom they encounter and seek to understand. Such a mode of knowing gives a voice to particular groups – patients, counsellors, church communities and so forth – and allows previously hidden life experiences and narratives to come to the fore and to develop a public voice. So, for example, one might choose to study a group of voluntary parish workers and to examine what it is that they are *actually* doing and what it is that they *think* they are doing. In wrestling with this tension between perception and reality, the practical theologian can begin to understand the complexities of the task of the parish volunteer and provide knowledge which will enable their work to be challenged and enhanced. The exploration of chaplaincy in Chapter 6 offers a useful example of the way in which this type of knowledge can be gathered effectively through the use of qualitative methods.

However, gathering such 'knowledge of the other' raises important questions regarding who owns that knowledge and who is the best person to collect it. Is an external, 'objective'

researcher the most appropriate person to gather such information, or should it be members of the group being studied
who should be doing the research work? The danger of subtle modes of colonialism is always present within this type of
research. Chapter 8 will explore some of the ways in which this
tension can be understood and worked with constructively.

Knowledge of phenomena relates to research done on particular categories of event such as, for example, the manifestation of the Holy Spirit within a church congregation, methods
of discipleship, and the impact of change on particular communities. Here we can gain understanding of the meaning of
phenomena and the various complex processes involved within them. The exploration of suicide in Chapter 7 provides a
perspective on this mode of knowledge.

Reflexive knowing occurs when researchers deliberately turn
their attention to their own processes of constructing the
world, with the goal of saying something fresh and new about
that personal (or shared) world. While this mode of knowing
is not explicitly explored within this book the idea of reflexivity is very important. We will explore that reflexivity in more
detail later in this chapter and, to a greater or lesser extent, all
of the research projects explored will contain elements of this
way of knowing.

An interpretative paradigm

Qualitative research takes place within what has been described as an *interpretative paradigm*. Lincoln and Guba put
it this way:

> The net that contains the researcher's epistemological, onto-
> logical, and methodological premises may be termed a *para-*
> *digm*, or an interpretative framework, a 'basic set of beliefs
> that guides action' (Guba 1990, p. 17). All research is inter-
> pretative; it is guided by a set of beliefs and feelings about the

world and how it should be understood and studied. Some beliefs may be taken for granted, invisible, only assumed, whereas others are highly problematic and controversial. Each interpretative paradigm makes particular demands on the researcher, including the questions he or she asks and the interpretations the researcher brings to them. (Lincoln and Guba 2000, p. 20)

An important underlying epistemological assumption within qualitative research is the perspective of *constructivism* (Lincoln and Guba 1985; Swinton 2001). Constructivism assumes that truth and knowledge and the ways in which it is perceived by human beings and human communities is, to a greater or lesser extent, constructed by individuals and communities. In distinction from the epistemology of the natural sciences that assumes a more fixed, stable and external reality, this understanding of knowledge does not assume that reality is something that is somehow 'out there', external to the observer, simply waiting to be discovered. Rather, it presumes that 'reality' is open to a variety of different interpretations and can never be accessed in a pure, uninterpreted form. Instead, constructivism and its various derivatives assume the existence of multiple realities. This is a rather odd way of stating the case. Clearly if there is no such thing as reality, one cannot have multiples of it. What is intended by the suggestion that there are 'multiple realities' is really to emphasize that there are various interpretations that can be placed on the same phenomena, all of which hold independent validity. Such an epistemological position means that the researcher will be involved with the research process not as a distant observer, but as an active participant and co-creator of the interpretative experience. The implications of taking seriously the horizon of the researcher is discussed in more detail in Chapter 4. At this point it will suffice to observe that within the constructivist paradigm the boundaries between the researcher and the subject of the research process are blurred and interconnected.

The constructivist perspective, then, proposes that meaning emerges from the shared interaction of individuals within human society. From this viewpoint, human behaviour and understanding are seen to be an active process of construction and interpretation in which human beings together endeavour to define the nature of their particular social situations and encounters and in so doing make sense of and participate appropriately in their social, psychological, physical and spiritual environments. 'The meaning and definition of reality is therefore flexible, and open to negotiation depending on circumstances, perception, knowledge, power structures and so forth' (Swinton 2001, p. 97). If there is controversy over particular meanings, for example, where several definitions exist for the same piece of reality, then the meaning of that reality is *negotiated*, and defined according to the interpretative framework which the individual uses to make sense of their experiences of reality (Eaton 1986, p. 2).

Does reality exist?

However, to adopt such a stance does *not* mean that one needs to assume reality is *nothing but* a social construction. What it *does* however emphasize, is that our ability to understand and define what reality is is always filtered through a process of interpretation and construction that is influenced by a number of social, cultural, spiritual and interpersonal factors. In making the familiar strange, the qualitative researcher acknowledges the polyvalent and interpretative nature of reality and seeks to describe what situations look like when phenomena are viewed from different frames of reference. Each story described, each experience recorded, reveals a different perspective on the particular reality that is being examined. Taken together these stories and experiences lead us closer and closer to an approximation of what reality might look like.

There are of course some proponents of qualitative research who would argue that reality is inaccessible and that constructivism is *all* that there is (Denzin 1997). This is not our position. In our view, the Christian tradition claims to have received revelation. If reality is totally inaccessible, then so is revelation, a suggestion that leads to obvious and complicated theological problems. We would therefore argue that reality is both real and, in principle, accessible. We will discuss further in Chapter 3 why this is and how it might be overcome. Here, it is useful to think in terms of a

> continuum between a naive realism that accepts that truth can be fully accessed through human endeavour, that is, that theoretical concepts find direct correlates within the world, and a form of mediated or *critical realism* that accepts that reality can be known a little better through our constructions while at the same time recognizing that such constructions are always provisional and open to challenge. (Swinton 2001, p. 97)

Uncovering an interpretative universe

For current purposes, the central idea that needs to be drawn from the perspective we are discussing is that for qualitative research, the idea of value-free, objective truth becomes at best questionable and perhaps unsustainable. All reality is interpreted and formulated via an interpretative process within which the researcher is inevitably enmeshed. This is not necessarily a bad thing, as we will see in the discussion of hermeneutics in Chapter 4. Indeed, the involvement of the researcher is a necessary and constructive dimension of the interpretative process.

With this epistemological framework in mind, it becomes clear why it is that within qualitative research the quest is not for objectivity and explanation (as per the natural sciences), but for *meaning* and a deeper *understanding* of situations. Within the interpretative paradigm, human beings are recognized as actively creative agents who are constantly interpreting situations and ascribing meaning and purpose to events; creatures who constantly create complex networks of narratives to explain the world and their place within it. The meanings and interpretations of these narratives form the 'maps of reality' which individuals, communities and cultures use to interpret their experiences and to decide on the nature of appropriate action. It is therefore not enough simply to naively observe what a person is doing or how they are behaving within any given situation. In order to understand what is *actually* going on within that situation it is necessary to understand the *meaning* of the actions, the way the situation is being interpreted by those performing within it and the reasons behind the ways individuals and communities act in the particular ways that they do. The quest for this type of understanding forms the heart of qualitative research and is a fundamental dimension of Practical Theology's endeavour to critically reflect on the nature of situations.

Narrative-as-knowledge

A key aspect of qualitative research is its frequent orientation towards narrative. Sometimes this is explicitly expressed as in the various modes of research which identify themselves as narrative qualitative research (Denzin 1997, pp. 231 ff.). However, narrative is an implicit dimension within most qualitative approaches. The telling of stories and the accurate recording, transcription and analysis of this data forms the heart of the qualitative research enterprise.

This observation brings us to a second, important epistemological point. For the qualitative researcher, narrative knowledge is perceived to be a legitimate, rigorous and valid form of knowledge that informs us about the world in ways which are publicly significant. Stories are not simply meaningless personal anecdotes; they are important sources of knowledge. This is a difficult thing for the modern mind to take on board. Within post-Enlightenment Western culture, it is the mode of knowledge that is revealed within the so-called 'hard sciences' which normally forms the bedrock of our understanding of what is factual and what is not. As Gorsuch (2002, p. 124) puts it, 'in the modernist perspective as developed in the mid-

1900s, the sciences were seen as *the* model for understanding the search for truth'. Within such a cultural context such things as narrative, experience and emotion become modes of 'soft truth' which are, to a greater or lesser extent, excluded from the realm of 'public truth' that has relevance beyond the experience or opinion of the individual. 'Soft knowledge' may make sense in the privacy of one's own home, but it has little to say about the way things function in the public sphere.

The idea of the 'scientific fact' as definitive of rigorous truth is so 'natural' to us that we rarely think beyond it. The general cultural assumptions which underpin much scientific research seem to be that facts and the nature of reality can be discovered through careful observation carried out via the application of a process of enquiry known as the hypothetico-deductive method (Popper 1959). This approach involves presenting a theory or hypothesis based on literature, observation or prior knowledge that can be tested using empirical data to which statistics of probability are applied. If an observation is contrary to that which is predicted, this is taken as evidence against the hypothesis. An observation which is in agreement with that which is predicted is taken as corroborating evidence to support the hypothesis. Competing hypotheses can then be compared and their explanatory value assessed according to their ability to sustain certain predictions. This understanding forms the basis of the 'scientific method' which we will look at in more detail below.

If we take as an example the developing evidence-based culture within health and social care services we will see some of the implications of this position. In the NHS and social work settings today, evidence-based practice is seen as the most appropriate and reliable method by which best practice can be achieved. The randomized controlled trial is commonly viewed as the gold standard of all methods. This is seen particularly clearly by using the testing of medication as an example. A particular drug can be tested by randomly assigning the new drug or a placebo to a group of people. The group who are taking the new drug (who do not know this) are then monitored for various effects and expected outcomes, as are the group who are taking the placebo. If the drug is for headaches a major outcome measure will be reduction in headache reported by the patient and monitored through the observation of brain wave patterns by the researcher. If the number of people in the study is high enough, and this 'power' can be calculated, the likelihood of the effects occurring by chance are minimized and the scientists are able to confirm their hypothesis that the new drug has the required effect. They can then move on to generalize these findings to a whole population based on the randomized selection of the sample.[1]

This mode of knowledge-seeking is of course useful for measuring what it measures. However, if we attempt to claim, as our evidence-based culture often seems to do, that this is the *only* way of accessing reality, knowledge and truth, then we move in a direction which is highly questionable.

Nomothetic truth

The model of knowledge that underpins this modernist perspective is *nomothetic* knowledge. Nomothetic knowledge is knowledge gained through the use of the scientific method. Knowledge must meet three criteria before it can be considered scientific truth. It must be: *falsifiable*, *replicable* and

1. Even in this case, however, there are problems with what are known as intervening variables. It may be that the people in the group taking the new drug, even though they do not know which drug they are taking, will take something else as well or act in ways that could mean that the effects measured in them are not reliably attributable to the drug. For instance the members of the group may see a programme on the TV which suggests that standing on your head alleviates headache, others may determine not to row with their spouse as it gives them a headache. These intervening variables are not always available to or under the control of the researcher. It is obvious that the less active the participant the more likely it is that these variables can be kept under control. Unfortunately human beings are inevitably active and interactive. They react to and work on their environment all the time. This makes them very difficult subjects to research because they cannot be 'controlled' in the same way as animals.

generalizable. It will be helpful to look at each of these aspects of nomothetic truth in turn.

Falsifiability

A basic premise of the scientific method is that if something is not falsifiable, it cannot be counted as factual. In other words, it must be possible, at least in theory, to disprove a statement or proposition. A statement such as 'there is a God' cannot be considered nomothetic truth as it is impossible to falsify. A good deal of religious and spiritual truth is not falsifiable and therefore not considered to be true or at least verifiably true within this model of knowledge.

Replicability

For something to become scientific truth (nomothetic knowledge), it must be possible to replicate it. Gorsuch (2002) points to the way in which the scientific paper functions to consolidate this dimension of the construction of nomothetic truth. The scientific paper begins with a hypothesis, moves on to a methods section, describes how the study was done, and from there moves on to a presentation of the results. All of this is concluded by a discussion on the research process. To be publishable, it needs to have a certain internal rigour that will allow anyone who wishes, and who has the necessary technical skills to replicate the study, to do so. If it is replicable then it is judged as nomothetic truth, that is, scientific fact. If it is not replicable, then it is deemed to be erroneous and therefore not factual in any kind of publicly verifiable way.

Generalizability

Closely connected with the previous point is the idea of generalizability. In order to be 'true' a piece of knowledge must be generalizable, that is, it must be possible to take the results of the findings of the study or the experiment and to generalize to a wider population. If a study or experiment does not meet this criterion, then it will not be accepted as public/ scientific truth.

Can a scientist love his wife?

It is certainly the case that nomothetic knowledge as it is embodied in the language and practices of science has become the public currency for knowledge and the verification of what is true and what is untrue. However, the fact that there are powerful forces within culture pushing for the supremacy of nomothetic knowledge does not make nomothetic knowledge the only plausible form of knowledge (although it may often look that way). A deeper reflection reveals the all-encompassing aspirations of nomothetic knowledge to be problematic. Take for example the assumptions and practices of a scientist. In the public/professional domain he is tied in to a model of truth that is fundamentally nomothetic. That is the language that makes sense to his profession and to those who fund his profession. So, within his professional life, the scientist defines fact and truth in terms of replicability, falsifiability and generalizability. However, when he goes home from work, he loves his wife and children, and he believes that love to be real. It is not possible for him to carry out a randomized control trial to test the theory and even if he did, the love he shows for his wife and family would more than probably be quite different from the love a stranger might show towards them, or even the love that he has showed them earlier on in their relationship. So he finds himself living in two knowledge worlds, one determined by nomothethetic knowledge and the other by a different type of knowledge which he knows intuitively is true, but which fails to fit the verification criteria of his professional/cultural expectations. This other mode of knowledge forms the bedrock of qualitative research and of Practical Theology. This type of knowing is *ideographic knowledge*.

Ideographic knowledge

Ideographic knowledge is of a different order from nomothetic knowledge. It presumes that meaningful knowledge
can be discovered in unique, non-replicable experiences. It
assumes that it is not possible to step in the same river twice;
that the very action of stepping in the river shifts the river
bed, displaces the water in ways which mean it will never be
the same again. Ideographic knowledge assumes that no two
people experience the same event in the same way; indeed no
individual will experience the same event in the same way
twice. Ideographic events can be profoundly life-changing.
The resurrection of Christ, St Paul's experience of blinding
and his subsequent conversion, or Moses' encounter with God
on Mount Sinai would be good examples of the power of an
ideographic event.

Importantly, as Thomas Kuhn (1970) and Michael Polanyi
(1958) have ably shown, nomothetic knowledge is always
approached ideographically, that is, even a scientist approaches
the process of constructing experiments, interpreting results
and seeking funding for developments from the perspective of
their own narrative, a particular research community with a
specific history, biases and assumptions. As Gorsuch (2002)
puts it: 'although we may theorize or even dream in a nomothetic world, we *never* live in it'.

Ideographic truth is important from the perspective of
Practical Theology because it is integral to the language of
scripture and tradition. God reveals God's self in and through
knowledge that is profoundly ideographic. The major events
of the Christian narrative – incarnation, cross, resurrection –
are clearly ideographic. Ideographic knowledge is also an
integral part of the experiences and situations that Practical
Theology seeks to reflect upon. Recognizing the epistemological significance of ideographic knowledge is very important
for the practice of Practical Theology.

Qualitative versus quantitative research

This discussion of the distinctiveness of ideographic and nomothetic knowledge relates closely to the ongoing debate within the social sciences between qualitative and quantitative methods. Quantative methods tend to assume the primacy of nomothetic knowledge while qualitative methods focus on ideographic knowledge. Table 1 draws out the primary differences between qualitative and quantative approaches based on similar models of understanding to those we have been looking at.

These two research approaches are not bipolar opposites and, in fact, in practice need each other for the development of thorough understanding. Our point in this discussion of nomothetic and ideographic knowledge is not to put down one at the expense of the other. Both are necessary for the process of research and the understanding of the way that the world is. The issue we want to highlight is the way in which, due to the power of the scientific model of knowledge-seeking, the nomothetic discourse has been prioritized at the expense of the ideographic, with the latter often being downgraded to mere opinion or 'only description'. Qualitative research has often been a victim of this process of downgrading. We want to suggest that within the lived reality of human experience people actually utilize both modes of knowledge with equal seriousness. As practical theologians who take the Bible seriously, we can do nothing other than take most seriously the authenticity and reality of ideographic truth.

The importance of understanding

Qualitative research then, finds its focus in ideographic knowledge. Because of this the research process has a quite specific dynamic and focus. The task of qualitative research is not to seek to *explain* the world in ways that will make sense across cultures to all reasonable people at any moment in history. Rather the task of qualitative research is to describe reality

Table 1: Traditional bipolar representation of differences between quantitative and qualitative methodologies

Quantitative methodology	Qualitative methodology
searches for general laws, empirical regularities	searches for meanings in specific social/cultural contexts; possibility of theoretical generalization
adoption of natural science (objectivity as ideal)	rejection of natural science (subjectivity is valued)
try to simulate experimental situation	natural settings
explanation = prediction of events, behaviour, attitudes ('statistical causality')	explanation = understanding, interpreting reasons for observable behaviour, sense given to actions ('historical causality')
large-scale studies (extensive research); random sampling	studies of small groups; case studies (intensive research); purposive sampling
deduction	induction or grounded theory
survey instruments with predetermined response categories based on theoretical framework (questionnaire)	open-ended research instruments (semi-structured intensive interview, life history, focus group, observation . . .) from which theoretical categories (may) emerge
numbers (measurement)	words ('thick description')

(Damaris 2001)

in ways which enable us to understand the world differently and in understanding differently begin to act differently. *Description, interpretation* and *understanding* are thus found to be key terms for qualitative research and the qualitative researcher.

The problem of generalization

'But,' one might rightly ask, 'what about issues of generalization?' 'How can qualitative research be of use if its findings cannot be transferred from one context to another?' There are two responses that one might offer to such a question. Lincoln and Guba respond to the question of generalizability in this way:

> The naturalist cannot specify the external validity of an inquiry; he or she can provide only the thick description necessary to enable someone interested in making a transfer to reach a conclusion about whether transfer can be contemplated as a possibility . . . Clearly, not just any descriptive data will do, but the criteria that separate relevant from irrelevant descriptors are still largely undefined . . . the naturalist inquirer is also responsible for providing the widest possible range of information for inclusion in the thick description. (1985, p. 316)

Their point here is that it is not the qualitative researcher's responsibility to generalize. Their responsibility is to provide as rich and thick a description of the situation in hand as possible. If people want to test that for generalizability, then that is a secondary task. The primary task of the qualitative researcher is to ensure the accuracy of their description. Qualitative research thus provides the data that will enable future researchers to explore the possibility of transferability and to find models that describe a situation and that have transferable structures.

While this position contains truth, we would not agree with

it totally. It is true that aspects of human experience are unique and unrepeatable. Nevertheless, there remains a degree of shared experience which we believe can, to an extent, transfer from one context to another. Perhaps the doubts over generalizability can be alleviated if we think in terms of *identification* and *resonance*. While the findings of qualitative research studies may not be immediately transferable to other contexts, there is a sense in which qualitative research should resonate with the experiences of others in similar circumstances. This resonance should invoke a sense of identification with those who share something of the experience. So, for example, during a feedback session on the chaplaincy project outlined in Chapter 4, several chaplains told us that they felt a resonance with the results of the study. That is to say, they identified with what we found and resonated with the perspectives that our study raised.

Again, in the study of depression outlined in Chapter 4 the experiences captured were clearly unique and at one level ungeneralizable. Nevertheless, when the findings were shared with other people experiencing depression, the researcher was frequently informed that the findings resonated with the wider experience of depression and that this resonance challenged people to think differently and to look at themselves and their situations differently.

Qualitative research can therefore claim a degree of transferability insofar as it often raises issues and offers insights which reach beyond the particularities of the situation. It frequently (arguably always), creates a resonance with people outside of the immediate situation who are experiencing phenomena which are not identical, but hold enough similarity to create a potentially *transformative resonance*. We might not be able to take a set of results from one context and place them straight into another. It is, however, possible to explore whether or not the phenomena that the researcher has been observing can find a resonance and a sense of identification with others experiencing similar phenomena. The important thing to note here is that while generalizability is not a required goal of qualitative

research, the data produced frequently has implications beyond the immediacy of the research context.

Theoretical generalizability

The issue of generalization is certainly problematic. Nevertheless, within some schools of thought there remains the
possibility of 'theoretical generalization'. Theoretical generalization means that the researcher does not simply document
the experiences of groups of people for their own sake, but
also because she hopes that her study will contribute to theory
development with wider implications for other individuals and
groups. Here 'the goal is to use a concrete and delimited situation to better understand the broader social processes which
structure it, and how they are mediated by the specifics of the
situation' (Sim 1998). The particular study is used to develop
a theoretical model that can, in principle, be applied to other
similar situations. Sim describes theoretical generalization in
the following way:

> [In theoretical generalization], the data gained from a par-
> ticular study provide theoretical insights which possess a
> sufficient degree of generality or universality to allow their
> projection to other contexts or situations which are com-
> parable to that of the original study. The researcher recog-
> nizes parallels, at a conceptual or theoretical level, between
> the case or situation studied and another case or situation,
> which may well differ considerably in terms of the attributes
> or variables that it exhibits. In other words, the compara-
> bility required between the two contexts is a logical or con-
> ceptual one, not one based on statistical representativeness.
> (Sim 1998, p. 350)

Figure 1 illustrates this point.

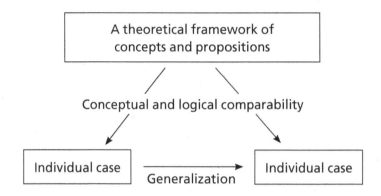

Figure 1: Theoretical generalization (Sim 1998: 350).

Continuing, Sim points out that:

> cases which are empirically *atypical* may provide an import-
> ant means of theoretical generalization ... Hence, whether
> two cases are empirically comparable depends upon their
> sharing certain attributes or variables in certain proportions
> or to certain degrees, largely independent of a *particular*
> theoretical perspective (i.e. the empirical regularities do not
> presuppose one theoretical explanation rather than another,
> even though analysis may ultimately show one such explana-
> tion to be preferable). In contrast, the theoretical compara-
> bility of two cases depends upon their embodying certain
> concepts within a particular theoretical framework, largely
> irrespective of any similarities or differences in the pattern
> of attributes or variables exhibited.

Theoretical generalization allows the qualitative researcher to
develop theoretical perspectives which, while not statistically
generalizable, have the theoretical potential to move beyond
the particularities of the situation being examined.

A multi-method research approach

There are many styles of qualitative research (Denzin and Lincoln 2000). Chapters 4–7 will explore the implications of a number of key methods, techniques and approaches. Here we will make some provisional observations that will help to provide an understanding of the way that the various methods are worked out within the process of carrying out qualitative research.

Some would argue for the importance of remaining within the acknowledged boundaries of particular qualitative research methods. We would want to argue for a much more fluid and flexible use of qualitative research methods. We suggest that the lines between the various methods used within the field of qualitative research are often thin and blurry. It is our opinion that the most effective way that practical theologians can use qualitative research methods is by developing an eclectic and multi-method approach which seeks to take the best of what is available within the accepted models of qualitative research, but is not necessarily bound by any one model.

Such a flexible approach to method emerges from reflection on the epistemological perspectives we have presented earlier. Uri Flick suggests that qualitative research is best done when it utilizes multiple approaches (Flick 1998, p. 229; 1992). We believe that he is correct. Individual approaches (grounded theory, ethnography, action research, etc.) are certainly useful as conceptual models. Nevertheless, in practice, a multi-method approach that utilizes the best of these methods, but is not necessarily defined or confined by any one of them may be the most appropriate way forward for the practical theologian. Denzin and Lincoln (2000, p. 5) argue that the use of multiple methods is an important aspect of the process of *validating* qualitative research:

> The use of multiple methods, or triangulation, reflects an attempt to secure an in-depth understanding of the phenomenon in question. Objective reality can never be captured. We can know a thing only through its representations. Tri-

angulation is not a tool or a strategy of validation, but an alternative to validation . . . the combination of multiple methodological practices, empirical materials, perspectives and observers in a single study is best understood, then, as a strategy that adds rigor, breadth, complexity, richness and depth to any inquiry.

For reasons that will become clear in Chapter 3, we would not agree with the implication that reality is 'nothing but' social construction. Nevertheless, Denzin and Lincoln's point is pertinent. If a situation is at least interpretatively polyvalent, then the more perspectives one uses to explore that reality, the richer the data and the deeper the understanding one will be able to obtain. When, later, we come to explore the various pieces of qualitative research, the way in which we utilize various aspects of different methods to respond to particular contexts and experiences will become clear. We would not of course want to suggest that 'pure methods' should be abandoned, only that by spreading our toolbox more widely and using it creatively and responsively, the practical theologian can find ways of accessing data that would be inaccessible if she were bounded by any single method.

Where does qualitative research start?

Having laid down these foundational insights into the nature and purpose of practical theology, we need now to move on and explore some of the ways in which this conceptual framework impacts upon the way that qualitative research is constructed and carried out. It will be helpful to begin by considering Ritchie and Lewis's (2003, p. 27) classification of the functions of research. They point out that considerations of the broader functions of social investigation help clarify the particular role of qualitative research in this broader process. They propose four major functions.

- *Contextual* – describing the form or nature of what exists

- *Explanatory* – examining the reasons for, or associations between, what exists
- *Evaluative* – appraising the effectiveness of what exists
- *Generative* – aiding the development of theories, strategies or actions.

Depending on the purpose of the research, there are a variety of means of achieving that purpose. It is therefore important to know from the beginning what the purpose of a piece of research is and be sure that the chosen method will achieve the stated purpose. A lack of clarity as to precisely what function one desires the research process to perform will result in confusion, lack of clarity and the generation of large amounts of superfluous data. It is therefore critical that from the beginning of the research process, the qualitative researcher is clear and focused.

The situation: establishing the problem

The locus of the qualitative research process is a particular situation that the researcher or the funding body thinks merits further attention because it is confusing or little understood. Unlike quantitative approaches, qualitative research begins with a general field rather than a specific hypothesis. As the research process progresses, material for the development of hypotheses begins to emerge. However, they tend to emerge *from* the data rather than be imposed on it by the researcher. It is therefore both usual and acceptable to pose a general question or to lay out an initial observation which later becomes the general field of study. In the studies presented later in the book, issues such as the nature of the emerging church, the purpose of hospital chaplaincy and the experience of depression all present as examples of explorations which did not begin with a hypothesis, but rather with a hunch and a sensitivity to a general field. Qualitative methods are thus seen to be at their most useful when little is understood or known about a situation. The initial task is to firmly locate the field of study and to clarify the purpose of the research. Both the field and the purpose may change in response to the data gathered, but if there is no foundational understanding of the starting place, then the study will risk implosion.

Having established these things, the researcher can move on to the next phase in study development: *developing the research question* (Figure 2).

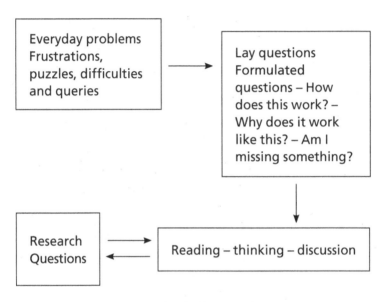

Figure 2: Developing the research question.

Figure 2 shows one way in which a qualitative research question can be developed. The process is initiated when the researcher recognizes that there is a particular interest that has prompted what could be called 'lay questions', that is questions which emerge not from 'professional looking', but from the everyday reflection on the world which is embarked upon often unreflectively by most if not all people. 'What do chaplains do anyway?' 'Can people with cognitive difficulties come to know God?' 'Why are men so prone to suicide?' The documenting of these lay questions and the researcher's provisional responses is essential for the effective development of the more formal questions that will steer the project. This process of documentation and reflection is the first step in the research process. It also provides a reference point for later in the research when the researcher may begin to wonder what it was that prompted the question in the first place.

Out of these intuitive reflections more formal lines of questioning emerge. 'What does the literature say about the nature of ministry within a secularized employment culture?' 'Is there a formal neurological link between cognitive ability and the ability to have religious experience?' 'What sociological evidence do we have to indicate why men commit suicide more than women?' These questions are then checked out and developed with reference to the appropriate bodies of literature. The formal research question may change through the life of the research because of the iterative and developing nature of the knowledge gained from the data collection. Referring to and interacting with other works and sources of information continues throughout the life of the research project and will inform and interact with each aspect of the process: the data collection, the analysis and the writing up of the project. The literature review is not a one-off search to make sure nobody has done the research before you. Rather the literature review becomes a tool of description, clarification and analysis at every stage of the research process (Green *et al.* 2001; Cooper 1998; Hart 1998).

John Howie gives very sound advice when he suggests that the research question should be:

- *important* – likely to contribute to an improvement in the situation you are interested in. This importance should also be located in the literature.
- *interesting* to others as well as yourself. The researcher may have a passionate interest in a topic which holds no interest at all to others either by word or in the literature.
- *answerable* in the time scale and with the resources the researcher has. This implies a 'cutting of the cloth'. Research

is only valuable when it is completed within a valid framework. A question may be fascinating but quite unanswerable given your own constraints (Howie 1989, p. 20).

We would want to make one addition to that list and that is that the question should be *simple and modest*. This should not be interpreted or misunderstood as uninteresting or simplistic. As will become clear, a simple question such as 'What do chaplains do?' can initiate a research process which is rich, complex and difficult. Nevertheless, a degree of common sense about range and complexity of the topic should be applied.

Data collection and analysis

Methods

Once the research question has been decided upon – and it is important to note that it may change as the research moves on – the researcher needs to clarify the method or methods of enquiry and analysis that best suit the chosen situation. The chapters in this book which document a variety of qualitative research projects demonstrate the way in which different methods can be used to collect different types of data. At this stage it is enough to note that there are different types of data collection methods and that these methods can be used in different ways also to analyse the data. The choice of method and the mode of analysis are deeply tied in with the epistemological positions that are assumed within the general outlook of the researcher and reflected in the research question. We have already discussed at length the implications of epistemology for qualitative research. It is, however, worth bearing in mind that the choice of method depends entirely on the research question and the situation under examination. To get at the lived experience of depression one requires a method which is phenomenological, giving a deep insight into the essence of the experience, and which is hermeneutical, providing the tools to interpret and understand that experience. To understand the spiritual experiences of a historically marginalized group of people such as people with learning disabilities, it is necessary to utilize a method which will empower people and genuinely allow their voice to be heard above the voice of the researcher. Again, in order to access ministers' views on suicide and the role of the congregation in preventing it and dealing with its aftermath, we need a method which will provide a forum that will enable ministers to speak safely and openly about issues that they rarely broach within a public context. If the correct method is not chosen it will not be possible to access the experience that the researcher desires to explore.

A common mistake within qualitative research is to feel an attraction to a type of data collection, for example the in-depth interview, and then, often too late, to discover that this method is not answering the research question or/and generating huge amounts of the wrong kind of data. For example, in Chapter 6 the research question was 'What is the role of the Chaplain?' In order to answer that question we had to decide which data collection method would help us most effectively. Asking chaplains directly would tell us what chaplains believed their role was and give us tangible examples. Using case studies would give us more material, and asking staff and patients would help us gain a different and deeper perspective. On the other hand, interviewing hospital managers, for example, might not have worked so well, since hospital managers viewed chaplaincy from a different angle. Indeed many had little idea of what the role of the chaplains actually was. That fact in itself was interesting and worthy of investigation. However, within the confines of the study and in line with the central research question, we had to make a number of decisions not to investigate questions that were interesting, but outwith the boundaries of the project's remit. The important thing to notice at this point is that the qualitative researcher must ask the vital questions: 'Who can help me address my research question?' 'How can I best help them help me in terms of method?' 'What questions can I *not* follow through on?'

Analysis

Put simply, data analysis is the process of bringing order, structure and meaning to the complicated mass of qualitative data that the researcher generates during the research process. It concerns the way in which interviews, text, reflexive diaries and all of the other data is collected and collated by the research. Analysis is a process of breaking down the data and thematizing it in ways which draw out the meanings hidden within the text. Analysing the data begins at the initial point of collecting the data. The interpretation and the reflective work of the researcher functions in conjunction with what Glaser has called 'theoretical sensitivity'. Strauss and Corbin (1990, p. 42) suggest that:

> Theoretical sensitivity refers to a personal quality of the researcher. It indicates an awareness of the subtleties of meaning of data. . . . [It] refers to the attribute of having insight, the ability to give meaning to data, the capacity to understand, and capability to separate the pertinent from that which isn't.

In the opinion of Strauss and Corbin theoretical sensitivity is developed through engagement with a variety of sources including the literature and the personal and professional experience of the researcher. Theoretical sensitivity is an important dimension of the rigour of a piece of qualitative research. Whether or not a piece of research is deemed credible or otherwise relates to the reader's confidence in the researcher's ability to retain a sensitivity to the data and make appropriate decisions as the project rolls out.

Silverman (2000) distinguishes different types of sensitivity that bear relevance to the qualitative researcher.

• Historical
• Cultural
• Political
• Contextual

The researcher must be aware of, and, as we shall argue below, be able to work within the boundaries that each dimension of sensitivity presents. Each dimension provides unique
and important insights which guide and inform the process of
interpretation and analysis. In particular Silverman raises the
importance of sensitivity in relation to the development of the
research question. As one is constructing the research question
one must be aware of and seek to recognize the significance
of these four levels of sensitivity. So, for example, we might
desire to develop a project exploring a situation within which
a particular church community refuses to accept the implementation of a new hymnbook. Without any knowledge of
the culture or the history of the congregation, we might simply
assume that a question such as: 'Why do church people refuse
to accept progress?' might be quite appropriate. Sensitivity to
the context and history might, however, inform us that they
are not refusing change, but a particular form of change, resist-
ance to which emerges from the unique culture and history
of the congregation. Subsequent chapters look at the issue of
analysis in some detail. For now, the importance of theoretical
sensitivity should be born in mind.

The role of the researcher in qualitative research

This focus on theoretical sensitivity brings us to one of the
most important dimensions of the qualitative research process:
the researcher. Unlike quantitative approaches to research
which can utilize complex tools of analysis such as statistical software or specialized laboratory equipment, the primary
tool of the qualitative researcher is herself. Within qualitative research it is the researcher who is the 'instrument of
choice' (Lincoln and Guba 1985). The key to good qualitative research does not lie in technical knowledge alone. Good
qualitative research requires a certain approach which is
dependent on the researcher's self-awareness and ability to
function effectively within an epistemological context which
is complex, rich, creative and sometimes dangerous. This

being so, paying close attention to the role of the researcher is vital.

What qualitative research is as a mode of knowledge-formation cannot be understood apart from the person of the researcher who carries it out. In concluding this chapter it will be appropriate to spend some time looking at the role of the researcher in qualitative research. A focus on the researcher as the 'primary tool' will allow us to work through and embody some final dynamics of the qualitative research and provide us with a firm foundation for the discussion that is to come.

Reflexivity

A key dynamic within the process of qualitative research is *reflexivity*. Previously we touched on the significance of reflexive knowledge. Here we want to begin to deepen that understanding by suggesting that reflexivity is perhaps *the* most crucial dimension of the qualitative research process. We would argue that reflexivity is crucial for every dimension of the qualitative research process from the selection of the question, the choosing of the methods and the writing of the final report. As such, we feel that reflexivity is not simply a tool of qualitative research but an integral part of what it actually *is*.

Put simply,

> reflexivity is the process of critical self-reflection
> carried out by the researcher throughout the research
> process that enables her to monitor and respond to her
> contribution to the proceedings.

Reflexivity is a mode of knowing which accepts the impossibility of the researcher standing outside of the research field and seeks to incorporate that knowledge creatively and effectively. Willig (2001) suggests that there are two types of reflexivity, *personal* and *epistemological*.

'*Personal reflexivity*' involves reflecting upon the ways in which our own values, experiences, interests, beliefs,

political commitments, wider aims in life and social identities have shaped the research. It also involves thinking about
how the research may have affected and possibly changed
us, as people and as researchers. (Willig 2001, p. 10)

Personal reflexivity urges us to take seriously the suggestion
that all research is, to an extent, autobiography. *Epistemological reflexivity* requires us to engage with questions such as:
How has the research question defined and limited what can
be 'found'? How has the design of the study and the method of
analysis 'constructed' the data and the findings? How could the
research question have been investigated differently? To what
extent would this have given rise to a different understanding
of the phenomenon under investigation? Thus, epistemological reflexivity encourages us to reflect upon the assumptions
(about the world and about the nature of knowledge) that
we have made in the course of the research, and it helps us
to think about the implications of such assumptions for the
research and its findings' (Willig 2001, p. 10).

The positivist paradigm of research would suggest that the
researcher should be a distant, detached and objective observer.
Within this model the researcher uses particular tools to
explore the *object* of research. Her task is to ensure that she
does not become part of the text in order that contamination
can be kept to a minimum. We have already argued that such
apparent objectivity is in fact a myth and that researchers are
participants and actors within the research process, whether
this is acknowledged or otherwise.

The reflexive qualitative researcher adopts a very different
position. She assumes that 'researchers both influence and are
influenced by the process of engaging in research. A reflexive
approach recognizes this reciprocal relationship and seeks to
make it explicit' (Northway 2000, p. 392). Rather than seeking after tools and methods that will distance her from the
research process, the researcher *becomes* the primary tool that
is used to access the meanings of the situation being explored.
In other words, the researcher does not simply access methods

and tools, but, as has been suggested, in fact *is* the primary research tool. Because of this, the need for reflexivity is paramount within the research process, especially when working with people who are in danger of implicit or explicit exploitation (Northway 2000). Reflexivity makes explicit the reasons behind particular modes of engagement, the choice of methods, the reasons for looking at this population or individual in this way, and the impact of the researcher's personal history and presuppositions on the situation. This in turn enhances the researcher's self-awareness and sensitivity to the moment.

Sensitivity and co-creation

Reflexivity and sensitivity are closely intertwined. Good qualitative research demands a high degree of sensitivity, and self-awareness for the accurate 'reading' of situations and the effective interpretation of people. While the researcher's primary task is to describe the encounter, in reality, she is inevitably a *co-creator* of the mode and content of the encounter. More than that, she is, implicitly or explicitly, a co-creator of the narrative that is the product of the research encounter. This idea of co-creation becomes sharply focused within the interview situation. Whether the interview is unstructured, semi-structured or structured (Robson 2002), the sensitivity of the researcher is paramount. The way in which a researcher responds, the follow-up questions asked, the researcher's intonation, their eye contact and body language will profoundly impact the way in which a participant tells their story (or doesn't as the case may be), and the way in which that story is heard and recorded by the researcher. In a very real sense the presence and verbal interaction of the interviewer with the interviewee is mutual and reciprocal. Sensitivity towards and awareness of the complex dynamics of the interview situation is crucial if this co-narration is not to turn into colonization. Chapters 4 and 8 will explore in more depth some of the implications of this aspect of the interview process.

Awareness of the significance of the present moment

The epistemological framework we have laid out thus far has
shown clearly the ways in which we consciously and uncon-
sciously create a multitude of meanings around the various
phenomena that we are investigating. In order to capture this
within the research process, the researcher must develop a deep
sense of the significance of the present moment. By this we
mean not only the respect that should be given to participants
for the honour they bestow upon the researcher in allowing
her to share in the intimacies of their lives, vital as this certainly is. Awareness of the significance of the present moment
is closely related to reflexivity and co-narration. It is to be
fully aware that the creation of meanings around the issues
being discussed may be contradictory, emotionally charged
and quite at odds with what the researcher initially thought
was going on. The process of building the narrative may shift
and change without the normal communicational bridges
that guide conversation. Sensitivity to the significance of the
present moment enables the researcher to move gracefully
with the rhythm of the encounter and to recognize the shifting uniqueness of experience. Such an awareness enables the
researcher to be open and sensitive enough to respond gracefully and creatively to this contradiction and confusion. By developing sensitivity to the significance of the present moment,
the researcher is able to shift direction and change gear as she
moves with the changing rhythms of the research encounter.
Openness, with sensitivity to and awareness of the obtuse, are
key skills that require to be learned, developed and honed. All
of them emerge from the practice of reflexivity. The interview
situations discussed in all of the case material illustrate this
point in different ways.

Reflexivity and the research interview

Reflexivity as described thus far is vital for all dimensions of
the research project. In order to illustrate this it will be help-

ful to explore some aspects of reflexivity as they relate to the interview process. This will both provide some vital insights into the nature and importance of interviewing, and illustrate the significance of reflexivity for this and every aspect of the qualitative research process.

Denzin and Lincoln suggest that:

> Qualitative research involves the studied use and collection of a variety of empirical materials – case study; personal experience; introspection; life story; interviews; artifacts; cultural texts and productions; observational, historical, interactional, and visual texts – that describe routine and problematic moments and meanings in individuals' lives. Accordingly researchers deploy a wide range of interconnected interpretive practices, hoping always to get a better understanding of the subject matter at hand. (Denzin and Lincoln 2000, p. 4)

This definition makes it clear that the nature of qualitative data is, by definition, wide and varied. Consequently there are a number of ways in which this data can be captured and analysed. However, a key tool of qualitative research that is obviously deeply linked to the researcher is the interview or, more precisely, the in-depth interview. Qualitative research seeks to create deep and rich insights into the meanings that people place on particular forms of experience. In order to access these experiences, it is necessary to engage in forms of deep conversation that will elicit this knowledge. Such conversation is necessarily deep, intense and rich, and as such committed and time-consuming.

Are interviews conversations?

Interviews are concentrated human encounters that take place between the researcher who is seeking knowledge and the research participant who is willing to share their experience and knowledge. Such encounters are designed to enable the researcher to access and understand the unique meanings, interpretations and perspectives that the participant places on the chosen subject. Interviews share similarities and differences with conversations. Both are open and dynamic modes of communication wherein the end-point is never totally clear until the verbal journey is over. Both are living things that evolve and change, and within which the participants themselves are changed both by what they learn, and by the nature and process of the I–Thou encounter that forms the essence of the interview process.

Nevertheless, we would suggest that interviews are not synonymous with conversations. Stephen Pattison (1989) suggests that

> Participation in a conversation implies a willingness to listen and be attentive to other participants . . . Conversations allow participants to discover things about their interlocutors which they never knew before; all participants end up seeing themselves and others from new angles and in a different light.

At one level there are strong similarities between interviews and conversations. The interview process is a meaningful human encounter within which both parties gain implicit and explicit knowledge about the other. It is a unique space for the creation and sharing of meaning. There are however important differences between an interview and a conversation. In distinguishing interviews from conversations there are two points that we would want to draw out.

The importance of power

First, a conversation is normally mutual, informal and has no fixed expectations attached to it. So, for example, one does not normally write up conversations and present reports on them that may be read by thousands of other people. An interview normally has at least a broad goal and an outcome that will be shared by many people. The interviewer is not simply chatting with the interviewee, but instead has an agenda that she needs to be very much aware of if she is not to impose that agenda onto the interviewee. The interviewer is in a position of power. She is an expert in the technicalities of the research process; she knows what is expected of her in her 'professional role' as a researcher and she has particular expectations about what the outcome of the research might be. She also has control over what is recorded, how it is recorded, what is deemed to be significant or insignificant and what will or will not end up as part of the final product. Having stated the goals she is trying to achieve (even the research topic sets some kind of agenda), the researcher sets up the parameters of the field of discussion and, through the nature of her questions and her responses to the situation, co-creates the narrative that emerges. She is therefore in a position where she can control, abuse and misrepresent the person she is encountering if she is not very much aware of these hidden power dynamics.

The interviewee on the other hand has considerably less power. He has signed a consent form stating that he is willing to participate in the study. But once the form is signed and the interview begins, his control over the project and indeed over his words begins to ebb away from him. He is, to a greater or lesser extent, dependent on the interviewer to represent him accurately, to record and interpret his words faithfully and to produce a report which, whether he likes it or not, in some sense resonates with their experience. The interviewee is therefore in a position of vulnerability which the researcher needs to be constantly aware of. Some of the implications of this and ways in which research design can overcome or at least recognize the importance of this are aired in the discussion on participatory research in Chapter 6. The interview is a dangerous gift that people offer to the researcher, a gift that can be received, treasured and accepted, or abused, manipulated and implicitly or explicitly discarded. Reflexivity and the recognition of the subtle and hidden dynamics of the interviewer's relationship to the interviewee are crucial.

Interviewing is not counselling

Second, interviewing is not counselling. Within a conversation it is very easy for one or both of the participants to begin to engage in implicit or explicit pastoral activities. When one party begins to speak about something that is emotional, difficult or unpleasant, a conversation participant can easily move into the role of counsellor. Most of us do this when we are conversing with our friends about difficult issues. An interviewer cannot act in this way. Our suggestion is not that interviews become cold and detached from the interviewee. Rather our point is that counselling is another role, one which the researcher has not been given permission to adopt even though they may be qualified to do so. So, for example, a student of one of the authors is currently working on a qualitative research project on bereavement among men. She is a qualified bereavement counsellor. However, the study has been carefully set up in order to ensure that this is not her role within the interview situation. The interviewees have been made fully aware of this, and clear lines of access to specialized bereavement counselling services have been arranged in case problems and issues arise within the interview situation which require further pastoral intervention. The key is to make sure that there are back-up referral mechanisms in place before the study begins, which can enable the researcher to pass on to an appropriate caring agency the interviewee who may have particular needs. Keeping the role boundaries between the participants in the interview process is vital for both parties. This will be explored in more detail as we move on.

Interviews, then, contain elements of similarity to conversations, but their focused nature, the necessary power dynamics and their non-clinical focus make them markedly different. The importance of reflexivity as a vital dynamic of this, and indeed of the whole qualitative research process, is clear.

Summary

In closing this chapter, it will be helpful to draw together the various threads that we have woven. Table 2 below outlines the key point we have put forward in this chapter.

Table 2: Features of qualitative research

Research question	Is it important, interesting, answerable and simple?	Select the topic with care and with sensitivity to the various dimensions of the situation.
Methodology	Are the basic epistemological and philosophical assumptions inherent in the research question reflected in the proposed data collection and analysis methods?	Establish the type of knowing that the research question elicits and requires: realism, critical realism, social constructionism, etc.
Method	How can I answer my question?	The range of qualitative methods available go from immersion and participation to semi-structured interviewing. Each carries with it advantages and difficulties. Make sure the method fits the research question.

Analysis	How am I going to analyse my data?	Establish: What kind of data you are going to collect, the research question, and the basic clustering mechanism. How will you present the data? Will you use data analysis software? If so, which package?
		The process of analysis: 1. The nature of the main categories derived 2. The themes that emerge from the main categories 3. Code the themes into sub-themes 4. Give meaning to the themes and sub-themes through interpretive and reflective work 5. Reflect on the interpretation

Sampling	Who can answer my question and how do I choose them? What kind of sample do I want? Is my sample theoretical, purposive, or opportunistic?	Theoretical sampling is staged and offers opportunities to collect data from a variety of sources that can answer the question. As the theory grows so the sample evolves. It is commonly associated with grounded theory.
		Purposive sampling is where the sample is specifically chosen because it offers the best chance of answering the question. The sample is usually taken at one point in time.
		Opportunistic sampling is the least accurate and implies that the sample is taken from people who are around at the time and who have some relationship to the research question.

| Validity | Will the methods I am using measure what is intended? Is the analysis related to data collection? Does the data collection process collect what it says it does? | This is helped by *Triangulation* – this is where either more than one method, more than one researcher or more than one analytic technique is used. *Feedback to participants* – this is sometimes known as member checking and helps confirm the analysis and contribute to it. *Identification of outlyers* – this involves finding examples of extremes in the data and cross-examining these rather than treating them as uninteresting because they are extremes. |
| Reliability | Could the same data and analysis be produced by another researcher? | This is helped by: *Careful records* of the Data collection process. *Researcher journal* kept from the start of the research and noting theoretical and practical developments as well as researcher insights. |

		Triangulation in analysis. *Independent* co-analysers.
Generalizability	Is there a mechanism for theoretical generalizability or transferability?	Qualitative research does not claim to be generalizable in the probabilistic sense as we have seen. However, it is expected that general analytical comments can be drawn from the data which throw theoretical light on similar but different situations. For instance, the implications of the role of the chaplain in Scotland may not be entirely dissimilar to the role of the chaplain in England or Wales or in a different form of chaplaincy.
Dissemination and feedback	How are the participants engaged in the findings?	It is not uncommon to invite respondents' comments as part of the final report. Workshops and presentation in some form is also a means of member-checking.

Conclusion

In this chapter we have tried to give readers a sense of what qualitative research is and how it is done. As our model has developed, the ways in which qualitative research can be effectively used by the practical theologian has become clearer. Qualitative research is a useful tool of complexification which can enable the practical theologian to gain rich and deep insights into the nature of situations and the forms of practice that are performed within them. It would appear that qualitative research holds a good deal of potential for practical theological research. However, before we move on to explore the research process in more detail, we need to spend some time working through some of the significant tensions between the two disciplines. It is clear that there are tensions and apparent contradictions, particularly with regard to epistemology and the ways in which the two disciplines define 'reality', which need to be addressed before qualitative research can be used faithfully in the service of God. The following chapter will draw out and explore some of the critical tensions between Practical Theology and qualitative research with a view to clearing the way for a critical examination of the qualitative research projects presented in the second half of this book.

3

Practical Theology and Qualitative Research Methods

Thus far we have constructed a model of Practical Theology and a perspective on qualitative research that has enabled us to see some of the possible areas of dialogue and integration. It would seem that qualitative research does have the potential to become a useful tool for the practical theologian as she goes about her task of analysing and reflecting theologically on complex situations. Nevertheless, there are areas of tensions and apparent contradiction, particularly over epistemology and the nature of truth and knowledge. The inherent tendency of qualitative research to assume a fundamentally non-foundational epistemology which is highly sceptical about the possibility of accessing truth that has any degree of objectivity, stands in uneasy tension with the theological assumption that truth is available and accessible through revelation. If the practical theologian is going to be able to work effectively and authentically with qualitative research, this tension will need to be resolved.

Also, we need to begin to look at exactly how qualitative research can be used by the practical theologian. How does it actually link with theology? What kind of conceptual structure will allow the two disciplines to come together in a way that prevents one from collapsing into the other? Precisely where does the information elicited by qualitative research fit into the process of practical theology research? We begin this chapter with an exploration of Practical Theology method. We examine critically one of the most prominent models for doing Practical Theology and integrating the social sciences: *mutual critical correlation*. This method seeks to bring together an interpretation of the religious experience and the contemporary situation in a way that enables both to engage in critical and potentially transformative dialogue. We highlight the pros and cons of this approach and offer a mode for integrating the social sciences into practical theological method that overcomes some of the inherent difficulties with mutual critical correlation. The key question we wrestle with in this chapter is:

> how can Practical Theology and qualitative research
> be brought together in a way that is both mutually
> enhancing and faithful?

Method and methodology

In Chapter 2 we discussed various methods that are used within the process of qualitative research. We have not yet defined precisely what we mean by the term 'method'. As we move on to discuss Practical Theology method, it will be useful to tie down a little more tightly the meaning of the term 'method' as we use it here.

There is a common tendency to use the terms 'method' and 'methodology' as if they were synonymous and interchangeable. In fact they are not, and it is important to be clear about the distinction between these two concepts. *Methods* are specific techniques that are used for data collection and analysis. They comprise a series of clearly defined, disciplined and systematic procedures that the researcher uses to accomplish a particular task. Interviews, sampling procedures, thematic development, coding and recognized techniques and approaches to the construction of the research question would be examples of qualitative research methods.

Methodology is connected to method, but in a particular way. The term 'methodology' has a number of different meanings. Formally it relates to the study of methods. More broadly, the term methodology has to do with an overall approach to a particular field. It implies a family of methods that have in common particular philosophical and epistemological assumptions.

Methods are carried out within a particular set of methodological assumptions. So, for example, within the social sciences the 'interpretative paradigm' that we examined in Chapter 2 provides a particular methodology. The various approaches to interviewing, reflexivity and data analysis used within that paradigm comprise the various methods. Within the natural sciences the philosophical perspective of 'logical positivism' provides a common methodology. Logical positivism is a perspective on knowledge which assumes that knowledge cannot be found in intuition or revelation, but only through perceptual experience. Within this model, which is closely associated with the scientific model critiqued in Chapter 2, such things as intuition or revelation are assumed, not necessarily as false, but certainly as meaningless. The particular scientific methods that emerge from this methodology are represented by the types of laboratory-based activities of traditional science and the more recent development of such things as randomized controlled trials. The important thing to bear in mind is the way in which the methodology determines the methods used. The methodology of constructivism does not sustain the method of randomized controlled trials. The methodology of logical positivism does not support the method of in-depth phenomenological interviews.

Practical Theology method

Practical Theology utilizes a variety of methodologies and a wide range of accompanying methods. The model of Practical Theology that we have developed here is deeply embedded within the hermeneutical/interpretative paradigm. It seeks to interpret a variety of dimensions – situations, scripture and tradition, Christian practices – and it draws on various hermeneutical perspectives in its attempt to understand God and human experiences. As such, the overall methodology within which Practical Theology sits and from which it develops its various methods is the interpretative paradigm as described in Chapter 2.

However, the overarching methodological framework within which Practical Theology takes place is theology. Theology offers a perspective on knowledge, truth and reality which constantly brings it into conflict with other methodologies, including the interpretative paradigm. This is no small point, bearing in mind the relationship between method and methodology. It is clearly necessary for the practical theologian to be aware that particular methods that it may draw from the interpretative paradigm may conflict in significant ways with the assumptions of the underlying theological methodology. For example, a methodology which assumes that truth is totally inaccessible, and that the social world is *nothing but* a series of ever-changing social constructions, clashes in fundamental ways with a methodology which assumes the reality of revelation and the reality of creation. The question then is: How can practical theology find a method that does not clash with its essential theological methodology?

The model of Practical Theology developed in Chapter 1 reveals it to be a discipline which is fundamentally hermeneutical, correlational, critical and theological. It is hermeneutical because it recognizes the centrality of interpretation in the way that human beings encounter the world and try to 'read' the texts of that encounter. It is correlational because it necessarily tries to hold together and correlate at least three different perspectives – the situation, the Christian tradition and another source of knowledge that is intended to enable deeper insight and understanding. It is a critical discipline because it approaches both the world and our interpretations of the Christian tradition with a hermeneutic of suspicion, always aware of the reality of human fallenness and the complexity of the forces which shape and structure our encounters with the world. It is theological insofar as it locates itself in the world as it relates to the unfolding eschatology of the gospel narrative;

a narrative that indicates that truth and the grasping of truth is possible. Any methods used by the practical theologian will need to reflect and hold in tension all of these dimensions.

The method of mutual critical correlation

One way in which Practical Theology has attempted to deal with this correlational dimension of its practice is through the development of a particular method: *mutual critical correlation*. Mutual critical correlation provides a way of holding together in critical tension the four components of the practical-theological task that we highlighted above. Mutual critical correlation sees the practical-theological task as bringing situations into dialectical conversation with insights from the Christian tradition and perspectives drawn from other sources of knowledge (primarily the social sciences). It is a model of integration which seeks to bring these dimensions together in a way which respects and gives an equal voice to each dialogue partner.

Tillich's method of correlation

The method of mutual critical correlation finds its roots in a modification of Paul Tillich's (1951) method of correlation. Tillich sought to correlate existential questions that were drawn from human experience with theological answers offered by the Christian tradition.

> In using the method of correlation, systematic theology proceeds in the following way: it makes an analysis of the human situation out of which the existential questions arise, and it demonstrates that the symbols used in the Christian message are the answers to these questions. (Tillich 1951, p. 62)

> There is a mutual dependence between question and answer. In respect to the content, the Christian answers are dependent on the revelatory events in which they appear; in respect

to form, they are dependent on the structure of the questions which they answer. (Tillich 1951, p. 64)

In developing an understanding of Tillich's approach it will
be helpful to draw on John Wesley's quadrilateral model of
theological sources of revelation. Wesley proposed that *scripture, tradition, experience* and *reason* provide the four primary sources for Christian truth. As we listen to each of these
we develop a holistic view of revelation which respects the
omnipotence of God. Within Tillich's method of correlation,
both reason and experience, as they are worked out within
particular situations, provide us with questions which we then
need to address to Christian scripture and tradition.

Reason and experience	→	Existential/theological questions	→	Answers from scripture and tradition

In this way the questions that emerge from human experience (the product of rational reflection) find their answers in
scripture and Christian tradition. Through this method Tillich
hoped to achieve a degree of relevance for the Christian tradition within a rapidly secularizing social context.

Tillich's model is helpful insofar as it opens up a constructive dialogue between Christianity and contemporary culture.
However, practical theologians working from within an interpretive methodology have noted that Tillich's model seems to
assume that it is somehow possible to distil 'pure theological
truth' which can then be applied to the questions produced
by the world without these questions in turn challenging the
theological response. His method is a uni-directional model of
reflection which applies Christian truth to the world without
allowing the world to significantly question particular interpretations of that truth.

In response to such a critique, subsequent thinkers within
Practical Theology such as Seward Hiltner (1954) and most
influentially David Tracy (1975) expanded the critical dimen-

sion of Tillich's model and incorporated a dialectical element which enabled the correlation between scripture, tradition, experience and reason to be *mutually* correlative and critical. This model critically correlates questions and answers drawn from the Christian tradition with questions and answers taken from other sources of knowledge that reside within and impact upon society and culture. It does not however assume that the answers given by the religious tradition have necessary priority within the dialogue. The conversation is mutual with all parties potentially having an equal say, and all parties in turn become open to radical transformation. We can sense here some resonance with the previous discussion on qualitative research and the idea of multiple realities or perspectives emerging from a single phenomenon or situation.

In this way Christian tradition and practice and other forms of theory and practice are brought together in mutually constructive critical dialogue, in an attempt to do justice to the insights and revelation that are gained through reflection on the socio-historical context and the theological/existential demands of Christian faith and practice. As Paul Ballard puts it:

> At the heart of this model is a dialogue between the tradition and (usually) the findings and theories of contemporary social sciences with a view to providing a theoretical basis for practice. Its strength lies precisely in its recognition of the need for theoretical dialogue. (Ballard 1992, p. 3)

David Tracy sees this method as central to the understanding of the essence of Practical Theology:

> Practical Theology is the mutually critical correlation of the interpreted theory and praxis of the Christian fact and the interpreted theory and practice of the contemporary situation. (Tracy in Browning 1983, p. 76)

This method has been used effectively in different ways by a number of contemporary practical theologians and forms the basic dynamic within the various models of the pastoral cycle which has become so popular as a mode of theological reflection within Practical Theology (Pattison and Woodward 2000; Willows and Swinton 2000).

Mutual critical conversation

One particularly clear and helpful model of mutual critical correlation is presented by Stephen Pattison in his paper 'Some straws for the bricks' (Pattison 1989). Pattison offers a model that he describes as *mutual critical conversation*. He bases his model of theological reflection on the metaphor of a conversation between friends; friends who have differences, but who also have much in common and much to learn from one another. This conversation takes place between the Christian tradition, the social sciences and the particular situation that is being addressed (or the possible hypothetical outcomes of particular understandings and practices). Such a conversation is necessarily open and 'dangerous'. Pattison points to the fact that conversation is:

> a living thing which evolves and changes. . . . The participants in a conversation are changed, both by what they learn and by the process of conversing with other participants. . . . Participation in a conversation implies a willingness to listen and be attentive to other participants. . . . Conversations allow participants to discover things about their interlocutors which they never knew before; all participants end up seeing themselves and others from new angles and in a different light. . . . The concept of conversation does not necessarily imply that participants end up agreeing at every point or that the identity of one over-rides the character of the others. . . . Conversations are often difficult and demand considerable effort because participants start from very different assumptions and understandings. Considerable energy may have to be expended to try and understand the relevance or importance of another participant's contribution. (Pattison 1989)

Thus it is in the spirit of an open dialogue, which genuinely seeks after truth, respects the perspectives offered by other disciplines and is prepared to invest appropriate quantities of intellectual energy in assessing and discovering the nature of that truth, that this model of critical conversation works itself out (see Figure 3).

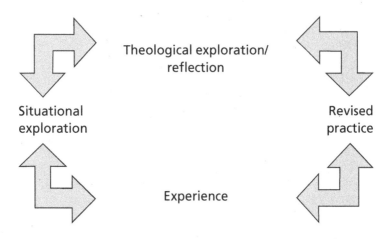

Theological exploration/
reflection

Situational
exploration

Revised
practice

Experience

Figure 3: A model of theological reflection: Pattison's 'mutual critical conversation'.

Figure 3 shows in simple form how this method of critical conversation functions and gives us an initial inkling of the role of qualitative research within such a conversation. A situation is identified within the contemporary practice of the Church or the world which the practical theologian decides is worthy of reflection and exploration. The practical theologian then begins to explore the situation using other sources of knowledge. It is here that qualitative methods can effectively be utilized in uncovering the hidden meanings within the situation and the practices that participants embark upon in response to their particular understandings of the world. This data with all of its challenges, contradictions and surprises is then taken into constructive dialogue with scripture and tradition with a

view to developing revised forms of practice that will impact
upon and transform the original situation. Within the model
of critical correlation, the data acquired from qualitative
research has an equal voice within the conversation and can
challenge theology and tradition in exactly the same way as
theology and tradition can challenge its findings. While taking
full cognisance of the findings of other theological disciplines,
the practical theologian has a necessary prophetic freedom to
challenge established interpretations of scripture and tradition in the light of the ongoing practices and experience of
the Church, and to challenge specific forms of practice in the
light of scripture and tradition. In this way it can be seen that
theory and practice are held together in critical tension with
each feeding into and off the other; each constantly challenging, enhancing and clarifying the other. The intention of this
method is to enlighten, broaden, deepen and if necessary challenge both ecclesial practice and theological understandings
in the light of current practice, Christian tradition and the
illumination which can be gained from other sources of knowledge. Theological understanding is assumed to be emergent
and dialectic rather than simply revealed and applied.

The danger of translation

In many ways these authors would be sympathetic to much
that is offered by the model of critical correlation. We believe
that Practical Theology is a constructive theological discipline
and that the Church has much to learn from what is being revealed in the present through the continuing work of the Trinitarian God in the world as well as from the past as revealed
in scripture and tradition. The model of mutual critical correlation opens up the opportunity to challenge interpretations
of scripture and tradition that may have become distorted,
forgotten or deliberately overlooked. The prophetic challenge
of this method is crucial to the overall practical-theological
task. We also believe that, given appropriate boundaries, the
social sciences have the potential to be useful critical dialogue

partners in the process of doing theology in ways that are challenging but necessary.

Nevertheless, we feel that the interpretative dimensions of the method of critical correlation can be theologically problematic if certain issues are not clearly addressed. The idea of mutual conversation is helpful, but it does beg the question as to whether it is theologically appropriate to give all of the dialogue partners equal weighting within the research process. If theology and theological knowledge is in fact open to radical change and transformation as it interacts with the social sciences, then there are important issues at stake. Can the social sciences *really* challenge theology at a fundamental level as the wider implications of this method would suggest? If so, this would indicate that the social sciences can be given, at least in principle, some kind of epistemological priority over theology. This raises the important question: *How can a system of knowledge created by human beings challenge a system of knowledge that claims to be given by God?* If mutuality truly means that both parties have an equal voice in the research process and that the social sciences can actually override theology on central issues, then the danger of idolatry becomes a real possibility.

A christological perspective on mutual critical correlation

How then can we hold on to the possibility of truth and revelation, while at the same time recognizing the inevitable interpretative dimensions of the way that we interact with scripture and tradition and the need to look to other disciplines to aid us in the process of spiritual discernment? In her book *Theology and Pastoral Counseling: A New Interdisciplinary Approach* Deborah van Deusen Hunsinger explores how it might be possible to bring together theology and the social sciences (in her case depth psychology) in a way which prevents them collapsing into one another. In order to achieve this goal, she draws on the theology of Karl Barth and in particular his thinking about the nature of Christ as laid down in the Chalcedonian

Creed produced by the Council of Chalcedon in AD 451. This council wrestled with the mystery of how Jesus could at once be fully God and at the same time fully human. This extended quotation from van Deusen Hunsinger will help sum up the Chalcedonian position as she wants to put it forward:

> The Council of Chalcedon in A.D. 451 was an ecumenical assembly that defined how the divine and human natures of Jesus Christ were to be conceived in the teaching of the church. The Council declared that the person of Christ was to be understood as 'complete in deity and complete in humanity' and that his two natures were related 'without separation or division' and yet also 'without confusion or change.' . . . According to Barth's interpretation of Chalcedon, Jesus' divine and human natures, each present in a complete or unabridged way, were to be understood not only as related without confusion or change but also with conceptual priority assigned to the divine over the human nature. While the divine and human natures of Christ remained conceptually distinct and were not to be confused with one another, they also could not be separated or divided from each other. They constituted the identity of Jesus Christ only as they occurred in differentiated unity. . . . only when the divinity of Jesus is assigned precedence over his humanity does Barth regard the relationship between them as properly conceived. (van Deusen Hunsinger 1995, p. 63)

From this christological position, van Deusen Hunsinger goes on to apply what she describes as 'the Chalcedonian pattern' to the relationship between theology and psychology (and by extension theology and all other sources of knowledge). She suggests that the relationships between the two disciplines/ sources of knowledge should be viewed as similar to the relationship between the divine and human natures of Christ, in that there should be:

- Indissoluble differentiation
- Inseparable unity

- Indestructible order
- Logical priority of theology.

It will be helpful to explore each of these dimensions in turn.

Indissoluble differentiation

The idea of indissoluble differentiation means that the two natures (of Christ) are related without confusion or change (van Deusen Hunsinger 1995, p. 65). When applied analogously to the relationship between theology and the social sciences, the suggestion is that the two disciplines have specific roles to play and that they reveal specific forms of knowledge which should not be confused with one another. So for example, we may be able to develop a model of health and human well-being from psychology. However, this is not to be confused with theological terms such as shalom or salvation, which may be connected, but which have different and separate theological meanings when understood within their own parameters. Put slightly differently, theology can identify itself with psychology, but psychology does not have the power to identify itself with theology (Barth 1956, p. 18).

Inseparable unity

By inseparable unity van Deusen Hunsinger means that the two natures coincide in an occurrence without separation or division. (van Deusen Hunsinger 1995, p. 65). Relating this to theology and the social sciences, she suggests that at the same time as their difference should be acknowledged, so also should their unity. The social sciences can offer complementary knowledge which will enhance and sharpen our theological understandings. Similarly theology will offer perspectives which will challenge and shape the perspectives offered by the social sciences. One does not discount the other; in a similar way to the way that divinity and humanity were held together in the person of Christ, so also theology and the social sciences hold together in critical complementary tension within the lived experience of the researcher or the practitioner.

Indestructible order

The idea of indestructible order is of vital importance. By indestructible order, van Deusen Hunsinger means that in and with their differentiated unity, the two natures of Christ are asymmetrically related, with one term having logical precedence over the other. While both theology and the social sciences are united and separate, the voice of theology has logical precedence within the critical conversation. Theology talks of ultimate issues, of life, death, God and the meaning of life. The social sciences do not have the capacity to deal with these issues. Thus theology has logical precedence within the conversation. We will discuss this more fully below. Here the important thing to notice is that within this structure, theology and the social sciences are differentiated, unified and ordered in a very particular way.

Logical priority

Within van Deusen Hunsinger's framework, any conversation between theology and the social sciences is by definition asymmetrical, with theology having logical priority over any other dialogue partner. Van Deusen Hunsinger wants to argue that such a position is not simply a faith stance (although that clearly and appropriately forms an aspect of her position), but is also a *logical precedent for interdisciplinary enquiry*. This is a big statement which requires further clarification. Drawing on the philosophical work of W. F. R. Hardie and S. L. Hurley, van Deusen Hunsinger describes the idea of logical precedence in this way: '*A* is logically prior to *B* . . . when the definition of *B* mentions *A*, but the definition of *A* does not mention *B*' (Hardie 1968, p. 52). Hurley clarifies and develops this point helpfully:

A conceptual account of X is an account of what we mean, understand, and intend ourselves to be talking about, when we talk or think about X. If X is not correctly thus accounted for in terms of Y, then X is conceptually independent of Y; if Y is accounted for in terms of X, where X is not in turn accounted for in terms of Y, then X is both conceptually prior to and independent of Y. (Hurley 1989, p. 10)

Following this line of argument and applying it to the subject matter of this book, we might say that theological concepts are conceptually independent of the data offered by qualitative research methods. Similarly, the data of qualitative research is conceptually independent of theological concepts. 'This conceptual independence of the two from each other [reflects] the "indissoluble differentiation" between them' (van Deusen Hunsinger 1995, p. 68). However, theology does not acquire its ultimate significance from the data of qualitative research. It is an independent source of knowledge that draws on qualitative research for the purposes of clarification and complexification, but has no need of it in terms of its self-understanding. Within the process of practical-theological research, qualitative research data *does* acquire its significance from theology. Theology's significance is therefore logically prior to and independent of qualitative research data. Qualitative research is thus seen to have a relative independence of theology and also an ultimate dependence on it. Qualitative research can describe events and processes within the world. To that extent it is independent of theology. However, it can only describe these event and processes as they relate to theology. Thus, to translate van Deusen Hunsinger's words about the relationship between theology and psychology, from a Barthian standpoint, although qualitative research data is both logically independent of and dependent on theological categories in different ways, theological categories are by definition both logically prior to and independent of psychological categories with respect to their significance (van Deusen Hunsinger 1995, p. 69).

A revised model of mutual critical correlation

Such an approach both challenges the potentially unfettered interpretative dimensions of the model of critical conversation and also enhances it. It challenges it insofar as it asserts that the dynamic within the critical conversation is not symmetrical and is not purely interpretative. It assumes that there is a realist dimension to the conversation that gives logical priority to theology and which must not be overlooked or ignored. While there remains much scope for critical dialogue and mutual reflection, the conversation is always inherently asymmetrical with theology having necessary logical priority. By insisting on the significance of a realist ontology, and affirming 'that God *really* speaks through the biblical witness; i.e. that there is such a thing as divine revelation' (van Deusen Hunsinger, unpublished personal correspondence), van Deusen Hunsinger's position enhances and protects the theological dimensions of practical-theological enquiry and helps prevent a drift into forms of relativism which ultimately risk removing the significance of the reality of God from the practical-theological endeavour, thus retaining a sense of urgency, telos and mission.

The significance of interpretation and meaning-making

However, while we would agree with the basic epistemic priority given to theology within the critical conversation, certain aspects of van Deusen Hunsinger's model are problematic. It is not clear how van Deusen Hunsinger's model would deal with the dimensions of theological knowledge which emerge from particular communities and which may challenge some accepted interpretations of divine revelation. Her position emerges from her own faith, based in the ecumenical councils and creeds. As such it is thoroughly embedded with the theology of the Reformed tradition. However, the diverse ways in which these creeds have been interpreted and the current fragmentation of the Church over issues of doctrine and the nature of revelation would cause us to have a hermeneutic of suspicion as to whether or not our interpretation of revelation is pure, faithful or otherwise. It is clear that van Deusen Hunsinger's position is a commitment of faith. This is of course not a bad thing. The significance of faith commitments for doing Practical Theology is a centrepiece of the argument of this book. Indeed, to suggest that her position is a faith position is not unusual or derogatory. All commitments to bodies of knowledge and epistemic systems are foundationally faith commitments, even within the so-called 'hard sciences' as people like Kuhn (1962) and Polanyi (1958) have ably shown and we have suggested in Chapter 2. The problem is not that we take up a position that is informed by faith. The question is, do we have enough self-awareness and reflexivity to be aware enough of our own commitment to a body of knowledge that we can recognize those dimensions within it which *are* social constructs and which *do* require a more critical and less dogmatic position? There is an important issue of reflexivity here.

We are in agreement with van Deusen Hunsinger that revelation is real and that God does speak meaningfully and uniquely through the witness of scripture. Nevertheless, in the light of our previous discussion, we cannot escape from the fact that doing theology is an interpretative enterprise within which divine revelation is interpreted by human beings who are fallen, contextually bound and have a variety of different personal and denominational agendas. Within the critical conversation which is Practical Theology, we recognise and accept fully that theology has logical priority; qualitative research tells us nothing about the meaning of life, the nature of God, cross, resurrection or the purpose of the universe. Nevertheless, the ways in which that revelation is interpreted, embodied and worked out are deeply influenced by specific contexts and individual and communal histories and traditions. These contexts, histories and traditions profoundly impact upon the types of practices that are developed in response to revelation and the degree to which these practices will remain faithful to that revelation. This being so, it is not inconsistent to suggest that even when given logical priority, theology itself can be and indeed should be the subject of critical reflection and challenge.

Such a position is consistent with Barth's general way of thinking. As John Webster observes:

> Barth is unremittingly hostile to any idea that some other science is necessary as a grounding for theology – he takes that as a denial of the fact that revelation is a sufficient basis for the knowledge of God. But that being said (and it is a big thing to say, and makes Barth very different from the correlationist styles of Practical Theology in the Tillich tradition), Barth is not in principle hostile to drawing on spheres of enquiry outside theology, and does it all the time in his work (philosophy, primarily, though also history). Nor does he think there is anything such as 'pure' theology – in his account of knowing God (Barth 1961–2) for instance, he is clear that there is no way in which we can step outside of ourselves and engage in some transcendental act of knowing which would lift us out of the creaturely conditions of knowing. But nor would he say that all theology is *simply* socially constructed, because he thinks that theology is an activity in the Church and the Church is a sphere in which the Spirit is at work. The work of the Spirit doesn't mean that theology is somehow immunised against outside influence or made infallible; but it *does* mean that the theologian can expect guidance, protection and chastening in order to think in ways which are appropriate to the gospel. For Barth, theology is not a citadel of achieved ideas, but a process, the event of being stripped of what is not in accordance with the truth of the gospel and of learning how to think in correspondence to the event of God's self-communication. (personal communication – unpublished)

We would suggest that Practical Theology can utilize qualitative research methods to aid in this process of ensuring that

Christian practice is in correspondence to the event of God's self-communication.

Hospitality, conversion and critical faithfulness

In the light of this we propose that bringing together situations, theology and qualitative research requires three things: *hospitality, conversion* and *critical faithfulness*.

Hospitality

Hospitality is an important Christian practice that relates, in essence, to the Spirit-enabled ability to show kindness, acceptance and warmth when welcoming guests or strangers (Hebrews 13:1–3). Here, we use the term to express an attitude within which Practical Theology can welcome and sit comfortably with qualitative research methods. The practical theologian shows hospitality towards the method she is working with. She welcomes it and takes what it has to say seriously. However, she welcomes these methods *as a Christian theologian.* In showing hospitality towards the research method the practical theologian does not need to compromise her position or pretend that she is something she is not. In being hospitable towards other forms of knowledge and alternative approaches to the world, the object is not to seek after the lowest common denominator within which dialogue can take place. It is rather to create a context wherein the voice of qualitative research can be heard, respected and taken seriously, but with no a-priori assumption that theology needs to merge, follow or fully accept the perspective on the world that is offered to it by qualitative research. Such an offer of hospitality is crucial for the development of the type of reflective conversation that, as has been suggested, is vital for the process of doing Practical Theology. However, the conversation takes place within the epistemological boundaries that van Deusen Hunsinger outlines and that we have developed in the previous sections.

Conversion

In order to achieve this there requires to be a change in the
way that the practical theologian views and uses qualitative
research. We would want to suggest that in order to be faithfully utilized, qualitative research requires to undergo a process of *conversion*. The metaphor of 'conversion' is evocative
and important. Conversion relates to a turning to God in a
way that decisively changes one's life from an old way to a
new way of life. In our case this means qualitative research
moving from a position where it is fragmented and without
a specific telos or goal, to a position where it is grafted in to
God's redemptive intentions for the world. God 'converts' the
field of intellectual enquiry outside theology, in this case qualitative research, and uses it in the service of making God's self
known within the Church and from there on into the world.
This of course makes sense in the light of the model of Practical Theology we have offered in Chapter 1. Conversion requires that certain things are laid aside and other things are
taken to the forefront. So, for example, the suggestion that
reality is *nothing but* a social construction requires a movement towards some form of critical realism. Above all, conversion relates to a movement which recognizes the reality of
God. This recognition means that certain dimensions of the
one converted are deeply challenged and changed.

Perhaps the primary thing that is laid aside when one is
converted is one's autonomy and freedom. The one converted
realizes that he or she is not autonomous or free, but is inevitably deeply dependent on God and God's grace for sustenance
and direction. In relation to qualitative research, this will
mean that the autonomy of the disciplines that make up this
field and their traditional insulation of themselves from God
is no longer sustainable. The practical theologian now views
them as in God's service. This does not mean that there cannot be critique and challenge of established Christian practices and ideas. Such critique is critical for faithful living. It
does mean however, that qualitative research methods now

seek to develop that critique *from the inside* and not as outsiders. Thus the epistemological framework that is adopted
within qualitative research methods is unalterably theistic, but
always open to the possibility of learning new things which
will develop our understanding of God and the practices of
the Church.

This notion of conversion applies also to the practical theologian. The practical theologian is converted by being taught
something new. Van Deusen Hunsinger's model tends to leave
the ancillary discipline untouched by theology, simply attrib-
uting it a subordinate role. The approach outlined here offers
ways in which theology can hold on to the reality of God's
revelation and engage critically with the dialogue partner in
ways that might be transformative for both partners. In this
way we can hold together the correlative dimensions of the
practical-theological task and take seriously the essence of
what van Deusen Hunsinger attempts to do in her asymmetrical model.

Critical faithfulness

This new knowledge born out of hospitable conversation
and creative conversion enables the practical theologian to
challenge forms of 'false consciousness' and to develop an
approach which is marked by *critical faithfulness*. Such a form
of faithfulness acknowledges the divine givenness of scripture
and the genuine working of the Holy Spirit in the interpretation of what is given, while at the same time taking seriously
the interpretative dimensions of the process of understanding
revelation and ensuring the faithful practices of individuals
and communities.

Such a position enables us to take seriously that which is
given within our traditions and to respect the centuries of tradition and reflection that have gone into establishing our understandings of divine revelation. It enables us to adopt a critical
and creative position towards qualitative research methods
and to begin to explore what the metaphor of conversion

means as we seek to re-imagine ways in which qualitative research methods can be sanctified and used appropriately. It also enables us to be realistic about the interpretative nature of our grasping after divine revelation and to recognize that truth is, at least to an extent, emergent and dialectic; emerging from committed, critical dialogue between situations, Christian tradition and the knowledge that we gain, *inter alia*, through the use of qualitative research methods. Figure 4 provides a framework which will tie together the things that have been discussed in this chapter thus far and provide a framework for the development of an emerging model.

Stage 1: The situation

At this intuitive, pre-reflective phase we begin to explore the nature of the situation and work out what we think are the key issues. Here we note the situation as we see it in the present and articulate in some initial form what *appears* to be going on. We may want to explore the literature that surrounds this area, we may decide to do some provisional historical and cultural explorations. All of this will help us to gain an understanding of the situation at this initial level. This process enables us to begin to articulate our initial observations and identify the primary issues that will be explored during the research process. All of this relates to the discussion of formulating the correct research question which we suggested earlier was crucial for the process of qualitative research. It is also crucial for practical-theological research for similar reasons. This initial analysis is not dogmatic or overpowering. Rather it is an attempt to make some initial sense of what is going on, why things are structured in the ways that they are and why people function in particular ways.

Stage 2: Cultural/contextual analysis

Here we begin to deepen our initial reflections by entering into dialogue with other sources of knowledge which will help us

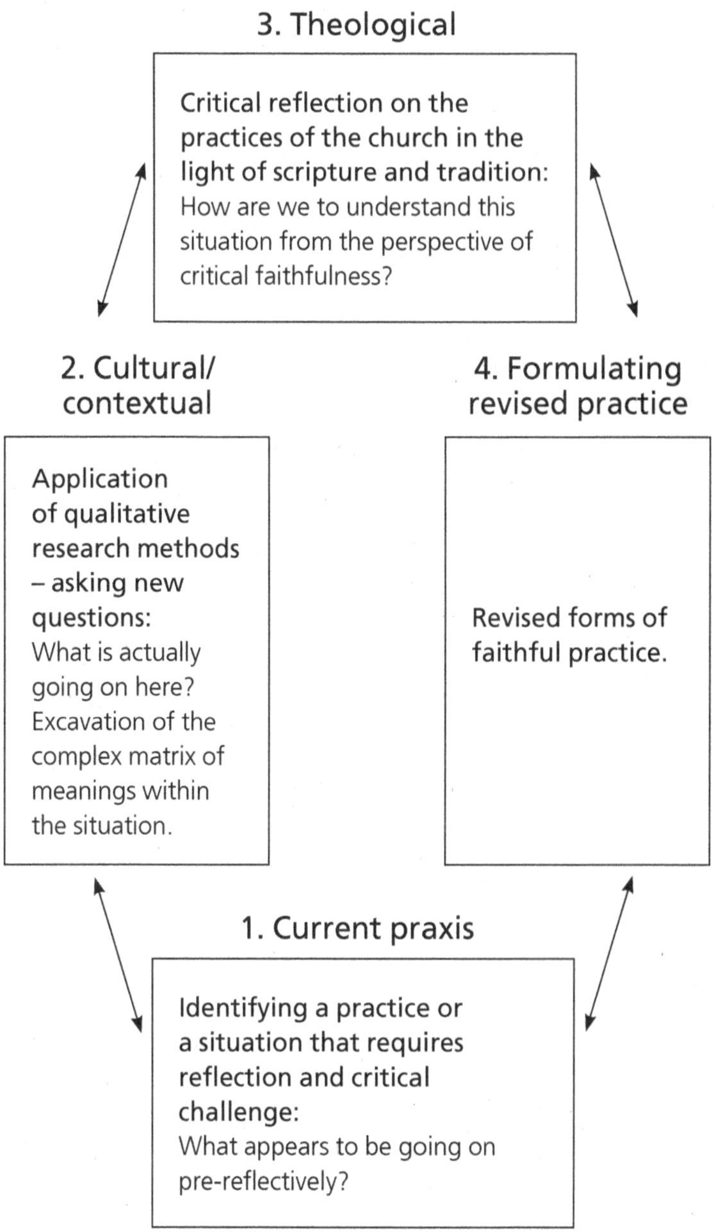

3. Theological

Critical reflection on the
practices of the church in the
light of scripture and tradition:
How are we to understand this
situation from the perspective of
critical faithfulness?

2. Cultural/
contextual

Application
of qualitative
research methods
– asking new
questions:
What is actually
going on here?
Excavation of the
complex matrix of
meanings within
the situation.

4. Formulating
revised practice

Revised forms of
faithful practice.

1. Current praxis

Identifying a practice or
a situation that requires
reflection and critical
challenge:
What appears to be going on
pre-reflectively?

Figure 4: Practical theological reflection.

develop a deeper understanding of the situation. At this stage
we begin to engage in a disciplined investigation into the various dynamics (overt and covert) that underlie the forms of
practice that are taking place within the situation. The intention here is to enhance and challenge our initial impressions
and begin to develop a deep and rich understanding of the
complex dynamics of the situation. It is at this stage that qualitative research has an important role. By engaging with the
complexities of the hermeneutical dimensions of the situation
new insights about its nature and structure begin to emerge.
Some of these will confirm our initial intuitive reflections, but
others will challenge and enhance that which we thought we
knew.

Stage 3: Theological reflection

At this stage we begin to reflect on what we have discovered
from a theological perspective. This is not of course to suggest
that theology has been absent from stages 1 and 2. It is simply
that at stage 3, we begin to intentionally reflect theologically
in a more formal manner. Here we begin to focus more overtly
on the theological significance of the data that we have been
working with in stages 1 and 2, and how it can be used to
develop our understanding of the situation we are exploring
and the practices which emerge from the various practices we
encounter. At this stage we begin to develop the conversation
by drawing out the implicit and explicit theological dimensions of the situation, sifting through the data and exploring the ways in which they complement and challenge one
another; searching for authentic revelation in a spirit of critical faithfulness and chastened optimism.

Stage 4: Formulating revised forms of practice

At stage 4 we return to the situation that we began with.
Here we draw together the cultural/contextual analysis with
the theological reflection and combine these two dimensions

with our original reflections on the situation. In this way the conversation functions dialectically to produce new and challenging forms of practice that enable the initial situation to be transformed into ways which are authentic and faithful.

This basic model, which some readers will recognize as based on the pastoral cycle, is helpful in locating the place and function of qualitative research methods and its relationship to the theological dimensions of the practical-theological task. Of course in reality the circle is not followed through step by step. There is movement in various directions as new insights raise fresh questions and enable us to see things differently. Nevertheless, Figure 4 offers a helpful conceptual map which allows us to locate qualitative research within the process of doing Practical Theology. Those who have been involved with qualitative research will also see similarities to the hermeneutical circle and to action research methods. We will explore this latter connection more fully in the conclusion to this book.

Conclusion

Having laid down an understanding of Practical Theology, qualitative research and how the two might effectively and faithfully be brought together, it is now necessary to begin to explore how, in the light of this, we might begin to engage in the process of qualitative research. Part 2 comprises an examination of five qualitative research projects that the authors have carried out. Reflection on these projects will enable us to come to a constructive understanding of what the conceptual framework laid down in the first part of the book might look like when it is put into practice. Each of the following chapters reflects particular ways in which Practical Theology and qualitative research methods can come together to enable the process of informed theological reflection on particular situations. The situations explored are as follows:

1 Researching personal experience
2 Researching a local church

3 Researching ministry
4 Researching pastoral issues
5 Participatory research.

Taken together, the various explorations of these diverse yet
interlinked situations will provide invaluable insights into
the ways in which qualitative research can contribute to the
practical-theological enterprise. The studies do not follow
the model presented above in a simple A+B=C manner. They
are written in a way which emphasizes the role of qualitative
research in the process of Practical Theology in the light of the
discussion presented thus far. Readers will nevertheless see the
ways in which the dynamics of theological and cultural reflection highlighted within the model work their way out in the
exploration of the situations that are presented. Each chapter
follows a similar pattern:

- *The situation* – An initial analysis of some of the complexities of the situation.
- *The method* – An examination of the particular methods
  deemed to be appropriate for gaining new knowledge about
  this situation.
- *Theological reflection* – An example of theological reflection on the data with a view to indicating how this might
  be done.
- *Suggestions for revised forms of practice* – Indicative suggestions for forms of revised practice based on the findings.

Taken together these pieces of research will provide a depth
and a clarity that will enable the reader to see clearly the complex processes at work in constructing and carrying out a
piece of qualitative research, in a way that enables the type
of faithful practice that we have suggested forms the heart of
Practical Theology's task.

Part 2

The Practice of Research

4

Researching Personal Experience: Depression and Spirituality

Introduction

At the heart of the enterprise of qualitative research is the search for meaning and the process of interpretation. The ways in which meaning is sought and discovered vary as does the understanding of what interpretation is and the role it should perform within the research process. In this chapter we will explore in some depth the nature of interpretation by focusing on a particular method of qualitative research which has come to be known as *hermeneutic phenomenology*. As well as giving us insight into an important qualitative method, a focus on this way of doing qualitative research will provide some vital hermeneutical insights and understandings that will help us understand the interpretative process as it relates to the other methods presented in this book. Our focus in this chapter will be on a study carried out by one of the authors that sought to understand the lived experience of depression. An examination of this study will provide some vital insights into the importance of hermeneutics for qualitative research and practical theology.

The situation: depression in Western society

The purpose of the study was to explore the lived experience of depression and to examine some of the ways in which a person's religious faith might function in enabling them to cope and live with this particular form of mental health problem. By drawing together hermeneutics and phenomenology in order to listen carefully to the voices of sufferers, it was possible to capture something of the essence of the experience of depression in a way that would be illuminative and transformative.[1]

The social context of depression

Depression is one of the most prevalent forms of mental health problem within the United States and Great Britain. Depression is most common in people aged 25–44 years, and 1 in 6 people will have depression at some point in their life (Mental Health Foundation). The World Health Organisation estimates that depression will become the second most common cause of disability worldwide (after heart disease) by 2020 (Samaritans). There is a tendency within Western culture to use the term 'depression' as synonymous with sadness. However, depression, particularly in its most severe form, is much more than sadness. Depression manifests itself in various forms and to varying degrees. People with *mild* depressive episodes find it difficult to continue with their work and social lives, but usually continue to function, albeit less well than normal. Those experiencing *moderate* depressive episodes have a wider range of symptoms, which are present usually to a greater degree. Sufferers find it very difficult to function normally at work or home. People living with *severe* depressive episodes typically may also include features such as: great distress and agitation, slowed thought and movement (psychomotor retardation), ideas of guilt (Gilbert 1992, p. 22), suicidal fantasies or plans which may be acted upon, pronounced somatic symptoms, psychotic symptoms (Gilbert 1992, p. 2). The people involved in this study had all experienced severe depressive episodes.

---

1 Some of the research presented in this chapter was originally presented in Swinton 2001. It is presented here in a different and much edited form with permission.

The cultural context of depression

An interesting feature of depression is the ways in which it is impacted upon and indeed to an extent constructed by culture. For example, Arthur Kleinman (1980) in his research on depression in Taiwan, discovered that within this culture which stigmatized depression and made it socially unacceptable, people tended to somatize their sadness. People experienced the same symptoms and feelings of sadness that are the marks of depression in the West, but, because it is a socially unacceptable disease, they presented to their doctors with sore backs, stomachs, etc. The same feelings, but with different manifestations due to different social circumstances.

Brown *et al.*, in their research into depression in women in the Hebrides Islands of Scotland, discovered that religious communities could be protective for women against depression. They offered support, friendship and a place where problems and concerns could be aired and worked through in community. However, culturally, men did not express themselves in this way and tended not to be involved in religious communities. Instead they drank to excess and became involved in acts of violence. The same feelings but a different social expression.

Research such as this sensitizes us to the ways in which a person's beliefs, contest and culture can impact upon and profoundly shape their experience of depression. It is not possible to understand the experience of depression apart from the unique individual who experiences it within a very particular context which is filled with specific meanings, values and expectations. In order to understand depression, it is necessary to understand what it means to that particular person within her particular context.

Spirituality and depression

An initial and intuitive reflection on depression reveals it to be an inherently spiritual condition. Its central features of profound hopelessness, loss of meaning in life, often perceived loss of relationship with God or higher power, low self-esteem and general sense of purposelessness, all indicate a level of distress which clearly has spiritual connotations.

Within Christian tradition, depression has frequently been recognized as having a spiritual dimension. St John of the Cross's *Dark Night of the Soul* offers deep insights into the nature of spiritual depression. The dark night:

> puts the sensory spiritual appetites to sleep, deadens them, and deprives them of the ability to find pleasure in anything. It binds the imagination, and impedes it from doing any good discursive work. It makes the memory cease, the intellect become dark and unable to understand anything, and hence it causes the will to become arid and constrained, and all the faculties empty and useless. And over this hangs a dense and burdensome cloud, which afflicts the soul, and keeps it withdrawn from the good. (John of the Cross 1959, ch. 16)

Commonly expressed feelings such as Why me? Why can't I find a point in living? My life has no meaning any more, in a real sense express the depths of meaningless which are the hallmarks of clinical depression. Meaning and the search for meaning are recognized as central aspects of human spirituality (Carroll 1993; McFadden 2000; Wong 1998). The crisis of meaning brought about by depression is thus seen to be a deeply spiritual experience. There is therefore a sense of spiritual crisis inherent within depression that will not necessarily be alleviated by psychotherapy or pharmacology, particularly if the true nature of the crisis goes unnoticed (Karp 1996). Describing precisely what that element of crisis comprised for the participants and how they found ways of finding resolution and hope, was one of the possible outcomes of the research project.

The Method

The particular method chosen for this study was *hermeneutic phenomenology*. It is interesting to note that hermeneutic phenomenology is, in a sense, both a methodology and a method in the sense that these words were defined in Chapter 3. It is a methodology insofar as hermeneutics and phenomenology provide an epistemological and, as we shall see, an ontological framework within which the process of qualitative research is carried out. However, they also comprise a method insofar as the concepts they supply can be used to provide specific tools of qualitative engagement which are crucial to hermeneutic phenomenological method. Hermeneutic phenomenology therefore sits on an interesting borderline between method and methodology.

The intention of this approach is to allow the researcher access into the inner experiences of research subjects. Although it has not been used extensively in the study of spirituality, significant studies have begun to emerge that explore the lived experience of spiritual distress (Smucker 1996), spiritual relationships (Stiles 1994), recovery from alcoholism (Bowden 1998), the essential elements of spirituality (Tongprateep 2000) and hope (Breitbart and Heller 2003). These studies provide rich insights into human experience and provide vital understandings which can significantly inform the practice of care. Before the present study, this approach had not been used to explore the experience of spirituality within the context of depression.

As hermeneutics and phenomenology are important underpinnings for all of the studies presented in this book, it will be helpful to spend some time exploring precisely what these philosophical frameworks are and how they function within the research process. John McLeod (2001) suggests that:

> Anyone who has ever completed a piece of qualitative research knows that doing *good* qualitative research is not merely a matter of following a set of procedural guidelines. The principal source of knowing in qualitative inquiry is the

researcher's engagement in a search for meaning and truth in relation to the topic of inquiry . . . in the end it is the capacity of the inquirer to see and understand that makes the difference. (p. 55)

It is the process of precisely how we come to see and understand that the philosophical perspectives of phenomenology and hermeneutics attempt to clarify.

How do we know what we know? – Phenomenology

Let us begin with some provisional definitions of the two central concepts. *Phenomenology* is a philosophy of experience that attempts to understand the ways in which meaning is constructed in and through human experience. This perspective views a person's *lived experience* (the thing in itself) of and within the world as the foundation of meaning. It 'seeks to set aside any assumptions about the object of inquiry, and build up a thorough and comprehensive description of the "thing itself"' (McLeod 2001, p. 56). The aim of phenomenology is to determine what an experience means to a person quite apart from any theoretical overlay that might be put on it by the researcher, and to provide a comprehensive and rich description of it (Moustakas 1994)

> [P]henomenology is the study of the lifeworld – the world as we immediately experience it pre-reflectively rather than as we conceptualize, categorize, or reflect on it. . . . Phenomenology aims at gaining a deeper understanding of the nature or meaning of our everyday experiences. Phenomenology asks, 'What is this or that kind of experience like?' It differs from almost every other science in that it attempts to gain insightful descriptions of the way we experience the world pre-reflectively, without taxonomizing, classifying, or abstracting it. (Van Manen 1990, p. 9)

Phenomenology does not attempt to build theory that can be used to *explain* the way the world works. Rather it seeks to present plausible insights that bring us in more direct contact with the world (Van Manen 1990, p. 9).

> Transformative experience alters action. Knowledge result-
> ing from phenomenological inquiry, becomes practically
> relevant in its possibilities of changing the manner in which
> a professional communicates with and acts towards another
> individual in the very next situation he/she may encounter.
> Phenomenological knowledge reforms understanding, does
> something to us, it affects us, and leads to more thoughtful
> action. (Van der Zalm 2000)

Phenomenological insight, in providing deep insights and understandings into the way that things are, enables people to see the world differently, and in seeing it differently to act differently towards it.

How do we know what we know? – Hermeneutics

Hermeneutics functions in quite a different way from phenom-enology. In hermeneutics, understanding is always from a par-ticular position or perspective. It is therefore always a matter of *interpretation*. The researcher can never be free from the pre-understandings and 'prejudices' that inevitably arise from them being a member of a culture and a user of particular modes of language. Indeed, as we shall see, the act of interpre-tation is dependent on such prejudices.

Hermeneutics relates to the general science of interpretation (Reedier 1988). It has to do with the ways in which human beings interpret and make sense of the world. It is important to note that in the perspective being developed here, hermen-eutics (the act of interpretation) is not simply something that people do. Rather, with Gadamer (1981) we would want to argue that hermeneutics is what people *are*, that is, human beings are by definition interpretative creatures. In other words, hermeneutics is an ontological rather than merely an epistemological position. We cannot be anything other than interpretative beings. Humans can only make sense of the world through utilizing complex and ongoing hermeneutical processes which are carried out implicitly and explicitly, reflectively and unreflectively. Within the research context, the practice of hermeneutics relates to making explicit and formal the ontological propensity of human beings to interpret the world.

Hermeneutics and phenomenology

There are clearly tensions and differences between these two perspectives: with one seeking to explain the world and people's experiences within it in an objective, unbiased way, and with the other, as we will see, claiming that interpretation, bias and prejudice are crucial to the ways in which human beings encounter the world. Nevertheless, while there are dissimilarities between phenomenology and hermeneutics, there are also important similarities:

1 Both assume an 'active, intentional, construction of a social world and its meanings for reflexive human beings' (Mcleod 2001, p. 57). While phenomenology seeks to explore the true meaning of a phenomenon, it does not rule out that that meaning may be the product of interpretative processes. So, for example, a phenomenological study of the ways in which ministers perform pastoral care will seek to get to the essence of the phenomenon being observed by seeking to exclude any biases or preconceptions by the researcher. It does not, however, rule out the fact that those being observed may construct their meaning of pastoral care through an interpretative process. It simply does not see an analysis of this dimension as part of its task.
2 Both 'deal mainly with linguistic material, or with language-based accounts of other forms of representation' (van Deusen-Hunsinger 1995). Central to the analytical task of both hermeneutics and phenomenology within qualitative research is the significance of language and the importance of analysing texts. Certainly the modes of analysis may

differ, but the central importance of language and text is shared and crucial.

3 Both are concerned with the development of *understanding* which may assist people to anticipate events, by sensitizing them to possibilities. In distinction to the perspective of the natural sciences and its primary task of explanation, both hermeneutics and phenomenology seek to provide modes of understanding which, while potentially transformative, are not necessarily explanatory.

It is interesting to note that each of these points of complementarity are also points which mark out the approaches as significantly dissimilar to the natural sciences. Indeed, the use of hermeneutics and phenomenology as research methods has emerged from a growing dissatisfaction with a realist philosophy of science based on the study of material entities with no reference to cultural or social context (Ryan 1996). Hermeneutics and phenomenology presents a significant challenge to positivism,

Hermeneutic phenomenology

In the qualititative research method of hermeneutic phenomenology, both of these perspectives are brought together in order to provide a rich description of the experience and a necessary interpretative perspective on lived experience.

As a method, hermeneutic phenomenology displays both descriptive and interpretive elements. It is

> *descriptive* (phenomenological) . . . because it wants to be attentive to how things appear, it wants to let things speak for themselves; it is . . . *interpretive* (hermeneutic) . . . because it claims that there are no such things as uninterpreted phenomena. The implied contradiction may be resolved if one acknowledges that the (phenomenological) 'facts' of lived experience are always already meaningfully (hermeneutically) experienced. Moreover, even the 'facts' of lived experience need to be captured in language (the human

science text), and this is inevitably an interpretive process.
(Van Manen 1990, p. 181)

The hermeneutics of Hans Georg Gadamer

There are a number of philosophical perspectives that researchers have used to inform the process of hermeneutic
phenomenology. In the study that is our current focus, it was
the philosophy of Hans Georg Gadamer (1981) that formed
the foundational perspective. For Gadamer hermeneutics is a
fundamental human act and a significant way of being in the
world. In line with the ontological position outlined above,
Gadamer argued that the act of interpretation is not 'just one
of the various possible behaviours of the subject, but the mode
of being' (Gadamer 1981, p. xviii). In advocating the ontological nature of interpretation, Gadamer indicated clearly that
he was not concerned with offering a methodology for the
human sciences (1981, p. xiii), but was more concerned with
clarifying the conditions in which understanding can take
place (1981, p. 263). From this ontological position he went
on to develop some key concepts that were important for the
method that was used in this study.

The limitations of method

Somewhat ironically, bearing in mind the way that his thinking
forms the heart of this qualitative research method, Gadamer
was highly suspicious of method. He argued that any perspective that a method offers necessarily imposes limitations and
boundaries. The particular questions that emerge from within
the plausibility structures of the method will allow the user
to access only a limited amount of knowledge, that is, only
the amount of knowledge that the method's questions will
provide. Methods are therefore inherently limited and limit-
ing. The main problem with methods is that those who utilize
them become embedded in a particular perspective and find it

impossible to see the limitations that that perspective enforces upon them. Gadamer's key point here is that we must become aware of our own embeddedness or historical situatedness and constantly reflect on the ways in which this situatedness influences the way that we interpret our world.

Bracketing?

The suggestion that the researcher must be aware of his situatedness contrasts with Husserlian phenomenology (Husserl 1963). Insofar as Gadamer discounts the possibility of bracketing, his position puts him at odds with phenomenology as previously described. Bracketing refers to the suspension of a person's beliefs and preconceptions in an attempt to look at the phenomenon 'as it is', that is, without any intrusion from the researcher. By adopting a stance of objectivity and neutrality, the phenomenon can be seen and understood for what it essentially is (Corben 1999). In rejecting the possibility of such objectivity or neutrality, Gadamer presents a perspective that assumes our pre-understandings or prejudices to be necessary in order for us to make sense of the world.

Experience

Gadamer develops a particular perspective on experience which it is necessary to understand. He suggests that the ability to remain open to new experiences which may be radically different from previous ones is of the utmost importance.

> [T]he experienced person proves to be . . . someone who is radically undogmatic; who, because of the many experiences he has had and the knowledge he has drawn from them, is particularly well equipped to have new experiences and to learn from them. The dialectic of experience has the proper fulfillment not in definite knowledge but in the openness to experience that is made possible by experience itself. (1981, p. 335)

The phrase 'dialectic of experience' refers to a quality of experience which Gadamer calls *negativity*.

> The fact that a particular experience once experienced can never occur to us in the same way again, that is, as new, leads us to understand that experience is a process which depends upon each new experience contradicting something which we already know or feel. For Gadamer, experiences which merely confirm something that we already know are not genuine experiences, but, rather, are repetitions of previous events. 'Every experience worthy of the name thwarts an expectation' (Gadamer 1981, p. 356). (Murray 2005)

Murray, reflecting on Gadamer's suggestion that the experiencing consciousness has 'reversed its direction', that the one experiencing has become aware of its own experience, makes an important observation:

> Clearly [Gadamer] has captured the recursive nature of experience, that is, the back and forth or dialectical movement of the hermeneutical circle. Just as true experience leaves one open to new experiences, each new experience also influences our understanding of previous experiences, which then, in turn, widens even more the horizon within which we may have yet more new experiences. As Gadamer points out, 'the structure of reflexivity is fundamentally given with all consciousness' (Gadamer 1981, p. 334). And it is this awareness of the recursiveness or reflexivity of thought which precedes and allows what Gadamer calls historically effective consciousness. (Murray 2005)

Thus, the process of knowing and the development of knowledge relates to a constant process of experience – surprise – re-encounter with renewed experience.

Prejudice

For Gadamer, understanding is not something that can be done by separating subject from object in the way that the natural sciences assume. Both subject and object are bound together and mediated by a common cultural and historical context, and *effective history*, that is, personal experience and cultural traditions. Gadamer refers to these pre-understandings as *prejudices*. When one approaches a phenomenon, one inevitably does so with particular prejudices and pre-understandings which inevitably affect the process of interpretation. However, prejudice is not something that is negative or that we should try to eliminate. Quite the opposite, prejudices are crucial for our developing understanding of the world. Gadamer understands prejudice as

> a forestructure or a condition of knowledge in that it determines what we may find intelligible in any given situation. [He] replaces the opposition between truth and prejudice with the assertion that prejudice – our situatedness in history and time – is the precondition of truth, not an obstacle to it. (Hekman 1986, p. 117)

In order to understand and assimilate new experiences it is necessary to draw on these pre-understandings. Indeed,

> to try to eliminate one's own concepts in interpretation is not only impossible, but manifestly absurd. *To interpret means precisely to use one's own preconceptions so that the meaning of the text can really be made to speak for us.* (Gadamer 1981, p. 358, my italics)

As well as being a swipe at Husserl's idea of bracketing in transcendental phenomenology, Gadamer's position here is also a reassertion of the ontological demand for the significance of contextuality in understanding.

Thus, the basic structure of a person or community's effective-history constrains and to an extent defines the range of possible interpretations, excluding some possibilities and calling forth others. It is therefore necessary for a person to be aware of their own historical situatedness and the ways in which it influences their interpretations of those texts, objects, people, and events we choose to seek to understand (there is a deep resonance here with the idea of reflexivity as outlined in Chapter 2). The *historically effective consciousness* is one which is truly open to experience (as previously defined), and which is aware of the influence and significance of their pre-understandings. Thus, for Gadamer, the image of the researcher as separate from the object of study is replaced by a dialectical understanding that suggests the need for dialogue and conversation between the text and the researcher; conversation that does not exclude the researcher's pre-understandings, but constructively draws them into the dialogical process.

The fusion of horizons

Gadamer argues that it is naive to believe that one can ever be truly detached from the object of interpretation. In order to understand a text we need a fusion between the horizons of the world of the researcher/interpreter and the world of the text. From this perspective, the task of the researcher is not to bracket their prejudices, but to fuse their horizons with the horizons of the research participants in a way that will deepen and clarify the meaning of the experience being explored. Horizons are closely connected with prejudice in that they contain an individual's and a society's underlying assumptions about the way the world is and how people and things should function within it.

Thus, the task of the researcher is to enter into a constructive, critical dialogue with the text within which a fusion of the two horizons is brought about. The fusion of horizons is a version of the hermeneutic circle (described below), in that it is a crucial dialogical process that takes place between interpreter and text. Understanding occurs when the horizons of the scholar intersect or fuse with the horizon, context or standpoint of the objective enquiry. Hekman (1986, p. 104) likens this process to Buber's (1958) idea of the 'I–Thou' relationship in the sense that it demands a radical openness to the experience of the other and a respect for experiences that transcend one's own horizons.

Gadamer explains the metaphor of the horizon as 'the wide superior vision that the person who is seeking to understand must have. In order to acquire a horizon means that one learns to look beyond what is close at hand – not in order to look away from it, but to see it better within a larger whole and in truer proportion' (1981, p. 272). This means that the horizon of the interpreter includes her entire forestructure, that is, what she finds intelligible given her specific cultural perspectives and her place in history (Thompson 1990). Understanding occurs when the horizon of the scholar intersects or fuses with the horizon of the object of enquiry (Smith 1996).

Thus interpretation and understanding is more than simply adopting an empathic stance with the text's author. Rather it is a creative process within which even the author's original assumptions concerning the meaning of the text may be challenged and deepened. According to Smith (1998)

> Gadamer suggests that in trying to understand a text, the interpreter is always performing an act of projection, that is, 'he projects before himself a meaning for the text as a whole as soon as some initial meaning emerges in the text' (1981 p. 236). These meanings only emerge because one is reading with particular expectations (guided by one's horizon), and there is a continual testing of rival foreconceptions as meanings emerge in the text. 'This constant process of new projection is the movement of understanding and interpretation' (p. 236).

Here we have the interaction of both hermeneutic circle with its dialogical movement from part to whole, and the fusion of horizons.

The hermeneutical circle

Both Smith and Murray have mentioned the significance of the hermeneutical circle. Before we move on to explore how these hermeneutical principles apply to qualitative research we must spend a little time reflecting on the importance of this final dimension of Gadamer's thinking. The hermeneutical circle refers to the interpretive process wherein the scholar moves backwards and forwards from 'whole to the part and back to the whole' (Gadamer 1981, p. 259). Single words only make sense within the context of a wider linguistic pattern. Likewise that wider pattern is determined by the specific meanings of individual words. It is out of this interpretive, dynamic movement that meaning and understanding emerge. For example, the word 'football' on its own can have a variety of meanings according to the context within which it is used. It is only within the context of a sentence that one can assess whether or not the word 'football' is referring to the sport as a whole, or simply the leather ball that is used as part of the sport. Depending on whether it is prefixed with the word 'American' or 'British' will to an extent determine the precise nature of the sport being referred to. If one introduces the word 'rugby', this again changes the meaning and shifts our understanding of the word football. Thus the meaning of the word emerges from its interaction with its wider context of other words or sentences. Similarly a sentence provides only partial information if it is viewed within a paragraph. A paragraph only makes sense within the context of a chapter, the chapter finds its full meaning within a book, and so forth. This circular exercise is an ongoing process, moving from whole to part and then back to whole. In order to make sense of the whole situation, it is necessary to move backwards and forwards between the meaning of the words and the meaning of the wider text (Swinton 2001). This is the type of movement that is present within the hermeneutical circle.

Research design

With this philosophical framework in mind, we can now return to the research project under discussion. The design framework used in the study was an adaptation of the research frameworks developed in the work of Smith (1996), Diekelmann *et al.* (1989) and Van Manen (1990). The research process moved through a series of ten stages that can be outlined as follows

1 A series of in-depth interviews were carried out in line with the general principles of phenomenological interviewing (Van Manen 1990; Moustakas 1994)
2 The interviews were recorded on minidisks which were then transcribed by the researcher, thus creating a text which could become the locus of the interpretive process
3 The texts were then entered into MARTIN, a software program specifically designed to assist in phenomenological research. MARTIN is a Windows tool aimed at facilitating analyses rather than generating new theories. In this sense it differs from other similar software packages such as NUD*IST[2] or NVivo, which are designed for grounded theory and theory generation. MARTIN was designed to reflect the ways a researcher thinks about and interacts with written texts. 'Utilizing object-oriented programming and Windows' graphics interface, MARTIN offers researchers an alternative to fixed labeling schemes by using the computer screen as the electronic equivalent of a desktop. Documents and interview texts are displayed in windows that can be moved, stacked, tiled, resized, or reduced to icons. Each text occupies its own window, and multiple texts can be displayed simultaneously, making it easy to work across texts. Notes can be attached freely and discarded at any time' (Swinton 2001, p. 105).
4 The researcher then began to immerse himself in the texts that had been created. This involved reading them over and over in order to get a feel for the content and for the subtle nuances of the interactions with research participants.

---

2. NUD*IST stands for Non-numerical, Unstructured, Data: Indexing, Searching and Theorizing. Put simply, it works with textual documents, and facilitates the *indexing* of components of these documents; is able to *search* for words and phrases very quickly; and claims to support *theorizing* through enabling the retrieval of indexed text segments, related memos, and text and index searches; and through the construction of a hierarchically structured tree to order index categories.

5 During this process of immersion, and moving between individual phrases, sentences, chunks of narrative and the entire text and context (the hermeneutical circle), themes began to emerge that appeared to incorporate something of the essence of the experience of depression and the role of spirituality in living with it. Van Manen (1990, p. 79) describes phenomenological themes as 'structures of experience'. In searching for and seeking to analyse a phenomenon, 'we are trying to determine what the themes are, the experiential structures that make up that experience'. Themes are not objects of generalization. Rather, they are 'like knots in the webs of our experience, around which certain lived experiences are thus spun and thus lived through as meaningful wholes. Themes are the stars that make up the universe of meaning we live through. By the lights of these themes we can navigate and explore the universes' (Van Manen 1990, p. 90). Themes do not necessarily represent the experience as initially interpreted and understood by the person themselves, but are a constructive product of the fusion of the researcher's horizons with those of the participants as together they embark upon the quest for meaning and understanding. All of the participants within this study commented on the way in which the themes that emerged from their transcripts made them aware of aspects of their experience that they had not reflected on or recognised previously. This being so, the emergent themes may participate in a process of consciousness-raising within which research participants discover new aspects of their situation.

6 These themes were then collected and organized using MARTIN, and representative phrases and statements collected to illustrate and elucidate the various themes and their meanings (Van Manen 1990, p. 30). The various themes were grouped together and the researcher embarked upon a process of dialogical reflection, moving between the extrapolated themes (the parts) and the text as a whole (the hermeneutical circle) in order to check the

authenticity of the themes, and to develop a deeper, fuller understanding of the meaning that was being expressed by the research participants.

7 The researcher then constructed a thematic analysis of each of the research transcripts. This involved structuring the themes in line with the various emphases within the text and developing an initial interpretation of the lived experience of each of the participants. Relevant extracts were taken from the text and used to illustrate and elucidate the various themes

8 These reconstructed, thematized narratives were then given back to the participants for validation. The author then spent some time with the research participants working through the transcripts and making any alterations necessary caused by obvious misunderstanding or misinterpretation. At this stage the participants became co-researchers, actively participating in the shaping and interpreting of the data. A copy of the original transcripts and their thematic analyses was also given to independent expert qualitative researchers, who were then asked to validate the themes identified by the researcher.

9 All of this data was collated, and the final process of interpretive reflection and narrative construction was embarked upon. This involved a return to the process of immersion, within which the texts were compared and contrasted in a search for constitutive patterns which unified all of the texts.

10 Writing is fundamental to this form of research. 'Creating a phenomenological text is the object of the research process' (Van Manen 1990, p. 111). Through the process of writing and rewriting, the interpreted accounts were brought together and a final account constructed

11 The research product was fed back to the research participants and their thoughts and comments were taken into consideration prior to the final draft of the account being produced.

The cohort

The research was based on six depth interviews with a purposive sample of three men and three women who had experienced depression for an extended period of time (at least two years). All were currently living in the community, and all were regularly in contact with the mental health services. As the purpose of the investigation was to create a rich description of their experiences, rather than to explain them, a small sample was deemed appropriate (Moustakas 1994; Smith 1996). The participants were volunteers who responded to the invitation of the researcher and a call for volunteers put out at a local day centre for people with mental health problems. Permission was granted by the local healthcare ethics committee to approach people with long-term mental health problems with a view to exploring the subject matter of the project.

The interviews

Data was collected using unstructured interviews. This was deemed most likely to elicit rich data that would enable participants freely to relate their personal narratives in ways that are uninhibited by the researcher's personal agenda and the boundaries of fixed questions. All interviews were initiated with the question: 'What is it that gives meaning to your life?' The interviews lasted for 45 minutes to an hour and took place at a number of locations: within Aberdeen University, at the local mental health drop-in centre and in the participant's own home. As well as these primary interviews, the researcher also spent time with the participants at the various stages of feedback and reconstruction. These feedback sessions also provided useful information and clarification that proved invaluable to the overall research process.

Issues of validity

The question of validity in qualitative research continues to be a matter for debate. (Koch 1996, 1998, 1999; Lincoln and Guba 1985). Some argue that the idea of validation is an inappropriate interpolation from the natural sciences, that is, that the idea of validation requires an assumption of normativity and generalization which is the antithesis of the essence of qualitative research in general and hermeneutic phenomenology in particular. While we accept the importance of such a critique, these authors nonetheless feel that issues of rigour and validity are of importance for qualitative research. Such issues as reflexivity and the idea of merging horizons require mechanisms that will ensure that the interpretative process does not diverge from the given 'script' in ways that are misleading, inappropriate and which actually misrepresent the phenomenon being explored. Prejudice and pre-understanding may well be necessary for the process of interpretation. However, if these elements of the researcher's experience serve to occlude or indeed exclude the horizon of the research participant, then there arise significant issues of ethics and authenticity. We therefore feel that a process of validation is a necessary dimension of the qualitative research process.

However, this process diverges significantly from the processes of validation that are found within the natural sciences. As we have suggested, the object of qualitative research is to gain *understanding* of the experience of research participants, rather than to *explain* the experience. Consequently, any form of validation process will need to reflect this perspective. Within this study the researcher drew on certain processes of validation that are well established and accepted within the literature.

Trustworthiness

Lincoln and Guba (1985) put forward the term 'trustworthiness' to indicate a possible way of identifying and defining rigour within the process of qualitative research. According to Guba and Lincoln (1994) the rigour within qualitative research emerges from the three dimensions of *credibility*, *auditability* and *fittingness*. One might analogously align these dimensions with the quantitative criterion of validity, reliability and generalizability. For a study to be trustworthy it must be credible, it must be possible for an external person to audit the progress of the work and it must have a sense of fit or resonance with the experiences of the participants or others experiencing similar phenomena. The trustworthiness of this study was achieved in a variety of ways based around the ideas of credibility, auditability and fittingness.

A thick, rich description

As we have mentioned, the idea of *credibility* is fundamental to the trustworthiness of a research project. Without such credibility in the eyes of the 'information sources',

> the findings and conclusions as a whole cannot be found credible by the consumer of the inquiry report . . . credibility is crucial and . . . cannot be well established without recourse to the data sources themselves. (Lincoln and Guba 1985, p. 213)

Credibility emerges from the richness of the research data and its ability to resonate with others who have been through experiences similar to the ones being described.

> For the study to attain credibility it must be able to present a thick, rich and recognisable description of the subject matter. A qualitative study is credible when it presents such faithful descriptions of a human experience that the people having that experience would immediately recognise from those descriptions of interpretations as their own. A study is also credible when other people (researchers or readers) can recognise the experience when confronted with it after having only read about it in a study. (Sandelowski 1986)

A thick description seeks to capture the essence of a phenomenon in a way that communicates it in all its fullness. It is therefore rich, vivid and faithful (Koch 1998). The implication of this for the research process as a whole is that the process of writing, reflecting and accurately interpreting the data is not simply epiphenomenal to data presentation and analysis. It is a crucial part of the process (Swinton 2001).

Participant validation

The transcripts and the interpretation of the data were returned to a sample of the participants for validation. In each case the themes were talked through and any suggested adjustments relating to inaccuracy were incorporated in the final text. A vital part of the validation process was the use of participants' own words and narratives as a prominent aspect of the final text. Participants were often surprised by the data shown to them and frequently expressed an awareness that while true, these dimensions of their experiences had not previously been reflected on consciously. This is indicative of the importance and efficacy of the merging of the researcher's horizons with those of the research participant. A study which was purely phenomenological, that is which sought to explore the person's experience objectively with no attempt at interpretation, would in fact have missed some vital dimensions of the experience.

Independent validation

The process of independent validation enables the researcher to reflect on and monitor possible distortions brought to the study and to ensure that the way in which the data is being processed and understood is true to the data that is collected. The interview texts were read and the themes checked by independent researchers with knowledge of the qualitative research method being used. Comments were noted and discussed.

Auditability

Auditability refers to the decisions made by the researcher at every stage of the research process (Koch 1998). This aspect is achieved when

> another researcher can follow the 'decision trail' of a study from beginning to end. . . . In this way, readers of a report may not agree with the author's interpretations, but at least they should be able to understand how he arrived at those interpretations. (Smith 1996)

This means recording the decisions and experiences encountered at each stage of the research process and recording them in the form of an 'audit trail' that can be followed through by others (Koch 1998). To this end, the researcher kept a research diary which noted the way the process was developing and the reasons behind the various decisions that had to be made along the way.

A recognizable final product

Finally the end-product of the research process should be recognizable as reflecting something of the essence of the experience being described (Lincoln and Guba 1985). Here we find the importance of the phenomenological dimension of this method. To this end, the final research findings were fed back to participants for discussion and further reflection (Swinton 2001).

Results

From the analysis of the data a number of key themes emerged:

- *The meaningless abyss of depression*
  The suggestion that depression is like being trapped at the bottom of a deep abyss with no possibility of rescue.

- *Questioning everything*
  A sense that all of life's certainties had gone and that everything was open to questioning, including a person's faith.

- *Abandonment*
  Feelings of being abandoned by others and ultimately by God.

- *Clinging on*
  A desperate need to cling on to faith and to God despite the ravages of the illness.

- *The desire to relate and the failure of relationships*
  A desperate inner need to relate but an outer experience of the failure and loss of relationships.

- *Being ground down*
  A sense that chronic depression is unrelenting and soul-destroying.

- *Being trapped into living*
  A deep tension between the desire to commit suicide and the moral obligation not to.

- *The crucible of depression*
  The idea that depression was a crucible wherein the person was being cleared out and purified through the ravages of the illness.

- *The healing power of understanding*
  A desperate need for others to understand their situation. The key for recovery and health was not simply therapy and medicine, but understanding and deep, resonant empathy.[3]

Here we will explore two of these themes with a particular focus on the theological issues that are raised by this piece of research.

---

3. For a full description of the results of this reasearch project see Swinton 2001.

Theological reflection

The meaningless abyss of depression

For the participants in this study, meaning, and the ways in which it can be lost and regained within the context of depression, was central to their experience of depression. If life had meaning, then it was possible for people to cope with the considerable difficulties that depression imposed upon their lives. As one participant put it:

> I don't depend on there being direct, individual meaning in my particular circumstances or situation and all the bad things that happen to me. I'm quite happy to live with the idea that, you know, in a fallen world there are things that happen to people just sort of through chance and circumstance. But what one does need to believe is that all of that is happening in an ultimately meaningful framework.

However, if that 'ultimately meaningful framework' collapses, as is the case when they tumble into the depths of depression, the person is catapulted into a deep, dark void that is deeply disturbing and spiritually devastating.

> When I'm in a phase that I am able to believe that there is a God who gives meaning to that universe, then I have hope. But there have been spells when I haven't been able to believe that, and that has been absolutely terrifying. That's been falling into the abyss. That is seriously nasty!

Depression is a profoundly, existentially lonely place. It is a place where even God is often absent. The resonance with the lament psalms is obvious:

> How long, O Lord? Will you forget me forever?
> How long will you hide your face from me?

> How long must I wrestle with my thoughts
> and every day have sorrow in my heart?

How long will my enemy triumph over me?
Psalm 13:1–2

The experience of depression is an experience of desolation.

The imagery of the abyss in the above quotation powerfully symbolizes the terrifying black pit of meaninglessness into which a person slides during the experience of depression. The only foothold out of the abyss is the possibility that there is meaning beyond the pain of one's present situation. If this foothold is torn away, there is as one participant put it: 'nothing but "nothingness" and darkness'.

> You would go to bed at night and it was dark outside, and it felt dark inside. All creative energy was gone, it just wasn't there. When I woke in the morning, although it was dawn, inside nothing had changed and it was still dark.

The abyss is filled with doubt about God, self, others and the order of the world. It is a meaningless void within which strength, hope and light are drained, leaving the person in a dark and lonely place. Even when well this woman felt like she was walking around the edge of the abyss, knowing that at any time she could tumble back down into the darkness. Even when she was well she was terrified. The experience was unrelentingly negative even when her depression was reasonably well controlled.

Trapped into living: the logic of suicide

When the experience of depression is understood in this way, suicide becomes an alternative which is considerably more logical than might normally be assumed. To live like this is to live with deep pain and hopelessness; modes of pain and hopelessness within which faith and religion are often absent but which, even when present, can function in unexpected ways. A person's faith can be an unwelcome preventative factor blocking the 'obvious' solution of suicide.

> It's a bad thing [not being able to commit suicide] when

you're feeling incredibly depressed and you're stuck in life. It's like ... em ... I just wish I didn't know about God. You know? 'Cause then it would be easier to actually just say 'That's it! I can't take any more!' But in the end when I feel better, I feel probably ... that, well it's probably just as well (laughs) that I knew him. You know? But I think there's always this em ... it's a double-edged sword I think.

It is interesting to note that here, the introduction of faith into a conversation intended to heal (for example a counselling session), might in fact be received in a negative and perhaps scathing manner. If the counsellor, pastor or friend is not aware of this hidden tension with regard to the role of faith in the experience of depression, significant issues may arise.

The idea that faith can be an unwelcome guest emerged on a number of occasions in various interviews. One man put it like this:

I've had experiences where faith was, at the time, the last thing I wanted, because I felt it *trapped me into living*, because I ... I suppose it was when I was most suicidal, and ... the only thing that I could think of was killing myself and so the fact that I knew God and had a faith made it very difficult for me because I knew deep down that God wouldn't particularly want me to kill myself, so I would be going against his word I suppose, to actually do it. And so it was like a trap (laughs) because I couldn't get out of that; I couldn't ... I suppose in a way it was fear, fear of the consequences of doing it, eternal damnation or whatever. You know this fear of, I've got to meet and ... I've done this, what's he going to say to me? (laughs) You know? So that's probably what's going on in my brain at the time was the fact that my greatest need and wish was to be dead, but I couldn't do it because God was there and I shouldn't I suppose.

Other themes that emerged from the study indicate that the knowledge of being loved by God provides the strength that enables people to cling on to faith and life in times of deep distress. However, at the same time, the fear of that same God acts to prevent self-harm, even though self-harm may be the (understandable) desire of the individual and the best perceived solution. Life with depression is lived in the midst of this tension between being pleased about being alive, and a feeling of being 'stuck in life', an experience which can be both frustrating and at times annoying.

Abandonment

A common theme that ran through the interviews was the experience of feelings of abandonment both by God and by those around the person.

> I know that God is in control, but, when one's emotions and mood and everything are up for grabs, it's actually exceedingly hard to feel that. That then gives rise to a conflict, because what you feel and what you know are not saying the same things. So you get . . . what I probably got a lot of was a sense of abandonment and the feeling that God's walked off and left me. Where is He now? What use is this faith thing anyway? So that then becomes an inner conflict.

The essence of this man's faith has to do with his perception of engaging in a loving relationship with God. 'Faith to me is not religion as such. It's a personal relationship with God.' Such a relationship cannot be maintained by intellect alone. As with any other personal relationships it demands emotion and feeling. Yet, during times of depression he cannot *feel* his relationship with God in the way that he has done in the past. This conflict between intellectual and experiential knowledge leads to a sense of abandonment by God. Like a lover who knows in his head that his partner cares for him, but in his daily life does not experience that care in either words or actions, so also this man finds himself caught up in a conflict between what he knows in his head and what he does not feel in his heart. If his faith were purely legalistic this might be easier. However, as his faith is deeply experiential and relational, this is a serious problem for him. He no longer *feels* loved by God. This experience is much more than a theological crisis. It is a crisis of being and identity.

The Scottish philosopher John Macmurray (1961) in his trenchant critique of Cartesian dualism points to the ways in which human beings are 'created' in and through their relationships with others. In a very real sense we are persons-in-relation. We depend on one another for our identities and understandings of the world. I am only a father because of my children, a husband because of my wife, a lecturer because of my occupation, and so forth. My personal identity and the way I view the world and my place within it is not a pre-set given, but rather the product of my relational interactions with other human beings and my social and cultural context, including the ways in which I interpret and utilize God.

This observation is helpful in interpreting and understanding feelings of abandonment. All of the participants in the study appeared to have an intrinsic form of spirituality, that is, their religious/spiritual tradition was considered to be a fundamental part of their lives, the foundational bond that they used to bind themselves to the world. Depression destroys this bond and leaves the person with a serious crisis of identity and spirituality. The sense of being abandoned by God is more than just a negative cognition. It is indicative of a serious existential crisis. 'If God has abandoned me, then what and who am I?' If a person can no longer relate to God, and if their self-image and interpretation of the world is dependent on their experience of God, then to experience such abandonment is, in a very real sense, to lose a part of themselves. The experience of being abandoned by God leaves them with a wide, gaping wound where once there had been a powerful source of hope, love, meaning and purpose. Thus the person is thrown into a void of unknowing that is much more profound and devastating than simply the lowering of their mood. In the midst of the sadness of depression, there is a significant loss of self which the person has to struggle to understand and come to terms with. Depression destroys that which is most dear and significant to a person. It challenges a person at the very core of their being and forces them to reconsider who they are and what their life is really about.

Conclusion

These abstracts begin to show how the method of hermeneutical phenomenology functions, the type of data it will provide and the implications for practice that follow from this. By providing deep and often surprising insights into the experience of depression, hermeneutic phenomenology has enabled us to see and to begin to understand the hidden spiritual dynamics within the lived experience of depression. Depression is clearly much more than simply a lowering of a person's mood. Depression is a condition that affects the person in their entirety producing a deep spiritual, existential, physical, psychological and relational crisis that embraces them in every dimension. Within such a context even faith and religion begin to function and be perceived in quite different ways. Irrespective of whether its roots lie within a person's biology, psychology or trauma within their social experiences, the consequences of depression permeate the whole experience of the person, and cannot be reduced to a single aspect.

Such reflections, insights and understandings provide useful data for rethinking and reframing the healing practices used by counsellors, pastors and friends who minister to people with depression. They also raise important theological issues. For example, bearing in mind the types of experience described above, the way that depression erodes faith and meaning and the clear logic of suicide when viewed from a different frame, how are we to understand the theological dynamics of suicide? Is it truly an unforgivable sin, or, is there a theological frame wherein it may be perceived as a breach of the gift of life that God gives to human beings, but an understandable and forgivable response to horrific experiences. This in turn raises issues and questions relating to the theology of suffering and whether or not the inability to sustain faith through suffering is a weakness or a biological or psychological inevitability. It is not our task to attempt to answer these questions within this book. Our point is that this method enables us to discover fresh insights into the experience of depression or any other phenomenon, insights which raise new and challenging questions for theology and practice. As such, when used in the service of God, this form of qualitative method holds much potential for developing faithful practices and transforming understandings.

5

Researching a Local Church: Exploring an 'Emergent Church'[1]

Within a social context where the church at least appears to be dying, the study of congregations takes on a new pertinence. While mainline institutional religion is struggling, there remain pockets of ecclesial activity that continue to buck the trend and which indicate possibilities for new growth and trans-formative change. Church communities are rich and diverse. They are filled with history and tradition, and recognizing and understanding why they are the way they are and how they became what they are is a difficult, complex and complexing task. Congregations represent unique cultures (Dowie 2002; Arbuckle 1991) with their own personalities, foibles and psychic processes. The task of analysing them, working through and working out the various issues, requires particular skills of data collection and analysis. In this chapter we will explore one way in which a local congregation can be researched. The study examined here will illustrate the way in which critical theological reflection and qualitative methods work together to produce rich, illuminating and potentially transformative data. Here we will consider the stages of research that are necessary for the effective study of the type of congregation looked at here. These stages comprise: the *research method*, *data collection*, *analysis* and *theological reflection*. We will show the interdependence of these various stages and how they worked

---

1. This chapter is written by Cory Labanow at the University of Aberdeen.

together to provide deep insights into a local church setting. The original study was done as part of a Ph.D. research project. It focused on one particular 'emerging church', which we have given the pseudonym Jacobsfield Vineyard, and its responses to the challenges of postmodernity.

The study was keen to investigate a local faith community participating to some degree in what many from within the movement have labelled the 'emerging church'. Though some recognizable networks have arisen in the past decade, there is no centralized hierarchy to the emerging church. In a dominantly descriptive fashion, Robert Webber has identified this new wave and heightened awareness of its presence in the evangelical community. He speaks loosely of three recent eras of evangelicalism: first, he points to the traditional evangelicals (1950–75), who hold to the worldview of modernism and an early twentieth-century style of church. This group has birthed the pragmatic evangelicals (1975–2000), who still hold to the worldview of modernism but place priority on reinventing their methods for communicating their modern interpretation of Christianity. The third, emerging group (2000–?) he labels the 'younger evangelicals', denoting them as 'anyone, older or younger, who deals thoughtfully with the shift from twentieth- to twenty-first-century culture. He or she is committed to construct a biblically rooted, historically informed, and culturally aware new evangelical witness in the twenty-first century' (Webber 2002). Pockets of the emerging church can be found in nearly every Protestant denomination, and its manifestations take many forms, from small, loosely arranged groups meeting in cathedrals to large-scale charismatic churches. What they share is a common dissatisfaction with twentieth-century Christianity and a more postmodern orientation to spirituality, but not stylistic homogeneity.

For the purposes of the study we defined the emerging church as

the identifiable network of Christian churches and individual Christians self-consciously dialoguing about and experimenting with the possibilities for reinventing the Church in order to survive in and engage with the emerging postmodern era.

Despite the helpfulness of Webber's overview, due to the emerging church's infancy and decentralization, very little serious research has been given to this group, thus warranting some disciplined attention which this study sought to give. Moreover, the emerging church was of special significance insofar as its uniting feature is a common commitment to proactively engage with postmodern culture; this created an ideal setting for exploring practical theological responses to the postmodern turn.

Aims of the research

The study set out to achieve three objectives:

1 To highlight the current challenges for 'emerging churches' by describing and understanding in detail one such church.
2 To identify the central theological question that seemed to be the focus of the church's mission and ministry.
3 To consider this theological question in light of current cultural and philosophical expectations and practices.

Method

Hermeneutic approach

The study adopted a hermeneutic perspective. It drew in particular from the work of Hans Georg Gadamer (1981) specifically as it has been utilized within Practical Theology by Don Browning (1991). Central to this hermeneutical perspective is a particular reflective pattern which moves from practice to theory to practice. This dialectical movement challenges the traditional theory-to-practice paradigm of Practical Theology and offers a dialectical approach which allows experience to challenge and be challenged by theology and the social sciences. The research intentions were to indicate some general challenges for 'emerging churches' by understanding the detail of one.

We have already looked in some detail at Gadamer's perspective on hermeneutics. Here we will revisit some aspects of his hermeneutic. Gadamer carefully argues that the interpreter is an inevitable part of the interpretive process, and that this dynamic is a prerequisite to understanding, not an obstacle to it. In this study, the researcher, though carefully aware of personal prejudices and pre-understandings, acknowledged himself as a participating member of the research process and proceeded carefully with this knowledge always in mind. Indeed his prehistory as a practical theologian was a vital dimension of his analytical horizon which was crucial for the process of analysis. We have seen previously the importance of understanding interpretation as the merging of horizons. Within this study, this process of merging horizons required a constant back-and-forth movement between practice and theory with interpretation not perceived as a one-time event in the research process, but rather as an ongoing process that continued throughout. This process entailed tentative construction, deconstruction and rebuilding of the data as an ongoing conversation between the horizons of (1) the researcher and the congregation and (2) the researcher and outside texts. Social science methods enabled the effective collection of the necessary data to allow this critical hermeneutical conversation to take place. In the study, two primary data collection methods were utilized:[2] *participant observation* and *interviews*, each of which we will describe in detail below.

----

2. Additionally, a one-time demographic survey was employed to gather quantitative data on church members' age, level of involvement, and previous church experience, but this was only used as a minor supplement to the qualitative data generated through the participant observation and interviews.

Participant observation

Pre-fieldwork: *gaining access and attaining ethical permission*

The initial role of the researcher was as a participant observer. Participant observation is characterized by an extended period of intense social interaction between a researcher and the members of a social group in the milieu of the latter (Bogdan and Taylor 1998). In the case of Jacobsfield Vineyard (JV), the researcher contacted and subsequently met with the pastor, in order to explain the intentions of the study and request permission to enter the congregation as both a full participating member and a researcher. At this point, ethical agreements were made. While the pastor obviously needed to grant permission for the researcher to use the findings in a Ph.D. dissertation, he was also asked to express any other concerns he might have. This was an important part of the research process which formally established the nature of the relationship between participation and observation. The pastor requested that the researcher should become fully involved in the life of the church in terms of offering service, attending services and meetings and developing community-based relationships. He also asked that the identities of church members remained anonymous and unrecognizable in the final drafts. This meant not only anonymity of names, but also the avoidance of any detailed description of specific church members which could lead to their identification. Finally the pastor requested that the study be, to some degree, a joint venture between the researcher and the leadership of the church. Since JV were also on a journey of exploring how to be church in the context of postmodernity, he felt that some occasional editorial collaboration would be mutually beneficial. This aspect of the research approach resonates with our previous discussion on the significance of participatory research. These ethical considerations were agreed upon and later drawn into a formal contract which also related to the allocation of pertinent publishing rights.

Though the pastor informed the church's lay leaders of the intentions of the researcher, the Jacobsfield Vineyard congregation was not publicly made aware of the researcher's role until several months into the study. Nevertheless, the researcher was open with JVers in conversations about his role as a researcher, and very clear with all interviewees of his intentions. Though there was some mild hesitation at first, after a few months of the researcher becoming assimilated into the weekly fabric of the church, JVers appeared to become desensitised to the researcher's presence. The researcher seemed to be perceived first and foremost as a fellow church member who participated in church ministries, served on monthly rotas, attended home groups and social gatherings and worshipped alongside them on Sunday mornings. The research project was acknowledged as part of his horizon, but his primary mode of identification came from the daily participation in the life of the church.

Recording the data

In this study a wide range of material, including formal pamphlets, conversational comments, and Sunday sermons, became data. Since the goal was to gather as much information as possible about the setting, the researcher was very keen to observe, read and listen as much as possible; systematic ordering and analysis of data were of secondary importance in the initial stages. This stage is sometimes known as *familiarization*.

The primary types of data collected in the first several months of the study were:

1 formal assertions,
2 congregational perspectives.
3 researcher reflections.

Formal assertions included things such as the church website, JV-authored leaflets describing their programmes and philosophy, Sunday sermons from Lawton (as either audio files or written notes), and newsletters mailed to congregants regarding events in church life. These data were pooled together and later formed a section in the final report entitled 'Leadership identity-claims'. These claims were contrasted against the second type of data, congregational perspectives, which accounted for the bulk of recorded information, and, arguably, the most influential data. These observations were drawn from every single interaction with Jacobsfield Vineyard, whether that interaction was an informal coffee rendezvous with a single JVer, a home group meeting, a volunteer day at their community service project, or the Sunday morning service. Of crucial importance was the researcher's faithful recording of these observations in his fieldwork journal. This was an important aspect of the researcher's reflexive practice. This was done as soon as possible, ideally during, but usually immediately following the events. This reflexive habit facilitated the registering of data which was rich, thorough, and vivid in detail. For this task, the researcher found it most helpful to take notes in a portable computer notebook which were later transferred to an online word processor (also *always* ensuring a backup source in case either the notebook or the file was lost).

Maintaining the fieldwork journal

Earlier we emphasized the importance of reflexivity for the process of qualitative research. It became clear early on that observations would not only have to be collected, but also collated into a manageable form. To this end, the meticulous maintenance of a fieldwork journal was perceived as very important. The researcher used the following heading format to shape the reflexive diary:

• Date
• Description

- Self-reflection
- Interpretation and investigation

Entries varied in length from a hundred words to over a thousand, depending on the length and complexity of the situation at hand. In the 'description' section, the researcher carefully logged various facts and observations drawn from the interaction and placed them, for the most part, in chronological order. The researcher's goal was to accumulate significant details which would be analysed later. To this end, a bulleted, informal format worked very well. The following is an extract from the fieldwork diary which reflects on a partial sample of one entry recorded in the early stages of fieldwork:

- Sunday service. Room seemed 70% full like last week. M mentioned that beginning this autumn they were going to set up the stage at a different end and expand the seating into an adjacent room to allow for more people.
- Some differences than last week: M present, worship band much different – [one JV worship leader] not participating, drums back, a woman on keys, acoustic led.
- [A female JVer] gave a notice about a newly begun women's prayer meeting.
- M chose to postpone the scheduled message (a copy of the outline was left on everyone's seat) entitled 'Jesus and Our Mistakes' in favour of one he wrote this morning loosely entitled 'What Kind of Church Are We Trying To Be?'
- A phrase by M kept coming up . . . 'do church work so we can do the work of the church'. It seemed to be a slogan he uses often. He also cited Karl Barth as one of his favourite theologians and used his phrase 'be the church for the sake of the world'.

After logging in these observations, the researcher spent some time writing in pre-analytical sections entitled 'self-reflection' and 'interpretation and investigation'.

Within the Gadamerian perspective which underpinned this

study, performing Practical Theology not only involves the experience of the subject(s) who are being studied, it also recognizes the inevitability and the validity of the researcher's own experiences and the interactions between these two horizons. Therefore, the latter section sought to give space to reflect upon how and why the researcher's own autobiography (in this case, a recurring factor was past disaffection with a pentecostal/charismatic upbringing) was being triggered by what was occurring. Sometimes this category was left blank; other times it contained a substantial amount of material. The final category, 'interpretation and investigation', provided space for brainstorming about those things which the researcher was 'smelling in the air' and strategizing about how to further develop the study. These hunches and intuitive sensings were an important part of the early stage of the data collection process. What was the flavour of that home group? What values dominate this ministry? Why did the leadership make the decision which was announced today and what consequences might it have? Was anything from the event today worth follow-up (e.g. in an interview setting)? An example of an entry that included ideas such as these is as follows:

> Some themes seem to be emerging: (1) *Re-education.*
> M makes a lot of explicit references to and directly
> addresses old forms of doing church, viewing God, and
> living the Christian life. In their place he speaks of ways
> of rethinking, redefining, and giving new meaning to
> old practices. It's not so much introducing something
> entirely new which exists completely outside of their
> framework, but rather a metamorphosis or maturation
> of meaning of things which are already there to a more
> biblical and postmodern worldview. (2) *Worship.* This
> continues to arise as a very huge value/theme. Yet what
> exactly worship means to the Vineyard and the emerging
> church is still somewhat unclear to me. (3) *Community.*
> It seems nearly all JV participants with whom I've
> spoken are eager to explain to me that Sundays are just

one of many activities throughout the week which give meaning to their church.

While these specific themes did not end up becoming the loci of the study, pondering emergent motifs in this way gave next-step direction which eventually led to the creation of a credible identity framework.

Interviews

After seven months of participant observation, the researcher was poised to explore the central themes of Jacobsfield Vineyard in greater depth. The rich data obtained from these interviews became the primary data as the researcher formed an identity framework by which to understand this local church and later engaged in theological reflection. To accomplish this, the researcher conducted 26 semi-structured interviews with a cross-section of JVers.

Choosing the sample

As noted earlier, a demographic survey was conducted of a Sunday morning service. This information provided a profile of ages, gender mix, and levels of involvement which served as a guide for the researcher in selecting interview participants. This entailed accessing both a wide spectrum of interviewees and one whose mean would reflect the typical profile of the JV congregation. For this reason, interviewees were approached with the intention of ultimately mirroring this profile. In many cases, the researcher had already established at least an occasional relationship with the potential interviewee; while this carried the ethical danger of reflecting the researcher's personal relational network, it did assure that the interviewee would be more at ease with the researcher and thus more transparent in the interview. In the end, the statistics of the 26 interviewees mirrored the demographic profile very closely and thus was considered to be a representative sampling.

Identifying the questions

The task of identifying questions began in the early stages of the fieldwork and evolved as the researcher's immersion in the church community increased. From the fieldwork journal there emerged recurring themes, phrases and motifs. Whether in an unstructured interview setting or a casual conversation, the researcher made a discipline of raising these issues with JVers to ascertain whether or not the issues really were central to JV's identity and also whether the questions were posed in a clear manner which prompted a usable response. Some queries were discarded altogether, some were rephrased, and others were reaffirmed as key components to be used in the more systematic format of the 26 semi-structured interviews.

This process informed a two-part interview schedule (see Figure 5). The first (questions 1–5) focused on the JVers' stories of involvement at JV and their general reactions to church practices and then (questions 6–10) their personal analysis on more interpretive issues. The chronology of the questions was also engineered with more biographical questions at the outset in order to give the researcher a narrative framework by which to understand the remainder of the responses and to put the interviewee at ease.

Many of the interviews – which lasted anywhere from 45 minutes to two hours – took place in the homes of the interviewees. Most interviews were one-to-one, with the exception of married or dating couples who chose to respond to the questions together; their responses were distinguished in the written notes for further analytical purposes. Before the interview, each participant was made aware of the specific nature of the study, the purpose of the questions, the anonymity with which the findings would be used, and their right to discontinue the interview at any time; additionally, the researcher ended each interview by asking, 'Do you have any questions for me?' at which time they were given the opportunity to voice further questions which might have arisen during the course of the interview. The interviews were not tape

1. Personal Information (i.e. age, marital status, duration of attendance, previous church experience, level of involvement)
2. How did you come to JV?
3. Why are you here? (i.e. What needs are being met by JV?)
4. Have you ever experienced a definitive crisis in your faith (or, identity as a Christian)? If yes, how has JV been involved?
5. Reflect on:
   a. the use of elements of historical Christianity, such as observances of the Christian calendar, creeds, prayers, and other ancient practices
   b. worship
   c. the use of the Bible
   d. the phrase 'doubts and questions'
6. What is 'spiritual maturity' at JV?
7. Where would JV be on a 'church map'? Would you describe it as a Vineyard church, an evangelical church, an emerging church, none of those, all of those, or something completely different?
8. Is there a central issue JV are wrestling with or a question they are striving to answer?
9. Sometimes Matt uses the phrase 'alternative basis for living'. What does that phrase mean to you?
10. Is there any difference in the way power is used at JV versus the way in which it is used, for instance, in the business world or wider society?

Figure 5: A two-part interview schedule.

recorded; the researcher chose instead to make shorthand notes which were then logged into a formal sourcebook as soon as possible after the interview. To ensure the accuracy of the responses, probing questions were used to confirm that the

Q4c. Reflections on the Use of the Bible	Number of Respondents	Percentage of Total
Would like to see more of the Bible used	15	57.7
Suggested a better mix between straight Bible readings and culturally relevant concepts and teachings	8	30.8
Expressed dismay at how to best use the Bible (as a tool for discipleship)	8	30.8
Recognize that lack is potentially harmful for new Christians	5	19.2
No problems with the use of Bible	5	19.2
Despite an apparent lack of overt Bible teaching, Lawton's teachings are saturated with biblical truth	4	15.4
Grateful that JV do not link spiritual maturity with Bible reading	1	3.8

Figure 6: Sorting interview data.

interviewer fully understood the JVer's views. Moreover, if it was felt that their response was not comprehended correctly, the researcher would repeat back to them the shorthand notes for that particular question and request confirmation before proceeding to the next question. This helped to minimize interviewer bias and error.

Sorting the data

Once a predictable spectrum of responses began to develop among the interview results (after 15–18 interviews), it was clear that the sample was nearing sufficient quantity to merit validity. This is usually known as 'saturation'. This is the position when no new data is emerging during the interviews despite purposive sampling. After all 26 interviews were performed and logged into a semi-structured interview sourcebook (using the above questions as headings), overlapping sentiments were identified for each question, concisely phrased, listed alongside each other, and then attached to the number of respondents who indicated that response. For example, the question pertaining to JVers' reflections on the use of the Bible produced the account shown in Figure 6.

Additionally, each question also received some follow-up commentary pertaining to intangible results from the interview questions, such as pointing out that one sentiment was mainly expressed by older JVers, calling attention to the noteworthy presence of a recurring word or phrase, or articulating why the findings surprised the interviewer in light of former assumptions. While the numbers were descriptive and meant nothing in terms of predictive analysis it did help to 'see the data'.

Analysis

As the data was collected and categorized, the process began of drawing out of the findings a functional framework for understanding the identity of JV. A framework was sought which would represent the JV situation in both its complexity and its simplicity. The analysis was not a one-time event in the research process. Instead, it was a cycle of tentative construction, deconstruction, and reformulation which occurred as an ongoing conversation between the researcher and the congregation, the researcher and outside texts and the researcher and the accounts given by the congregation. The use of outside sources of input greatly contributed to the process of making sense of the data. In this study, the primary texts used were Alan Jamieson's *A Churchless Faith: Faith Journeys beyond the Churches* (2002) and Robert Webber's *The Younger Evangelicals: Facing the Challenges of the New World* (2002). This theoretical sensitivity noted particularly by Glaser (1978) comes from extensive reading and self-conscious cultural awareness.

Extracting the themes

It was at this point in the research study that techniques of progressive focusing were useful. The aim is to identify a handful (three to six) of key elements which, due to their centrality, can be linked with every aspect of the congregation's life. Pooling all data gained from conversations with observations of, and specific identity-claims by JVers aided by the external voices, the researcher grouped and classified the findings in order to discover common motifs which emerged, reformulating them time and time again. A central aim of the research was to highlight the current challenges for 'emerging churches' by describing and understanding the detail of one such church. The interpretive process described here yielded four dominant themes which were able to explain current challenges and questions described at Jacobsfield Vineyard.

1 Safety through honesty and openness
2 Experimentation, particularly in communication with culture
3 Maturity
4 Relationship to evangelicalism

Exploring interrelationships

However, these four themes represented uniformly alongside each other did not capture the essence of the congregation's self-identity. This being so, the researcher sought to discover what the relationships between these themes might entail. What was discovered at JV was a roughly equal-plane relationship between the first three, but a unique difference given to the fourth theme regarding the JV relationship to evangelicalism (or lack thereof). The other three motifs seemed to directly contrast with it; JVers consistently viewed evangelicalism

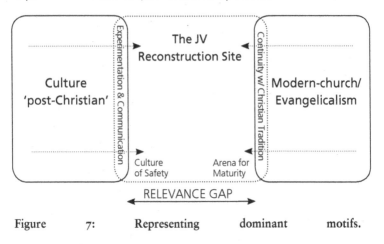

Figure   7:   Representing   dominant   motifs.

as their point of reference/departure as they described their experiences at Jacobsfield Vineyard. Aided by the feedback of congregants, the researcher produced a diagram by which to articulate these themes and how they interacted with one another (see Figure 7).

This task of deeply understanding the interrelationships between dominant motifs worked towards a more holistic grasp of the church, a necessary task for the final link in the analytical process: the central theological question.

Arriving at a central question

For the study at JV, the researcher adapted Don Browning's ethic of congregational research (Browning 1991). This ethic works towards a culmination in one meticulously-generated and meaning-laden 'central theological question' which seeks to encapsulate the church's core concerns; this is the spring-board, then, for later theological reflection (Browning 1991). Since the researcher had located JV at a liminal position between mainstream culture and evangelicalism, the notion of *reconstruction* seemed to present itself as a helpful idea for a central theological question. Essentially, JV seemed to be trapped between the necessity of change (both internal and external) and the fear of losing that which made them who they were. Questions such as 'What does make us who we are?' 'Can we change what we do and still be who we are?' and 'What do we reject and what do we keep?' were implicitly central in such a context. For JV, the central theological question was identified as

> What are our communally accepted and critically held criteria for reconstruction which result in relevance to ourselves and those to whom we are trying to credibly represent the Christian faith?

Central theological questions are the vital link between the social excavation of a group and the theological horizons with which it must converse. By narrowing a church's concerns to a finely-tuned question, one is able to engage in theological reflection in a focused and ultimately effective manner.

Rigour and validity

The fact that the researcher was intimately engaged in the research and interpretive process also provoked issues of validity. How can any reader of this study credibly interact with its findings when the prejudices of the researcher have been unashamedly involved in the process? The researcher, aware of the inevitability and necessity of pre-understandings, was also quick to recognize the potential downfalls of such 'bias' as well. Consequently, the researcher sought to counteract these dangers in the following ways:

1 obtaining JVers' own sentiments in such a manner as to minimize observer/interviewer bias and error;
2 presenting an account of the study of Jacobsfield Vineyard in such a way that the reader had access to the same information with which the researcher made interpretive judgements;
3 providing detailed rationales for analytical decisions in

order to enable the reader critically to agree or disagree; and

4 including an appendix section in the final report in which JV leadership personally responded to the interpretations generated by the research.

As discussed above in 'Interviews: Identifying the questions', great care was taken to ensure that the responses of JV interviewees were accurately recorded to reflect their thoughts as closely as possible. Since the semi-structured interviews were the most specific data collected in the study, this was crucial. Additionally, the researcher made frequent use of informal interviews as a type of member-checking to bring rigour and integrity to the data collected through participant observation. Informal interviews take place in the context of short, casual conversations; the participant observer employs these as a means to 'seek clarification about the meaning or significance of something that took place' (Robson 2002). In essence, they are used to link a researcher's perspective on particular events or ideas with those of other participants in order to decrease the likelihood that the researcher will overlook or misread key elements of a situation or issue. (For example, 'Did you sense a negative reaction to the Sunday talk this morning? If so, what caused it?') Such interactions in this study were frequent and quickly noted in detail in the fieldwork notes. They provided a more immediate dialogue for observations than the semi-structured interviews, albeit much less thorough and systematic.

Second, writing up the account in rich detail also contributed to the validity and trustworthiness of the study. Providing vivid descriptions of Sunday services, special meetings, and various ministries alongside ample self-descriptions from JVers themselves gave the reader the opportunity to become a secondhand observer and an interpreter herself. While of course the researcher's choice of what to portray and what to omit is an interpretive act itself, a thick depiction of the setting, inclusive of as many dimensions of the church as possible, goes a long way in boosting the confidence of the reader in the respective analysis.

Regarding such analysis, equal priority to thick description was given to the processes of interpreting and constructing a framework for understanding JV. The researcher did not simply portray the diagram representing JV's major themes and the interrelationships thereof without a thorough account of how this was derived from the data. This included an explanation of how the data was sorted and categorized, snapshots of JV life (stories from the participant observation period or direct quotes), and the rationale behind each interpretive decision made. For instance, in justifying the claim that one of JV's central themes was experimentation for the purpose of communication with culture, the researcher cited statistical evidence and quotes from the semi-structured interviews, some insights from Webber's *The Younger Evangelicals*, and two representative scenarios – one from a home group meeting and the latter from a large discussion group on the *Passion of Christ* film – which the researcher personally observed. It was the aim of the researcher not only to provide compelling evidence for the claims of the study, but also to facilitate the generation of challenging or complementary perspectives to emerge from the reader's interaction with the research.

Finally, the researcher sent the final drafts of the study to the pastor for his review, with a request that he write a response to be included in the final product. This enabled JV leadership to have an unmediated voice in which to express their perspective on the research and its conclusions, thus granting the reader an inside voice by which to achieve greater understanding of the church.

Theological reflections

The data generated many intriguing findings, and when set in conversation with theological voices, produced a very rich synergy. Some of these discoveries included the following; hopefully the underlying central theological question concerning the dilemma of reconstruction will be evident as a common denominator throughout the process of reflection.

The effects of permitting doubts and questions

To many JVers, feeling free to be who they are – especially with their weaknesses – is the very quality which makes JV different from other churches, and becomes the starting point for their development. 'If there's one word to describe JV,' one interviewee said, 'it's "real" . . . You can't possibly go through anything in life without having doubts, otherwise you're just fooling yourself. At JV we're just normal people trying to figure life out.' On one hand, making space for doubts and questions pertaining to faith was a core value: JVers continually attested to the need for respecting others' right to be uncertain, to question even the most basic claims of truth, to doubt anything they chose. Yet on the other hand, there was not a great deal of overt 'doubting' occurring among their ranks. When the semi-structured interviewees were asked about crises of faith, a few per cent shared a story of when they endured a season of doubting the Christian faith, questioned the meaning of life, or endured some other notable time of trial. The resolution to this tension became clear during one interview, as one JVer explained how the space for doubt created a culture of safety at JV:

> Other churches imply doubts mar one's character and indicate a weak faith. [JV's acceptance of doubts and questions] helps people feel accepted. It creates a culture of acceptance . . . Everyone has small [doubts], and since big ones [at JV] are OK, small ones don't become big ones. Because at most churches, small ones aren't accepted and then they turn into big ones.

Consequently, JV's acceptance of doubt was directly linked with their acceptance of people. Since human thoughts are the most central thing which constitutes individuality, respecting one's ability to think differently is possibly the deepest expression of holistic acceptance of that person. By creating a safe space for doubts, JV created a safe space for people to be themselves, thus spawning a tremendous evangelistic effect. As a result, JVers had a more relaxed view on propositional truth; for them, believing in dogmatic religious truth was not a necessary prerequisite for belonging to their church, though it did prompt confusion as to what it meant to be Christian. Needless to say, such findings provoke further exploration on how effectively to view the role of propositional truth in the life of church communities.

Reconstructing evangelism

One of the most commonly held values at JV which frequently manifested itself in all aspects of fieldwork (observation, semi-structured interviews, casual conversations, etc.) was an avid rejection of 'hard sell Christianity'. The researcher came to four conclusions regarding JV and evangelism:

1 They had a strong distaste – even an *abhorrence* – for modern evangelistic techniques (even the word itself was quite uncomfortable among JVers) such as handing out tracts or offering simplistic Christian sales pitches.
2 They still wanted to communicate 'the message of Christianity'.
3 They did not have a clear method. How could they communicate this message.
4 What that message is if it is more than 'pray this prayer'.

This setting produced a prime opportunity for theological reflection on the motivational basis for evangelism.

To arrive at a deeper understanding of why JVers felt this way, the dynamics of social institutions as explicated by Peter Berger and Thomas Luckmann (1991) were brought into the conversation, revealing that JVers felt a strong hesitation towards modern evangelistic techniques due to their preference for relating to outsiders with an attitude of announcing 'who is in' rather than a habit of defining 'who is out'. Therefore,

JV's tension point concerning evangelism was treated as an opportunity for a fresh encounter with the culture of inclusion as experienced in Jesus' vision for the kingdom of God. This interface with the kingdom of God prompted the question of how to be *intentionally evangelistic* without trespassing on the Other's right to be Other.

The struggle to redefine Christian maturity

During one season of the fieldwork, L gave an extended series of Sunday talks based on Mike Yaconelli's (2001) *Messy Spirituality: Christianity for the Rest of Us*, a book which L recommended all of JV to read over the corresponding weeks of the series. Remarkably, many did, and the book became a frequent topic of discussion in group encounters which the researcher witnessed over those months. Essentially, the book stressed the need for grace for others' problems, acceptance of one's own mistakes, and spirituality found in life's 'ordinariness' and 'oddness'. The stance was a reaction against the hypocrisy and legalism often associated with conservative evangelicalism, manifested by a surplus of narrative illustrations about people who had been rejected by supposedly 'spiritual' Christians and subsequently 'redeemed' by messy spirituality. The series created a lot of energy, partly due to JV's relationship with evangelicalism, but also because it prompted them to consider what spiritual maturity was (as opposed to what it was not). It appeared that while there was (1) an implicit expectation for maturity at JV, there was also (2) a very individual orientation to it and (3) a wide diversity of definition concerning it. 'What we're finding', one JV elder remarked, 'is that people want boundaries. Sure, they want to reposition or move the traditional ones, but they don't want the absence of boundaries.'

As this theme was set against the backdrop of current cultural and philosophical dilemmas around the specifics of maturity, it became obvious that JV were not alone in their struggle; moreover, JVers' definitions of spiritual maturity were very reflective of generic skills for living, sometimes entirely devoid of any overt religious orientation. Yet due to their priority on retaining the Christian identity and appropriating that in their lives, they were very eager to explore how traditional Christian resources – the Bible, observances of historical Christianity, and congregational worship – fit into their desire to become more mature individuals. In essence, they did not want to make an end out of the traditional means for spiritual growth, nor did they want to throw them out altogether.

6

Researching Ministry:
What do Chaplains Do?

Introduction

In this chapter we want to explore some of the ways in which qualitative research can be used to explore a specific group of people, in this case professional full-time clergy working within a specific context. There has been some interesting research on the clergy exploring various aspects of the nature and purpose of ministry (Francis and Jones 1996). Some of this has utilised qualitative research methods to some effect. There is however one group of clergy within the United Kingdom who have not been the object of a great deal of research: hospital chaplains. The work of Helen Orchard (2000) and Giles Legood (1999) has begun to open up this area of ministry for research and reflection. Legood's general overview of the field and initial explorations into the various types of chaplaincy and their relationships with one another opens up some interesting areas. Orchard's (2000) qualitative research on chaplains in England sheds some very useful and challenging light on the nature, purpose and function of hospital chaplaincy, as does Woodward's 1998 study. However, particularly with regard to a Scottish context, there has been very little research on what chaplains do and why they do it (Mitchell 1999). The study described in this chapter sought to address this imbalance by focusing on the work of hospital chaplains within the National Health Service in Scotland.

The recent implementation of national chaplaincy guidelines in Scotland (Scottish Executive 2002) which place an onus on Trusts formally to address the 'spiritual dimensions' of care, combined with the growing movement within chaplaincy that seeks to develop chaplaincy as a formally acknowledged healthcare profession on a par with other healthcare professionals (doctors, nurses, etc.), means there is a pressing need for the development of an evidence base that will provide tangible answers to the crucial question: 'What do chaplains do?'

The situation

Chaplaincy within the National Health Service in Scotland has been and continues to be an important dimension of the Service's drive towards a more holistic perspective on care which recognizes and respects both spirituality and religion. There is a general acceptance of the need for chaplaincy and an acknowledgement that it provides a valuable service. Nevertheless, when one gets down to issues of precisely what needs chaplains are actually expected to fulfil, things become much less clear.

The need for the development of an empirical base for chaplaincy has been noted by the Scottish Executive (the devolved parliament of Scotland), and in 2003 the Quality Health Care Division of the Scottish Executive funded the authors of this book to engage in an 18-month study exploring the role and function of the hospital chaplain within the National Health Service in Scotland. The study was carried out in 2003–4 and involved all of the full-time hospital chaplains working for the National Health Service in Scotland.

Complexifying the situation: cultural analysis

The increasing interest in the relationship between spirituality and health

An examination of the spiritual landscape in Scotland throws up some interesting observations. In line with much of Western Europe (Davie 1994) there is a significant decrease in adherence to traditional, formal institutional religion. The decreasing number of people regularly attending places of worship evidences this (Scottish Church Census 2002). However, while traditional religion appears to be in decline, there is a corresponding *increase* in the number of people expressing the importance of spirituality (broadly defined) for their lives and claiming to have significant spiritual experiences and beliefs (Hay 1990). Thus spirituality appears to have migrated from the overtly religious towards a more individualistic and subjective quest that has no necessity for formal structure, doctrinal belief or any form of anchoring community of like-minded believers (Heelas *et al.* 2005). People now want to *believe* in things spiritual, but no longer wish to *belong* to traditional religious institutions (Davie 1994).

This broadening understanding of spirituality is reflected in healthcare settings by the increasing focus on spirituality within the literature surrounding medicine, nursing, social work and occupational therapy, a rising interest in complementary and alternative medicine (Austin 1998) and a developing holistic view of health and illness within which the role of chaplaincy is rapidly gaining recognition as a significant dimension (*Scottish Journal of Healthcare Chaplaincy* 2003).

Expanding spirituality from the universal to the particular

In a healthcare environment that values highly the role of the 'specialist', such a holistic view of health presents very particular challenges to individual professions and to the ways in which multidisciplinary teams perceive themselves and their function. As medicine and healthcare advance in knowledge of the micro-mechanisms of the 'sick body', so the need for greater specialization increases. In tension with this emphasis is the practical need expressed by people encountering illness, to be treated as whole persons who require the generalizable aspects of their illness and their unique experience of it to be held in critical tension throughout their experience of illness. Within such a context spirituality becomes of foremost importance.

To provide authentic holistic, active, total care requires that attention be given to providing appropriate services that meet the *actual* needs of patients and their carers, that is, not simply the needs that healthcare professionals may perceive or/and assume, without reference to the wishes, desires and experiences of patients. The concept of patient-focused care is currently central Scottish and UK Government healthcare policy, which stresses the importance of patient and carer views informing service developments (Scottish Executive 2001 and 2003) and there is a good deal of evidence to suggests that patients want to have their spiritual needs met within a healthcare context (Murray *et al.* 2004). Developing strategies to meet such expressed needs is therefore very much part of the current governmental approach and, obviously, of the discipline of chaplaincy.

Religion and health: the known research

In the light of these cultural changes it is not coincidental that spirituality and religion (understood as related but not synonymous concepts), are fast becoming recognized as a significant aspect of the healthcare research agenda, even among those more inclined towards the biomedical end of the research community spectrum (Fry 2000). The data from studies produced thus far is suggestive of associations between religious and spiritual observance and well-being (Koenig *et al.* 2001, Larson *et al.* 1997). For example, Koenig *et al.* (2001) report their examination of the relationship between religion and

health in about 1,200 studies. They rated the quality of those
studies, and on a 1=poor – 10=excellent scale, they found
29 they rated as 10s and 84 that were 9s. Their conclusion
(in part) was that: 'in the vast majority of the cross-sectional
studies and prospective cohort studies we identified, religious beliefs and practices rooted within established religious
traditions were found to be consistently associated with better
health and predicted better health over time' (p. 591). It has
also been suggested that religion and spirituality may be beneficial on a number of levels and in relation to a wide variety of
conditions, including:

• Lower blood pressure.
• Reduced serum cholesterol levels.
• Reduced levels of pain in cancer sufferers.
• Protection against depression and anxiety. (Larson *et al.*
1997).

While there is little research within this area which is done
specifically on chaplaincy, a recent good example of the potential this area holds is the study by William Iler *et al.* (2001). Iler
reports on the effects of daily visits by a chaplain to patients
with COPD (Chronic Obstructive Pulmonary Disease), and
compares their health outcomes with a second group with the
same diagnosis who were not visited. Results: by comparison –
the visited group were less anxious at discharge, their length
of stay was significantly less; their satisfaction with the hospital was significantly higher. One conclusion that might be
drawn is that the support of a chaplain has a demonstrable
effect on the hospitalized patient, certainly with that particular diagnosis.

   A similar evidence base to that being produced within the
United States has still to be developed within the United Kingdom and Europe. It is therefore not possible to draw direct
comparisons across cultures. Nevertheless, the evidence that
does exist is helpful in locating some potential benefits that
spirituality and religion could offer at a clinical as well as a
pastoral level. While this area of research was not a primary

focus of this project, it does provide some useful background information and enables us to begin to grasp something of the essence and complexity of the situation.

The current situation in Scotland

Patient focus and public involvement

In Scotland, a succession of Ministers of Health have promoted the philosophy of patient-focused care. This refers to the recognition of the importance of meeting patients' holistic needs and the importance of inclusion and choice at a number of different levels. Part of this initiative manifested in the Patient Focus and Public Involvement programme and the setting up of a funded unit (Scottish Executive 2003). The Patient involvement programme is seen as part of the core business of each of the hospital boards and will be judged in similar terms to the clinical standards audit. Another vital component of the patient-focused perspective is that of *cultural competence*. This is being developed in the Ethnic Minority unit, where inclusion of all and a holistic perspective is pursued.

Spiritual care guidelines

At the same time and in response to the types of changes and developments highlighted earlier, a steering group was set up to explore what was required in terms of enabling chaplains to provide effective spiritual care. This group produced a set of guidelines for good practice in chaplaincy. This process resulted in a Health Directive Letter to all Health Boards (Scottish Executive 2002), two conferences aimed at senior management, the setting up of a Chaplaincy Training Unit and the production of draft policy statements which are being agreed on at the time of writing and which are being steered and developed by chaplains.

Spirited Scotland

In tandem with this development, the Scottish Executive also funded an initiative known as Spirited Scotland which offers a broad perspective on spirituality and health in Scotland. It acts as a networking point, hosts a website and issues a regular newsletter focused on spirituality and health. In practical terms Spirited Scotland has participated in supporting the development of confidence among health-care staff to deal with spiritual issues by offering educational initiatives within the boards. The Centre for Spirituality, Health and Disability at the University of Aberdeen, is also pursuing a research and development agenda that promises to make a significant contribution to the area of spirituality and healthcare.

It is clear then that, within Scotland, there is an important movement to take healthcare in directions which meet the types of spiritual need which are prevalent within contemporary culture.

Changes in chaplaincy

Within the field of hospital chaplaincy, important shifts are taking place in response to the context of societal and political changes discussed above. The shifts relate to the theological and philosophical roots of chaplaincy, as well as to the texture of the care that is offered by chaplaincy under the banner of 'spiritual care'.

A brief historical reflection on chaplaincy in hospitals

One of the main changes for chaplains relates to the movement from being a specifically *religious* carer, to being a deliverer of *spiritual* care, which is defined as a distinct form of care that is not solely focused on religion. It will be helpful to think this through in relation to the development of the definition of the term 'chaplain'. Traditionally, the word chaplain refers to a clergyperson who has been commissioned by a faith group or an organisation to provide pastoral service in an institution, organisation, or governmental entity. Chaplaincy refers to the general activity performed by a chaplain, which may include crisis ministry, counselling, sacraments, worship, education, help in ethical decision-making, staff support, clergy contact and community or church co-ordination. (Smith 1990, p. 136)

The chaplain, normally an ordained member of the clergy, is thus seen, at least traditionally, to be the representative of a particular faith community who is sent to work within a specific setting. Chaplaincy is both vocation and Christian ministry. This pattern of chaplaincy has been represented within the development of hospital chaplaincy in Scotland. Historically, full-time Scottish healthcare chaplaincy has been linked exclusively to the Christian church. More specifically, the vast majority of full-time hospital chaplains have been ministers ordained into the ministry of Word and Sacrament within the Presbyterian Church of Scotland. Hospital chaplaincy within a Scottish context is thus seen as a particular mode of Christian ministry emanating primarily from the Protestant churches, the primary intention being to represent the Christian church within a healthcare context. This full-time presence has been and continues to be complemented by part-time ministers from other denominations and priests from the Roman Catholic Church who spend time (paid and voluntary) working within the hospitals, while at the same time maintaining responsibilities within their own parishes.

Until relatively recently, full-time chaplains were *employed* by the Church, but *paid* by the Trusts. Within this arrangement, the chaplain was able to maintain his or her status as ministers who worked directly for the Church. The Trusts, who were the receivers of chaplaincy services, were responsible for the financial arrangements. Very few hospitals employed their own chaplains directly. This tension between the Church as employer, and the boards as the purchaser and user of chaplaincy services has, arguably, meant that clear lines of communication, authority accountability and supervision have been difficult to establish. In an increasingly bureaucratic, competence-based and accountable environment, this has been recognized by some as a growing anomaly. There is currently a move to consider direct employment of chaplains by the NHS. Some chaplains have taken up this option, and discussions continue as to whether or not this should become common practice.

Changing roles

The traditional denominationally oriented model of chaplaincy is being challenged, not only at the bureaucratic level, but also by the spiritual changes highlighted previously. With the general cultural movement away from religion, narrowly defined, to a more generic understanding of 'spirituality', understood as a diverse human universal, there has emerged a redefinition of the spiritual positioning of chaplaincy. Chaplains now tend to refer to themselves not as 'Christian ministers', but as 'spiritual carers'. Departments of 'spiritual care' are now replacing 'chaplaincy departments' within a number of Trusts, indicating the transition from 'chaplain' as defined in religious terms above, to the more generic term: 'spiritual carer'. Healthcare chaplains are now required to think about, interpret and act upon considerably wider definitions of spiritual care than previously assumed. This has important theological and practical implications that will be explored below. One of the key questions that chaplains have to tackle is the issue of what healthcare chaplaincy actually is in the midst of the cultural, professional and spiritual changes and transitions that are shaping Scottish culture and healthcare practices. This project was aimed at beginning to find an answer to this question.

A brief methodological note

Readers may be wondering at this point why there is such a long preliminary analysis of this particular situation. The reason for providing such an extensive background for this particular study is that in order to fully understand the reasons for the methods chosen and the research question that was developed, it is necessary to have a firm grasp of the cultural, spiritual and political context from which this piece of research emerged. Such an approach relates directly to Gadamer's (1981) concept of the importance of prejudice and effective history in the process of interpretation that was described in Chapter 4. The current situation with regard to hospital chaplaincy is complex spiritually, culturally and historically. The results of this particular study would not make sense without an awareness of the complexity of the situation and the nature of the prehistory and prejudices which lie behind the data thrown up within the research process. It is with an awareness of this effective history and the prejudices that it creates within the researcher and the research participants that this study began to gather and analyse data on chaplaincy.

The method

The background and context of this study reveals that healthcare chaplaincy, like many other professions in healthcare, reflects a profession in transition. The purpose of the research was to examine the meaning and manifestation of the shifts in perspective and self-identification being experienced by chaplains in Scotland. We intended to capture something of this dynamic in the main research question: 'what do chaplains do?' We hoped that the data would tell us something about how the chaplains saw their current and changing role and the ways in which they were managing these changing horizons in practice. The challenge for the method of this study was to capture the philosophical tensions in daily practice.

Research aims

The broad aims of the research were

- To describe the current role and function of the hospital chaplain,
- To build on the existing knowledge around the areas of chaplaincy, spirituality, religion and their relation to the process of healthcare within the Scottish National Health Service.
- To explore the various perceptions of the work of the chaplain held within the healthcare context
- To identify what patients perceive as the most beneficial approaches to spiritual care and support.
- To put these findings into the context of the national guidelines on spiritual care and subsequent policy documents produced by the healthcare Trusts.

Ethnography

The original study design was based around the use of ethnography as its core data collection method. Ethnography and its less intense sociological bedfellow, 'participant observation', both attempt to get at the 'truth' of a situation by living in that situation and gaining deep understandings from within. The researcher becomes part of the setting and in so doing begins to understand that setting, sometimes in ways which challenge and confront those who are 'natural' to the setting with new insights, knowledge and truths. The researcher is required to hold both the position of *outsider* and that of *insider* within the particular setting.

The method of ethnography has a good deal of resonance with the Gadamerian framework presented in Chapter 4, and in particular the metaphor of the merging of horizons. Dowie (2002) makes the point that ethnography is a particular form of hermeneutics:

> Ethnography is hermeneutically grounded in that it takes account of the intersubjective nature of understanding,

the role of language in constructing meaning, and the role played by the participant observer's own horizon in the hermeneutical conversation. (p. 37)

Ethnography sits comfortably with hermeneutics and resonates with the type of hermeneutically oriented methodological framework we have outlined previously.

Perhaps more than any other method, the ethnographic study seeks to capture the 'strange in the familiar'. Its purpose is to challenge and complexify situations and accepted views of the nature of truth and reality and, in so doing, to 'render the familiar strange'. Ethnography takes its meaning and philosophical assumptions from the discipline of anthropology, where ethnography is the traditional research tool for that discipline. Within anthropological studies ethnography involves prolonged and close contact with research subjects. The ethnographic method gives the best possible chance to understand the participant in their own setting. True ethnographic method however is difficult to achieve in healthcare settings for a variety of reasons (Carlisle and Hudson 1997).

The question of truth and knowledge

In Chapters 2 and 4, we saw that the interpretive/hermeneutical position has a tendency to questions the fundamental basis of truth and reality. In Chapter 3 we explored how the implications of this issue might be addressed theologically. Nevertheless, it should be acknowledged that, even within the social sciences, the lack of certainty over the possibility of truth, knowledge and reality raises serious issues. In his book *The New Ethnography*, Norman Denzin (1997) highlights a number of these issues. Chief among them is his challenge to the idea that it might *never* be possible to understand the meaning of others' actions or to agree upon a version of 'reality'. He argues that understanding will always be subject to interpretation on the part of the ethnographer, who inevitably brings with her her own background knowledge and assumptions. Thus any hope of understanding another becomes a lost cause, and the ethnographic account is best read as an account of the ethnographer rather than the topic of study. Even then it can only be an account of the ethnographer on that day at that time rather than an account that stands outside the immediacy of interpretation.

We have already addressed some of the implications of such a suggestion in our discussion on hermeneutics and Chapter 3's critique of such an over-emphasis on the interpretative dimensions of human life. Here it will be enough to bear in mind that the ethnographer's bringing of her own pre-understandings to the research situation does not necessarily discount the possibility of discovering knowledge. Indeed, such prejudices are the necessary context for the movement towards knowledge.

If we take Denzin's critique seriously, we are left with two main alternatives. We can accept the suggestion that there is no such thing as a universally acceptable true account of a situation. In the case of the chaplains study this would mean that there is really no way of answering the question 'What do chaplains do?' Every data collection approach would be an interpretation either by the chaplain or by the researcher. This would mean that we could only answer the question 'What does this one chaplain say he/she does?' Indeed we could only answer this question for that moment in time because the chaplain might answer it differently at a different time of day, or in a different situation. A morning that was full of paperwork and frustrating administration might cause the chaplain to assert that the dominant task was to fill in forms. On another occasion the chaplain may have spent a morning with one patient in deeply personal and spiritual conversation. He/she might then assert that the primary task of the chaplain was to comfort and be a spiritual guide. How then might we present the data? The most honest way would be simply to choose to present data for all 44 Chaplains featured in the study in its raw state and ask the reader to interpret the data, in the knowledge that the interpretation is itself a reflection of the reader rather than the data.

Alternatively we can seek to reclaim a position that suggests that there can be a workable and shared reality or set of meanings that constitutes a response to the question: 'What do chaplains do?' and that it is possible to describe this set of meanings following a process of careful collection of data from a number of sources that yields, in time and with careful analysis, a picture of the role of the chaplain that is coherent and agreed upon until proved otherwise.

This second position is helpful but problematic. Taken to its natural conclusion, this second alternative appeals to a rather crude form of empiricism which assumes, until proven otherwise, that chaplains do what the hospital says they do (or what their formal job descriptions say that they do). If this is so, there is no problem in simply asking the hospital manager in charge of chaplains what chaplains do and recording this. There is assumed to be no complexity within the language used; prayer means prayer whoever uses it and whatever context it is used in. If the hospital manager says the chaplain says prayers for patients who have asked him to do so, then the researcher records that the chaplains say prayers and it will be clear to all what that practice means. Data collected in this way is not seen as problematic, either as a piece of valid and reliable information or as an activity in itself. However, the extreme of this position does not take into account the possibilities (borne out in reality) that many chaplains do not have active managers in the hospital systems, that if there are managers they have no idea what the chaplain does and the fact that the understanding of prayer differs greatly from chaplain to chaplain and indeed person to person. Without further excavation of the meaning behind the word 'prayer' there is little point in pursuing the line of enquiry.

A third way?

As with most areas of life what we need to find is a balance between the two extremes. A 'third way' in this difficult methodological minefield is to agree to suspend disbelief in a shared reality until proven otherwise. In other words we enter the situation with a hermeneutic of suspicion regarding the possibility of discovering shared truth. Then, through a careful process of observation, interpretation and analysis, move towards clearer and clearer approximations of the truth. As in our discussion in Chapter 3, this assumes that there is shared truth and a meaningful reality which can be moved towards. This position acknowledges that the search for truth and knowledge within the research context is a journey wherein both are emergent and dialogical rather than clearly given and immediately available to all.

This perception of knowledge is also an acknowledged dimension of the practical-theological enterprise which perceives truth as given, but understanding of that truth as dialogical and emergent. In terms of qualitative research method, this perspective on the emergence of knowledge is supported by the idea of triangulation (Denzin and Lincoln 1998; 2000, p. 391), wherein similar data is collected using a variety of data collection techniques, researchers and analytic methods. This concept is now being extended into the idea of crystallization, which actively encourages students of research methods to use a variety of different disciplines, tools to enhance their own interpretive skills, and literary expression (Denzin and Lincoln 1998). In this way the researcher is able to capture multiple perspectives on the phenomenon under observation and in so doing to build up a deeper and clearer understanding of the situation. It was within this perspective of critical realism and triangulated methods that this study took place.

The study design

The original design which was focused on ethnographic study was subject to almost immediate revision. There were a number of reasons for this: methodological and practical. In the case of this study there were three major considerations.

• The ethnographic work could not be carried out by an

experienced ethnographer.

- The ethics application process was in a state of transition just at the moment that the Chaplains Study research was being presented for ethical approval.
- The write-up and presentation requirements – to make the research accessible and easily available to busy hospital staff – precluded a laborious presentation of data for interpretation by the reader.

It was therefore decided at an early stage to rethink the data collection strategies within the qualitative framework. It is important at the outset of a piece of research to have in mind the research question at all times. Can the data collection techniques provide material that can answer those questions was a key question in our devising of a more workable data collection framework. Our assumptions based on our own experience of qualitative research and hospital chaplaincy, were from the outset that the chaplains would not be able to give simple accounts of their role in the hospital. We therefore required a mode of exploration that would allow us to capture the complexity of the accounts. To this end we employed three data collection techniques:

- Stage 1: Carry out telephone interviews with all 44 full-time chaplains.
- Stage 2: Carry out case studies using observation and informal interview techniques. Here we would draw upon ethnographic techniques and approaches as outlined above, but use them outwith a formal ethnographic framework.
- Stage 3: Re-interview chaplains, once again by telephone.

Table 3 outlines this process in more detail.

Table 3: A framework for data collection

Telephone interviews	Case studies	Telephone interviews
Initial interviews of 44 full-time healthcare chaplains in Scotland	Observation, interviews and informal discussions with chaplains, patients, staff and family members in three chaplaincy sites.	Second set of interviews with full-time chaplains pursuing themes derived from telephone interviews (stage 1) and observational data.
Use of a four-item structure to guide the interview	Sites were chosen for their variety and geographical spread. Sixteen characteristics/ descriptors were identified from the data and these were given scores for each chaplaincy site. Five sites were initially chosen and three were finally used.	Themes pursued
• Personal journey into chaplaincy – who is the chaplain? • Typical day of the chaplain • Working arrangements within the Trust • The nature and development of chaplaincy		• Leadership • Professionalization • Spiritual needs of patients • Spiritual needs of chaplains • Religious and spiritual care • Spiritual correctness • Teamworking • Working in institutions
	Ethical permission was gained for the observation case studies. This took a very long time. This project was one of the first to engage in the new system which involved more paperwork, more screening bodies and uncertain protocols.	
	In the end it was practical to look at three sites and re-interview. The re-interview was not in the original protocol but was indicated by the content and flow of the research.	

Stage 1: Telephone interviews

Background knowledge of chaplaincy in Scotland and reading of other studies allowed us to devise four key areas of interest that guided the first set of interviews. These interviews were mainly conducted by a research assistant following piloting and training from the grant holders. The four key categories probed for information were

- The personal journey into chaplaincy – Who is the chaplain?
- The typical day of the chaplain
- The working arrangements for chaplaincy within the Health Boards
- The nature and development of chaplaincy as understood by the chaplain

Stage 2: Case studies

Case studies include observation, interviews and informal discussions with chaplains, patients, staff and family members in three chaplaincy sites. The selection of the sites for the case studies was important. The rationale behind the sample always needs to be explicit. In this case sites were chosen according to their variety and geographical spread. Sixteen characteristics/descriptors were identified from the data and these were given scores from 1 to 5 for each chaplaincy site. Five sites were initially chosen which offered a range of scores and thus variety, and three were finally used. The realities of the research timetable and the extreme length of time it took to negotiate the ethics application process accounted for the reduction to three sites.

Ethics

Ethical permission was gained for the observation and interviewing of patients in the case studies. This took a long time and, because of this, became a significant problem. This project was one of the first to use a new system which involved more paperwork, more screening bodies and uncertain and at times unsuitable protocols. Frequently the information required in the application forms for ethical permission was couched in very 'scientific' language, leaving little room for explanation of the qualitative method. This problem for qualitative methods is noted by Stephenson and Beech (1998). At its heart is the implicit assumption that 'good research' can be identified primarily via questions about sample size, statistical power and harmful interventions. From the perspective of qualitative research, for the reasons outlined thus far in this book, these are clearly the wrong questions to be asking in relation to good qualitative research. Greenhalgh (1997) provides a useful description of qualitative research and the relevant questions to ask with it and of it.

We are not, of course, arguing that qualitative research should not require ethical permission. Qualitative research is neither innocuous nor inherently benign. Qualitative research techniques can be disturbing for participants, particularly when they explore and unpack unwelcome insights into situations or experiences. There are also complex power dynamics that always need to be acknowledged and born in mind. As Becker (1967) has pointed out, researchers will inevitably find themselves taking sides. The risks must be understood and accepted by participants in order that the research is ethically sound and as safe as possible. The point we would like to raise is not that ethics are unimportant in qualitative research, but that there may be a systemic bias towards quantitative research which serves to make it difficult for ethics committees to understand and work with proposals relating to qualitative research.

Stage 3: Second interviews

The second set of interviews were not in the original protocol but were indicated as necessary by the content and flow of the research and the nature of the emergent data. These interviews with full-time chaplains pursued themes that were derived from the first set of telephone interviews and the case study material. These included:

- Leadership
- Professionalization
- Spiritual needs of patients
- Spiritual needs of chaplains
- Religious and spiritual care
- Spiritual correctness
- Teamworking
- Working in institutions

In this way through these three stages, we were able to gather rich and meaningful data which provided a diverse and full interpretative context for the continuing task of analysis.

Analysis of the data – the interpretation

The analysis is always the heart of any research project. It is that point in the research process where the mass of data that has been generated begins to be formed into meaningful units which will illuminate the complexities of the situation. The process of analysis is not a once-only event. It would be an error to assume that within qualitative research the method of data collection is in some way sequential to the process of analysis. The analysis should always be firmly linked to the research question and carried out simultaneously with the collection of the data. As this dialogical process unfolds, it may be that eventually it becomes clear that the research question is the wrong question. In the case of the chaplains study, the research question remained robust throughout the process of analysis and reflection: 'What do chaplains do?' seemed to be a solid question which related well to the collected data.

In the chaplains study the analysis took place throughout the process of data collection, and each step of the analysis informed the next phase of the data collection process. This caused some difficulties for the process of gaining ethical permission for the case studies, due to the fact that it was not possible to be specific about the precise nature of the case study and the next phase of the focus of the enquiry. We could not, for example, be certain as to the exact nature of the questions to be asked of the staff, patients or chaplains in the case studies since they were dependent on prior analysis and thinking. Again, the purpose of the case study related closely to the early process of analysis. This lack of certainty caused the ethics committees to be reticent and slow in granting permission for the study. The problem was not, however, that the project was ethically dangerous. Rather the problem was in persuading the ethics committees that qualitative research requires and indeed demands a degree of flexibility and openness with regard to its structure and design and that this flexibility did not open up the possibility of ethical infringement. Such flexibility was not built into the system, which was primarily geared towards empirical research from within the natural sciences.

The process of analysis

The actual process of analysis of data starts from the moment that data collection commences. Indeed, it could be argued that the analytic process starts earlier than this! In this case we embarked first on a general sweep of the 'situation', involving ourselves in an excursion into the world of the chaplain via the literature and informal discussions with chaplains and people involved with chaplaincy. This allowed us to set up our original categories for the first interviews. The data was collected by telephone interviews which were then immediately typed up and entered into a software package called NVivo. NVivo is a Windows-based software package designed specifically to enable the effective manipulation and analysis of qualitative data. NVivo is used to encode and interrogate coded data. The software allows the qualitative researcher to analyse text collected during interviews. It works with data which is either structured or unstructured. It can also be used to analyse other forms of document. The way in which the data can be coded with NVivo and its powerful searching capabilities means that the researcher can view the data in many different ways, leading to a rich and creative analysis (QSR NVivo 2002). This package is quite sophisticated and flexible, and at this stage we tended to use it as a data sorting device, rather than a specific tool of analysis. Once the data was entered, a process which involved transferring files from Word into Rich Text Format and then into the package, we were able effectively to begin the process of sorting the data into its initial categories.

A primary task of analysis is for the researcher to read the data and become very familiar with its content; to *immerse* herself in the data. It was necessary for this activity to take place before the data was re-sorted into the categories that would guide the ongoing analysis. It cannot be emphasized strongly enough that within the process of analysis, familiarity with the original text of the data is *essential*, as themes are sought and developed. Once the data is absorbed and understood by the researchers the categorization can begin.

It will be helpful for us here to look in some detail at one aspect of the data analysis for the chaplains study. One of the questions that we asked the chaplains was what their idea of a 'typical day' might look like. This question referred to the particular actions and practices which made up a day which was representative of what chaplains did on most days. All of the answers to this question 'What is a typical day?' were sorted into a 'typical day' file. We analysed the responses to this question for themes that would tell us something about the nature of the typical day. These themes were then re-analysed so that we were able to produce what the package calls 'trees' of categories and nodes that are linked together. These can be produced as a visual aid, laying out clearly the various themes and their related sub-themes. The software helped us sort out our ideas into manageable chunks. It meant that we could use the different ideas and themes that emerged to interrogate the first round of questionnaires. The ability to interrogate depended to some extent on how the data (the transcripts) were marked. For instance, through the initial readings of the interviews we saw clearly that the chaplains found it helpful to think about their typical day in relation to how parish ministry 'used to be'. This turned into a node for analysis within itself. As nodes such as these began to emerge, so a thematic pattern became apparent which provided us with an overview of the connecting themes which made up the practice of chaplaincy.

Software packages such as NVivo are of course only as sensitive as the researcher doing the analysis. In this case, the interpretation and meaning of the themes, nodes and categories required further excavation via reading, thinking and discussion. The package helped us organize the material, but it was this wider reflection and interpretative process which formed the heart of the analysis.

The intellectual job of the researcher participating in such a process of analysis is to *make sense* of the emerging categories and to make sure that the categories are derived from the data rather than imposed upon the data (reflexivity). This is the critical task and requires checking preferably by more than one person. It also reinforces the importance of an original understanding and knowledge of the 'raw' interview data that is then deconstructed into categories. The analysis is only ever as good as the analyser. It can be seen from this that there is great value in the process of triangulation as described in Chapter 2.

Theological reflection

Out of this analytical process emerged a variety of important insights and perspectives that provided new understandings of what chaplains do. Here we will examine two interesting issues with particular import for theology and practice:

1 The distinctiveness of chaplaincy as a form of ministry perceived as separate from parish ministry.
2 The suggestion that chaplains should be perceived as spiritually neutral.

What is distinctive about the chaplain's role compared to parish ministry?

It has been noted that historically the majority of Scottish hospital chaplains have been and continue to be ministers of the Church of Scotland. Yet, within the hospital setting, the perception and goal of ministry were perceived as different from those in the parish. Reflecting on whether this difference was real or imagined was an interesting aspect of our findings.

The analysis explored the tensions and complementarities that the chaplains highlighted, between the role of the chaplain and the role of the parish minister. In doing this we were able to explore some of the ways that chaplains sought to distinguish themselves as professionals with a discrete mode of ministry that was different from parish ministers. It became clear during the analysis of the first set of interviews that rather than having a positive perception of what their role was as hospital chaplains, there was a tendency for chaplains to describe their role in terms of the ways in which it differed from parish ministry. In other words, chaplains tended to identify themselves not by what they do, but by what they did not do. This related to a general tendency of chaplains to distance themselves from institutional religion.

All but two of the full-time chaplains who participated in the study had come from parish ministry. Some had been in the parish for many years. The analysis of the perceived differences between parish ministry and healthcare chaplaincy allowed a significant debate to emerge. Using the chaplains' own categories, we were able to create a table which showed the perceived differences reported by the chaplains (see Table 4). This is just one category that 'emerged' from the analysis of the data. While it was the respondents (the chaplains) who volunteered this distinction, it was the researchers who chose to highlight this category as of importance. Sometimes 'important' is understood to be linked to 'numerous'. In qualitative research there is little reference to 'How many?' and most reference to 'How?' This question of the distinction between hospital chaplaincy and parish ministry prompted a *how* question – rather than how *many* chaplains said what. This is a crucial distinction to make.

Table 4: Perceived differences between parish minister and healthcare chaplaincy

Parish	Chaplaincy
Central figure	Peripheral figure
Having to have your finger on the pulse in parish ministry in case some things went pear-shaped Int C26, s4.1, p72–5	In Church may know what is going on but here may be last person in this setting . . . Focus being on medical care . . . Int C14, s6.3, p112
Clearly defined and understood role	Less understood role/isolated
Faith community, identity of minister Int C4, s2.4, p16–18	In hospital have to prove yourself more, earn respect of people' Int C4, s2.4, p16–18
Knew you could be isolated in parish ministry but was different isolated . . . in a different sense, affinity with people, talking same language, importance of pastoral and spiritual care, although people (in chaplaincy) are supportive its recognized in parish and don't have to work at it Int C17, s4.2, p59	In chaplaincy could be more easily isolated . . . profile of being a chaplain to be worked at . . . can be isolating Int C17, s4.2, p59

Parish	Chaplaincy
Competitive	**Supportive**
When arrived in parish local minister phoned him, wished him well but not that well because if he did really well could take people away from his church Int C31, s4.1, p39–41	In chaplaincy at the beginning there wasn't a week that went past when other chaplains didn't phone and see how they could help Int C31, s4.1, p39–41
Agenda	**Different or no agenda**
Parish ministry . . . is like achieving target, bums on seats, like running a business, falling numbers Int C29, s.4.2, p56–7	Chaplaincy meets people where they are and more fits the gospel picture and ministry of Christ. Int H6, s2, p9–11
Meetings	**People**
More people centred in chaplaincy. Don't have building, finances to worry about. Dealing with people in deeper level Int C22, s41, p58–9	More frontline dealing with patients, staff, families at time of need. Int C2, s4.2, p55
	More deeper conversations here in a week than did in a month in the parish Int C7, s4.3, p59–62
Less able to get away	**More office hours**
Could have wedding on a Saturday and if that was day off, half day gone . . . five phone calls through teatime. Int C7, s.4.3, p59–62	Don't know when had Saturday commitment . . . when he goes home, they phone the switchboard Int. C7, s4.3, p59–62

Parish	Chaplaincy
More control over time	**More intense**
To control work as it came in in a sense, if lots going on, could go through to study and read some theology books Int C27, s2.2, p14	Come in till you go home, constant (at hospital feel like 'fire fighting' responding to need. Int C27, s.2.2, p14 Time. None of it. In parish ministry time was always a problem but at least there were elders one could delegate to (hopefully) Int H7, s3.1, p18–20
Longer-term contact	**Shorter-term contact**
Parish ministry working in context of longer-term relationships Int C21, s 4.1, p40–2 See people grow up, marry them, baptize their children. Int C1, s6.6, p70–1	Major adjustment in full-time chaplaincy, contact much shorter Int C21, s4.1, p40–2 Have to make an encounter count, no second chances Int H2, s5, p37–55
More balance	**More focus/crisis**
Parish obviously working with people in broad context of home life Int C19, s5.1, p49–50 In parish he worked in buried one child Int C12, s 3.12, p66	In hospital much sharper focus Int C19, s5.1, p49–50 Hasn't a clue now how many child funerals conducted Int C12, s3.12, p66

Parish	Chaplaincy
Church people	Non church people
Not just involved in religious club Int. C16, s4.1, p61–2	Working in real world, providing service for folk with no religious faith . . . still appreciate and look to chaplain Int C16, s4.1, p61–2

There are some interesting characterizations in this data that may indicate an implicit or overt effort by chaplains to move away from seeing themselves as parish ministers, towards a self-understanding as a distinctive group called 'chaplains'. This is tied in with the concurrent movement of chaplains from religious carers to 'spiritual care-givers', with one very much rooted in the Church and the Christian tradition and the other much more fluid, uncommitted and open to wide variations in what spirituality means and what spiritual care entails. The movement from parish minister to chaplain may also be perceived as part of the naturally occurring process of professionalization. (Abbott and Meerabeau 1998). Becoming part of a distinct group (in this case chaplains) requires distinctions such as these to be made, in this case the unique work of the chaplain as distinct from other forms of ministry. In the light of this it is worth looking in more detail at the implications of the data presented in Table 4.

Chaplains see themselves, on the whole, as more peripheral to any particular community than parish ministers do.

Parish ministers have an identifiable group of people for whom they are responsible: *a parish*. Offering care for the people within a particular parish sits well with their religious calling to the ministry of Word and Sacrament. They also have a role that is fully legitimized by those who choose to be-come part of the church communities that sit within particular parishes. Chaplains' perceptions of the parish minister was that he or she is a central figure within their community. It is true the authority of the minister is not as strong as in previ-ous times and that the church communities are considerably smaller than they have been. Nevertheless, parish ministers within the Church of Scotland are called to care for entire parishes which contain religious and non-religious. (It is inter-esting to note that at the level of being called to serve religious and non-religious populations, there is in fact a strong similar-ity between chaplaincy and parish ministry.)

Chaplains are seen as optional extras within a hospital setting

Chaplains do not have such a clear-cut official role within a healthcare setting. Their constituency is mobile and transient and their perceived place within the healthcare team is much less clear or well established.

Chaplains are marginalized and over-stretched

The remit of the Church of Scotland parish minister is to be responsible for every person within the parish boundary. However, in reality, it is only a small number of people who actually engage with parish ministers. Similarly, the role of the chaplain is, in principle, to care for the spiritual needs of every-one within the healthcare system. However, again, in reality it is a relatively small number of people with whom chaplains engage. Both chaplains and parish ministers are in different ways marginalized and over-stretched.

Chaplains have a different agenda to that of the parish minister

The primary task of parish ministers within the Church of Scotland could be summarized as being to proclaim the gospel, administer the Word and the Sacraments, and to enable people to find a meaningful spiritual home within their particular congregation. These are primarily *religious* needs.

Chaplaincy, as we have seen, has a more general focus on *spiritual* needs, a focus which chaplains suggest does not require overt proclamation of or adherence to specific religious beliefs. Indeed, in this study, some chaplains went so far as to suggest that their work is *agenda-free*, and that the nature of their discrete profession could be specifically identified by its agenda-free basis. This is of course a highly problematic suggestion. The hermeneutical perspective outlined previously in this book would strongly suggest that the idea of agenda-free engagement is neither possible nor desirable. Nevertheless, in the views of this study's participants, the distinction between chaplaincy and parish ministry over this issue is clear: parish ministers had a religious and theological agenda which was central to their work; for chaplains this was not necessarily the case.

Less emphasis on church buildings, church groups and leaky roofs

A number of chaplains applauded the freedom chaplains have from certain administrative and financial aspects of parish ministry. Chaplaincy was perceived to be liberating and much less bureaucratic. However, the increasing administrative burden now placed on chaplains as they become a more recognizable group within the healthcare setting appears to be impinging on this freedom.

Easier to escape from the role of minister

While the chaplains thought their role was more intense, it was also easier to escape from the role of 'minister'. Their experience of parish ministry was that parish ministers were assumed always to be available. The chaplains thought that, on balance, they had more time for relationships than the parish minister.

The myth of difference

In the data chaplains present themselves as having a distinctive position as clergy, separate from parish ministry and operating on the axis of spirituality and religion. They are charged with responding to both religious and spiritual need. While it is clear from the data why they think that their role is quite distinct from parish ministry, it is not completely clear that this distinction stands up to scrutiny. This 'myth of difference' may be a useful device to establish their own credentials, but the situation is in fact more complex than some seemed to assume. If chaplains are not religious carers and if their specific theological and ministerial training has only tangential significance, then why is it necessary for chaplains to be ministers at all? This point is emphasized further in the following discussion on the idea of 'spiritual neutrality'.

Spiritual neutrality

A dominant discussion within the spirituality and healthcare debate as it relates to chaplaincy has to do with the importance of *spiritual neutrality*. Chaplains believe that spiritual care has to be available to people of 'all faiths and none'. The Chaplaincy Guidelines are quite clear on this point and the sensitivities surrounding these issues are well recorded. As we have seen, the majority of full-time chaplains in Scotland are ordained Christian ministers. There therefore appears to be a clear tension between the chaplain's vocation, calling and training as a specifically Christian minister, and the political ideal of 'spiritual neutrality'. As we reflected on the data, it became clear that chaplains were in a position where they had to develop implicit or explicit forms of *spiritual correctness* which were in some ways comparable to the idea of political correctness. Political correctness has of course been a useful concept that has been used in the process of sensitizing society to the implicit prejudices it shows towards certain groups (women, people of colour, people with disabilities, etc.); this prejudice is present in the language we use, the attitudes we have and the social structures we create which make equality and inclusive citizenship problematic for these groups. 'Spiritual correctness' relates to the chaplain's recognizing implicit prejudices in the way that spirituality is understood and spiritual care is instituted within healthcare practices. It involves the chaplain moving beyond the boundaries of their own religious or denominational position and beginning to recognize the ways in which the more generic model of spirituality might be occluded by a primary focus on religion. In response the chaplains have begun to model a new way of being spiritual and in so doing hope to raise people's consciousness to a more inclusive understanding of spirituality.

Personal faith

However, positive as this is in some ways, in practice negotiating the tensions between the various expectations is complex. While the chaplains in our study enjoyed being free of the denominational party line, they nonetheless felt that their faith made a difference to how they worked as chaplains. It gave them a reason for what they were doing as well as supplying them with spiritual support, strength and encouragement. While there was a general push towards a generic understanding of spirituality, a number of chaplains stated that they were reluctant to lose the 'Christian bit'. The general theological position was to believe that God's role could be implicit in the ministry of chaplaincy without the need for it to be mentioned directly.

For many chaplains, the Bible was a source of inspiration, comfort and guidance for practice rather than a rule book. The 'road to Emmaus' was mentioned several times as a good example of biblical support for the chaplains to model. (On the road to Emmaus the risen Christ spoke with some of his disciples, but they didn't recognize him.) The chaplains also spoke about the importance of praying, quiet devotions or meditating as part of their personal, routine self-spiritual care. The idea of being 'upheld in prayer' by others was also viewed as important and offered comfort and support during difficult times. It is worth noting that these spiritual expressions are personal rather than communal. There is no need for a community of faith. In this sense the chaplain's expressions of spirituality and spiritual care revealed strong similarities to contemporary postmodern individualistic spirituality.

Dissociation from institutional religion

Some chaplains noted that their own faith or their attitude towards faith issues had changed or been challenged over the years. This may be what leads someone into chaplaincy and it may also happen during his or her time in chaplaincy. This 'journey' was highlighted as important within the majority of the interviews. The chaplains also indicated that they had theological doubts, uncertainties and difficulties. They felt that they were becoming less identified with the institution and doctrines of the Church. Chaplains also felt it was important to know their own base and boundaries while being open to others. Their own faith base motivated and determined their ability to be spiritually neutral with others.

> She does what she does in Christ's name, she wouldn't enter a conversation desperate to mention Jesus. (2nd Int C11)

Having a strong foundation was seen as making a difference

to practice. Faith gives support, strength and encouragement to the chaplains, but it does not necessarily affect the modes of practice they chose to adopt.

> gives strength and perspective on suffering, illness, loss, doesn't believe this is part of God's ordained plan, it's stuff that happens to folk. (Int C16 s2)

The chaplains faith informed their whole attitude, their whole being. God's role was implicit and present in encounters with people.

> Don't need to use traditional God language or mention God, for God to be present . . . is more hazy not as easily definable but just as authentic. (1st Int C37)

A needs-led theology

There is no doubt from the data that the majority of chaplains saw themselves as Christians with a foundational faith based in that tradition. Freed from the concerns of the parish, they saw themselves as more able to practise and live the gospel and be more 'Christlike' in the hospital setting. The idea of being 'like Christ' for those whom they encounter emerged with some frequency. At one level this seems like a straightforward affirmation of the compassionate nature of their ministry. However, a deeper reflection indicates that acting 'like Christ' is not as straightforward as it first appears. The emergence of this ideal poses a tension with the chaplains' expressed desire to be providing a service which is person-centred and 'needs-led'. When chaplains talk about being 'Christlike', it is not evident that this is a clearly thought-out theological position. Which dimension of Christ is it that they are seeking to reflect? The preaching Christ, the healing Christ, the condemning/judging Christ, the angry Christ? The prophetic Christ? The Christ whom chaplains wanted to be like was very clearly and usually unequivocally distinguished from the idea of evangelism and proselytizing. Indeed one of the difficulties for some of the whole-time chaplains was that they saw their part-time colleagues as much more evangelical and religiously orientated, a position which they viewed as problematic within a healthcare setting. This stands in tension with the ministry of Jesus, which had a primary focus on bringing people into right relationship with the *one and only* God of the Jews.

Chaplains saw their work as Christian and Christlike but only in certain dimensions. Where then does their image of Christ come from? In a needs-led culture, it would appear that the content of being 'Christlike' is derived from the particular needs of the individual before them, individuals who have no necessary knowledge of the Christian tradition. So, the content of being 'Christlike' is often determined not by theology, but by *secular humanism* as it is communicated to the chaplain in the pastoral encounter. To be 'Christlike' is an expression of a desire to act acceptingly and compassionately, but the image of Christ tends not to be taken from a thorough exegesis of the Christian tradition, but rather from the expectations of a needs-led healthcare culture. We highlight this important theological point not as a criticism of chaplains but as a challenge to assist them in clarifying the actual nature of the knowledge base that they work from and that underpins their practice and professional ideals.

Conclusion

Ministry is a complicated and multifaceted enterprise which is currently encountering new and unknown challenges and issues within contemporary Western culture. Our exploration of one aspect of ministry, chaplaincy, has yielded some interesting findings and has revealed some complex tensions between chaplains and parish ministers, chaplains and the established church and chaplains and the way that healthcare is currently practised within a Scottish context. Qualitative research methods have enabled us to engage in a process of complexification which has allowed us to reveal and understand some of the deep theological understandings and challenges which sit at the heart of the developing and changing discipline of chaplaincy. The specific methods used here – ethnography, telephone interviewing, computer-assisted data analysis – have worked together to provide a reflective context within which theological reflection can be done clearly and effectively and in a way which challenges chaplains to reflect on the nature of faithful practice and the place of their religious heritage in the process of ministry.

7

Researching Pastoral Issues: Religious Communities and Suicide

Introduction

As we have moved through this book it has become clear that the exploration and analysis of situations is a fascinating and demanding enterprise. At first glance situations appear to be relatively straightforward. However, once we begin to scrape the surface and examine the rich complexities of meaning, history, culture and spirituality that are involved with even the simplest of situations, we find exciting and challenging new understandings and possibilities. The area of pastoral care with its roots in the complexities of human beings, relationships and communities is a particularly complex area of investigation. A good deal of the pastoral literature focuses on techniques for caring aimed at particular individuals with discrete and easily identifiable problems or concerns. Some pastoral theologians have highlighted the need for a wider social and sometimes political analysis of pastoral situations in order that effective and appropriate pastoral care can be offered to individuals and communities (Pattison 1994). These theologians recognize that the pastoral task is much deeper and more complex than the individualistic therapeutic paradigm would allow. We would most certainly agree with those who take a wider perspective on the pastoral task. We would argue that in order to care for the individual, one needs to have an awareness of her social positioning, the context within which her problems emerge, the spiritual and political values and assumptions that structure her expectations and values. All of these things combine to make up the experience of particular challenges and problems. Earlier we suggested that, to an extent, depression was socially structured. Here we would want to suggest that all human illness and the problems and challenges we encounter have a crucial social structure which, if omitted from the 'caring equation' can mean that pastoral carers miss the mark in significant ways.

In this chapter we will explore one particularly pressing pastoral issue, which demands an understanding which is socially, culturally and spiritually informed: the rising rates of suicide, particularly among young men. This is a pressing and increasing problem throughout the Western world. It is particularly pressing within the Highlands of Scotland which has the highest rate of suicide among young men in the country. Critical reflection on this situation using insights from qualitative research will enable us to access some hidden dimensions of this pastoral situation and will allow us to look carefully at precisely what pastoral strategies might be most appropriate.

The situation

Suicide among young men in the Highlands of Scotland

In 1981 the rate among UK men aged 15–24 was 10.6 per 100,000 population. In 1997 it stood at 16.4 per 100,000. The rate among men has therefore increased by 55 per cent in 16 years. Young men are now four times as likely to kill themselves as young women (Morton 2000). Recent Scottish suicide figures show a reversal of rates in Scotland compared with England and Wales. (Stark *et al.* 2004). There are now higher suicide rates in Scotland than in England and Wales for both sexes, even allowing for differences in the way that suicides are defined. There is a consistently higher rate of suicide in the area of Highland than in other areas of Scotland.

The social and cultural context

The phenomenon of suicide is particularly complex and multi-faceted. Suicide and deliberate self-harm affects individuals, families, communities and society and confronts us with the stark reality of a variety of social, economic and spiritual issues. It lays bare societal problems such as social deprivation, poverty, mental illness and attitudes towards people with mental illness. It confronts us with deep spiritual questions of meaning, hope and social cohesion and poses important theological questions which are pastorally highly significant.

In 1897, Emile Durkheim, a founding father of the discipline of sociology, suggested that suicide was a social response or social act (Douglas 1967). He classified suicide into three types: anomic, egoistic and altruistic. Both anomic and egoistic suicide involves the detachment of the person from his/her social setting to the point where normative values are no longer relevant. The individual becomes adrift from a socially cohesive setting. Durkheim was particularly interested in the relationship between the individual and society.

His work on suicide was a reaction to the emergence of individualism in nineteenth-century social thought. In his seminal work on suicide he suggested that this rise in individualism and consequent movement away from religious collectivity creates a crisis within the individual. Durkheim explained religion from the perspective of its social function. It is an integrating factor in society. 'Religion is the symbolic expression of human dependence on society' (Heitink 1999, p. 41). Usually when society is in crisis, religion and the unity of society is reaffirmed. If this does not happen a state of anomie (detachment from societal values) occurs. Anomic societies are a serious threat to both the individual identity and social order.

While Durkheim's study was primarily intended to demonstrate the importance of sociology and, more specifically, the importance of the need for an independent scientific discipline concerned with human societ, the content and his analysis of the nature of suicide resonates down the generations. The concept of anomie seemed to have particular pertinence for the study discussed here. Could there be a similar sense of disconnection and anomie among the young men who were taking their own lives in Highland?

What do we already know about the Church and suicide?

Problems with social and gender roles

It has been suggested (Swinton 2000) that the values and gender expectations mediated by modern Western culture are implicated in the phenomenon of suicide. An emphasis on material success and traditional gender expectations puts significant pressure on young men. In a society where social value is determined by employment and income-generation, those unable to compete at this level are vulnerable to the types of crises of worth and identity that may well form a significant dimension of the processes leading up to the act of suicide. In a rural area like Highland, with its shifting patterns of unemployment and social insecurity, the potential for the development of feelings of exclusion from the mainstream and cultural expectations of 'success' are always on the horizon.

Coupled with this is a general uncertainty about what it means to be a man. Traditional role models of manliness have been eroded in significant ways. As Paul Thomson puts it:

> The face of men in Scotland has been burnt off and needs to be filled in again. For many young men today, their role models are violent, bullying and contemptuous, rather than strong, caring and affirming.

This uncertainty about gender roles and expectations works itself out in other ways that are important in terms of understanding suicide:

• Showing vulnerability, asking for help and acknowledging personal problems contradict many young men's view of what it means to be a man.

- Loss of traditional male roles (for example 'breadwinner'), poor health and identity problems (linked for example to unemployment, fathering, terminal illness, sexuality or imprisonment) all substantially increase the risk of suicidal behaviours.
- There is also evidence to suggest men's belief that surviving the suicidal act is somehow 'unmasculine' and a sign of failure.
- Young men are particularly poor users of virtually any health or related services on a voluntary basis. Men do not use primary healthcare in the same way as women – and this is particularly the case for young men.
- Counselling and advice services are used at least three times more often by women than men. (Morton 2000)

All of these factors play together to create the type of anomic experience that was highlighted by Durkheim.

The spiritual nature of the problem

If we understand spirituality broadly as the search for meaning, purpose, hope, value, love and a sense of the Holy, then it is clear that the crisis being described has significant spiritual elements. This being so, religious communities may well have a positive role to play. There is evidence that access to strong and coherent social meaning can act as a preventative factor for suicidal behaviour (Stack 1983; Stein *et al.* 1992; Wright *et al.* 1993). Religious communities hold the potential to offer such modes of social meaning and coherence. These communities contain formal systems of beliefs centring on some conception of God and expressing the views of a particular religious group or community. Faith communities, in essence, seek to answer the following questions:

> Who am I? Where did I come from? Where am I going to? Why?
> Who are you? Where did you come from? Where are you going? Why?

What is this world? Where did it come from? Where is it going? Why?

They can provide forms of relationship and social support which the research literature suggests are missing from the lives of many young men who commit suicide (Morton and Francis 2000). There is some research evidence to suggest that this hypothesis contains truth and that people with religious beliefs and an active involvement in religious communities are less likely to commit suicide. There is therefore existing evidence to suggest that religious beliefs and religious communities can act as preventative agents for people who feel suicidal. The problem is that, for the reasons outlined above, young men are less likely to access them.

The situation in Highland

However, while there is general evidence to suggest the pastoral potential of religious communities in dealing with suicide events, we know little of how communities in Highland utilize this resource and whether or not these communities function positively within that context. We do know that Highland and the Western Isles have a history and contemporary experience which is profoundly influenced by strong religious and spiritual traditions. We also know that although the national church attendance rates continue to drop, a strong and rising percentage of the population continue to acknowledge the importance of their spiritual lives.

What we do not know about the Church and suicide

While we know some things about suicide, there remains a great deal that we do not know. How do ministers of the Church and their congregations react to and work with attempted suicide or the families of people who have committed suicide? What is the extent of their knowledge of mental health problems? How do they 'construct' suicide in their

own thinking? Is this is an issue for them or the communities?
If it is, how do they respond when faced with a suicide? Is their
response different if a person belongs to their religious community? How do their religious beliefs shape their pastoral
responses to the experience of suicide? How do they perceive
suicide to impact upon families and the wider community or
what their training needs might be? These are the types of
questions that we used as we developed the reflective context
for the current study. The situation as laid down above indicates the possibility that religious communities and ministers
(perceived as primary pastoral carers) may have a significant
role in suicide events. Having done this initial work and developed some foundational understandings we needed to begin
to sharpen our thinking about the research questions. Here we
found Jennifer Mason's 'five difficult questions' to be a useful
conceptual framework for development.

Five difficult questions

Mason (1996) suggests that there are five difficult questions
that have to be addressed before any qualitative research
project can be embarked upon:

1 *What is the nature of the phenomena or entities or social reality (situation) which I wish to investigate?*

This question relates to *ontology*. It challenges the researcher
or research team to spell out the particular way in which they
see social reality. Mason argues that the way the researcher
sees social reality will determine how the research question is
formulated and the way the method is chosen and developed.
This is a difficult question to begin with and it may be that the
researchers have to return to the question again and again as
they 'mature' in their thinking. She suggests that there are two
extreme ontological positions. At one pole is the position that
sees the world (reality) as unproblematic made up of visible
component parts which have a clear and identifiable logic. The

opposite pole on the ontological spectrum is to view the world (reality) as profoundly problematic and made of complex and intricate patterns which are not essentially 'knowable'. We have previously explored something of these dynamics in Chapter 2. Everyone has an ontological position and clarifying what these positions are to ourselves is a necessary beginning point for any research project or investigation. We can only move with the research process when we have come to an understanding of our assumptions about ontology. In the case of the suicide study the researchers' ontological position presupposed that we could distinguish a thing called suicide from other forms of death, i.e. that it was a recognizable and discrete object of investigation, and that this understanding resides in the minds of the person committing suicide, their relatives and friends and the ministers.

2 *What might represent knowledge or evidence of the entities or social reality which I wish to investigate?*

This is a question about *epistemology*. How do I know what I know and how can I be sure that I can gather knowledge about the 'situation'. Do I for instance believe that if I ask people questions about the 'situation' they will give me answers that are meaningful and that I can understand? Or do I believe that a better source of knowledge lies in documents from the coroner or procurator fiscal or health statistics? It is obvious that the ontological and the epistemological questions are linked and this is noted by Mason (1996, p. 13).

3 *What topic, or broad substantive area, is the research concerned with?*

The research under discussion here sought to discover what the ministers of the church in Highland saw as their role in suicide events given the increase and alarm around suicide events and the possible association between suicide and anomie.

4 What is the intellectual puzzle? What do I wish to explain?

Mason suggests three types of intellectual puzzle: *developmental*, *mechanical*, and *causal*. The suicide study posed a puzzle which relates to all three of these categories:

- How have ministers responded to suicide over the last decades? How have present-day responses come about?
- How does the minister manage his/her response to a suicide event? What works as a useful response in the experience of ministers?
- What influence does ministers' involvement in suicide events have on the families and friends and on the suicide attempt itself? Can ministers' involvement influence a suicide event?

These questions eventually became the research questions which dominated the development of the methods intended to answer the questions.

Mason's final 'difficult question' is, in our view, the most taxing:

5 What is the purpose of my research? What am I doing it for?

This will depend on the context from which one is doing the study. In Chapter 5 we examined a study which was related to the gaining of an academic qualification. This goal shaped the design and intention of the study. Chapter 8 relates to a piece of research which sits within a research programme designed to empower the lives of people with learning disabilities. Again the shape and structure reflect the intention. Most practical theologians working within an academic context are not dependent on external funding for their research. Any such funding tends to be a (welcome) bonus, but not normally an essential element of their jobs. There tends therefore to be a freedom and a sense of choice over which areas to research which may not be available within other areas of societal scientific research where people's careers, jobs and future possibilities are dependent on income-generation. The motivation for this study related to the urgency of the issue, one of the authors' background in mental health nursing and the personal experience of suicide among friends. It was important to reflect on these background issues as part of the continuing process of reflexivity. Mason's questions helped us to narrow down and to focus in on the central issues that emerged from our pre-research reflections.

The Method

Since the study was concerned specifically with the role of ministers of the Church, the obvious first line of enquiry was to ask ministers to talk about and describe their own experiences of this situation. Our ontological and epistemological position assumed

a that it was the ministers' attitudes and behaviours that constituted the ministers' role in suicide events; and
b that these attitudes and behaviours are identifiable through discussion and interview with the ministers.

We assumed that the ministers could tell us something about their role. We also assumed that their specific experiences could greatly inform the general issues that emerged. It was proposed to interview ministers of the Church using a semi-structured interview as the main data collection technique.

Data was gathered from 16 ministers in the form of one-to-one interviews and from 12 churchgoers and ministers in a focus group meeting (Litosseliti 2003). Before the interviews for the main study took place a pilot process of interviewing was carried out which identified the general topics to be covered in the main interviews.

Stage 1: Pre-pilot generation of categories

Pilot questions were agreed upon through discussion with the grant applicants, and with the wider research group, and with reference to literature and parallel experience in other settings. The initial topics of importance were thought to be:

- The theological position of the minister.
- The actual practice of ministers in real situations of suicide or attempted suicide.
- The degree of connectedness to medical services – integration of church into community.
- The timing of the approach and its connection to ministry.
- Whether or not the role was preventative, or supportive post-suicide.
- The nature of the communities served.
- The training received in mental health issues.
- The minister's understanding of suicide and its link to mental health problems.
- The idea that ministry might be a public health intervention.

Stage 2: Pilot interviews

Three pilot interviews were conducted using these topics as a guide. These were analysed using NVivo (see Chapter 5) and then discussed by the research team who had carried out the pilots. This allowed a calibration of the researchers and the topics that were most likely to yield material which could help address the research question.

Stage 3: Analysis of pilots

The analysis yielded 24 categories or themes that came directly from the respondents' interviews. A framework for the main interviews was then developed.

Stage 4: Main Interviews

Choosing the sample

The next set of decisions related to how to identify and justify the main interview sample and to make sure that the sample of people chosen were in a position to answer the main research question, 'What role do ministers of the Church have in suicide events in Highland?' The population was clearly the ministers of the Church in Highland. However, decisions had to be made about the number, the denomination and the location of these ministers. In short, who could help answer the research question most effectively? The main criteria for suitable respondents was the experience of a suicide event about which they could talk. This allowed actual life events to inform the discussion. All the respondents were to be ordained ministers of the Church, working in Highland or having experience of having worked in Highland. In the event, there was one exception to this. One respondent had worked in another rural area in the UK with similar characteristics and cultural issues. It was agreed that his particular experiences were relevant and helpful to the compilation of a picture of the minister's role.

There were three main considerations.

Numbers interviewed: Often in qualitative research the numbers interviewed are very small, and this can sometimes be a cause of incredulity and astonishment in more positivistic researchers.

Geography: Highland is large and diverse in its communities and its faith traditions. Highland people who live in Wick view Inverness as foreign to them in the same way as they view London as foreign to their culture and traditions. Geographical spread was important to the credibility of the research sample.

Denominations: It was thought important to interview ministers from across the Christian denominations since it was suggested that ministers from different traditions would view their role differently. Thus ministers were chosen who had different backgrounds and denominational roots.

The sample size

Let us consider the vexed question of how many is enough that plagues qualitative researchers. In research using nomothetic knowledge we have seen that there are three criteria that must be met before 'truth' can be established. The knowledge must be falsifiable, replicable and generalizable. The size of the sample is of great importance to the ability to make generalizations. In research appealing to ideographic knowledge the size of the sample is of less importance than the nature of the sample. Can the people being interviewed offer something that might represent a general view and offer opportunities for theoretical generalization? (see Chapter 2). While often the final decision about numbers is based on the time and money available for the research, the number of interviewees is also related to the method for sampling. There are commonly understood to be three types of sampling applied to qualitative research. Purposive, opportunistic and theoretical.

Opportunistic. This is the least satisfactory type of sampling and as the name implies suggests that the sample is comprised of people who were available. The opportunistic sample however is a reality in time-limited and resource-tight projects. The opportunistic sample in the suicide study would have been any minister who agreed to be interviewed no matter what their denomination, location or experiences.

Theoretical. Here interviewees are chosen at a number of different points in the data collection period. The data is analysed progressively and new recruits are sought as the data yields categories that need further investigation. The interviewees are chosen progressively for what they can add to the data set. Eventually the data analysis does not produce any new categories and saturation is achieved. This means that there comes a point when the interviews do not yield anything new in terms of insight and there is no need to interview further. This is associated with grounded theory (Glaser 1992; 1994; 1995; 1998).

Purposive. A single-point purposive sample means that all the interviewees are chosen at the same time with specific criteria that are explicit and clarified in terms of the ability to answer the research questions. This was the sampling used in the suicide study. It was thought that up to 20 interviews with ministers could be conducted in the time available, within the budget available, and that 20 interviews would yield enough information to achieve the aims of the study.

In the end 16 ministers across different denominations were interviewed. These interviews were tape recorded and transcribed. One interview proved to be unusable because of poor technology. The interviews were conducted by four different researchers over the fieldwork period of 10 months.

Issues of confidentiality are clearly most important in this kind of work. All potential respondents were written to and asked to participate. At the first approach ministers were sent the research proposal. Prior to the interview itself ministers were asked to confirm that they had read the research proposal and were content to be interviewed. No minister was interviewed who expressed any concerns. Some ministers were concerned that their example could be identified, and for that reason no details that distinguish the case studies are included. The case studies were used as triggers for a wider discussion related to the topics on the research schedule. The sample was generated as a purposive group who were derived from recommendations from the first row of interviewees. Each interview was transcribed by a secretary and anonymized.

The focus group

The focus group was conducted in the latter part of the research process because it became clear that there was a group of churchgoing people who had heard about the research and wanted to meet to discuss the role of the Church rather than that simply of the minister. These were people who were highly motivated to attend the meeting and had worries and concerns about suicide levels in Highland from a number of perspectives. The research question regarding the role of the minister was not capturing enough in terms of the role of the church community.

The focus group involved a staged process of discussion similar to consensus group techniques (Murphy *et al.* (1998). These techniques aim to produce a negotiated understanding of the 'situation'. They allow participants to discuss and clarify with each other what their understandings of the key issues around the Church and ministers' role in suicide are.

The combination of these data resulted in a set of findings which are reported in full elsewhere (Swinton and Powrie 2004).

The analysis of the data

Once the data had been collected the interviews were analysed using the framework for the main interviews as the key categories. These were then re-coded according to the emerging themes and the data then presented as a series of categories, sub-themes and clusters. These 'data sets' were then cross-analysed so that common themes across the different original categories were identified and data from the different sets used to interpret the themes. As we have noted before, the analysis, interpretation and discussion are intimately linked. The researcher moves between the data, the interpretations and the literature trying to engage with the data reflexively and as a process whereby crude findings are given some context and meaning by the researcher/analyst.

Analysis as process

In an attempt to illustrate this process of analytical thought, we will now look at a particular aspect of the findings in the light of the three types of knowing discussed in Chapter 2: knowledge of the other, knowledge of the phenomena and reflexive knowing.

Ministers were asked to identify a particular example of a suicide attempt or completed suicide with which they became involved. Once they had told the story of this event they were then asked to reflect upon the nine categories that had been established for the main interview schedule.

To show the process of analysis we are going to focus on the findings around strategies for help and ministers' theories of suicide. These two categories are linked. How ministers think about suicide, how they construct reasons for suicide and moral opinions of suicide, will influence what help they can and do offer.

Ministers were asked to discuss strategies for help in relation to their particular example and also more generally. From these responses some 20 sub-categories emerged and these were clustered under five headings. The focus group also produced a series of points under a general heading of 'To be done' which emerged as part of the consensus group technique. These responses were placed alongside the ministers' responses.

In creating the clusters great care was taken to adopt the words (*in vivo*) used by the ministers or the focus group respondents rather than those of the researchers summaries. It is very easy to create categories which sound convenient and snappy but which actually are not representative of the data. In Table 5 it can be seen that under the general category 'strategies for helping' there seemed to be five types of situation called themes, in which help could be/was offered. These are expressed as headings at the top of the table. The 'logic' to these headings is then shown by listing the different textual supports for these headings.

Table 5: Responses to 'Strategies for Helping': Themes and the associated clusters. Focus group responses in italics.

For families post-suicide	For individuals who are feeling suicidal	Preventative strategies – long-term	Collaboration with other professionals	Acute preventative work – emergency
helping with closure	express unconditional love	set up an awareness group	parish nursing volunteers	targeted visiting
helping the families	show what the individual does have to give and live for	express unconditional love	links with professionals	parish nursing
helping cope with the feelings of it all being unexpected	show the person is not alone	change the Church's response *Prayer sessions for the congregation*	working together	*Group therapy*
express unconditional love	show the person that the Church 'is here' – like St Paul and the gaoler	confirm the love of God	teamwork and support for members of team	

listening and being there	listening and being there	long-term spiritual support	Prayer sessions for ministry teams
allow natural coping mechanisms to emerge		give education in spiritual matters and purpose	
Follow up, presumably to families and people who have attempted suicide		*A plan for suicide education for senior pupils*	
Doing the funerals		*Encourage projects*	
		Information distribution to schools (through the pulpit and through social groups)	
		Building faith	

These textual supports both justify the headings *and* offer explanation of the ideas within the headings. For instance, under the theme 'support for families post-suicide' is written 'helping cope with the feelings of it all being unexpected'. Ministers commonly reported in their interviews that the families saw the suicide as completely unexpected. Families seemed completely taken by surprise by the suicide. It was unexpected and unexplainable. This caused enormous sorrow and grief. The ministers saw their role as offering understanding about this feeling of surprise and the unexpected. They also reported having the same feelings themselves. The discussion helped the researchers understand that the suicide event produces shock in both ministers and their communities. We concluded that shock and surprise was a shared common emotion within the community, and ministers helped by being prepared for these emotions both in themselves and in others.

We then considered why the suicide was so often seen as such a shock and so unexpected given that the case study data also suggested that with hindsight the signs of distress were not so difficult to spot. We turned to the theories of suicide that ministers offered us.

The social construction epistemology (Berger and Luckmann 1979), which is the perspective that this research has adopted, suggests that we all hold theories about our social worlds which allow us to operate within the social world. These theories are based on what we as individuals understand to be reliable knowledge. This is itself negotiable. Some theories are difficult for us to change no matter how much evidence accrues to negate a theory. Other theories change as evidence mounts to disprove them. We are all, therefore, theorists trying out evidence-based practice in our social world (Berger 1963). We will all therefore have theories about why people commit suicide generally and theories about why a particular person committed suicide. These theories will determine our behaviour and actions. Ministers are no different.

In Tables 5 and 6 it can be seen that the ministers are offering descriptive, prescriptive and theoretical information which tells us about their ideas for improving the situation, their theories about why the situation is the way it is and their own personal constructs for understanding it. By linking these data sets and generating further themes we are able to move on to an interpretive understanding of the role of ministers in suicide in Highland.

The final part of this chapter looks at the question of knowledge as discussed in Chapter 2. This is of great importance in presenting a qualitative study. How can we know that what we have found is what we have found? Chapter 2 suggests three types of knowledge that are relevant to this process.

Knowledge of the other

This type of knowledge occurs when the researcher focuses on a particular individual or group and explores in depth the ways in which they view and interact with the world. In the suicide study we interviewed in depth a number of ministers to examine what it was that they were actually doing and what they thought they should be doing in relation to suicide events, using their own experiences as the starting point. This gave voice to this particular group who are dealing with this particular 'situation'. However, we cannot know that this knowledge is true, only that it was truthfully spoken, and we cannot know that it will remain the same. Indeed we can be almost sure that it will not remain the same. The knowledge we gain from individuals is what they choose to give us at the time of the interview or focus group. A different day, a different moment, different feelings, a different interviewer, may well have produced different responses. How then, can we say that our information is valuable and can help us understand the situation better? Can we say that our knowledge is true?

Some of these questions are impossible to answer. It would be correct to say that the knowledge was given to the researcher. The words are recorded and agreed. In order for

Table 6: Ministers' theories of

A cry for help	Disconnection/ Disillusion	Opportunity
it could be anyone	isolation	alcohol abuse
thin line	not fitting in	expediency/ unexpected
	difficulty with relationships	aggression
	dashed hopes	
	despair	
	facing dead ends	
	internal grief	
	like a physical blow	
	lack of self-esteem and worth	
	cycle of dysfunction	
	destructive lifestyles	
	lack of hope	

why people commit suicide

No faith	Brokenness	To stop pain	Mental Illness
see death as the end	marital breakdown	to protect family	distorted state of mind
no belief in afterlife	lack of affection	search for peace	acute depression
misinterpretation of church views		to stop hurting others	unspotted mental illness
misinterpretation of theology			
lack of strong church lead			

the meaning of the words to be understood and explored skilled research interview techniques are required. Teasing out the inconsistencies and the half sentences in particular requires attention. Asking the supplementary question, 'What do you mean by that?' 'Can you give me an example?' often produces a different response and an *in vivo* reworking of the point being made. The respondent works out his or her understanding of the situation as part of the interview process rather than separate to it. The interview is not an outcome but a process. It is the job of the interviewer to track these changes and unfoldings as part of both the interview and the analysis. The interview is itself a journey. The importance of the researcher as skilled voyager on the journey cannot be overestimated. Good data is only as good as the researcher who collects it. The researcher should be starting to analyse the data as the interview starts. We have noted that the characteristics of the researcher are of importance in the outcome piece of research and the reflexive nature of the piece.

One way in which some of the dangers of imposition or supposition of knowledge can be avoided is through feedback loops. The data can be fed back to the participants as part of the agreed research process. An interview transcript can be returned to the interviewer for comment, or an initial analysis can be returned to all participants for commentary. In the suicide study the draft of the final report was returned to the participants and their commentary formed a further section of the report. This allows ownership of the knowledge to reside more formally with the participants but raises practical issues of time and energy.

Knowledge of the phenomena

This relates to research done on particular categories of event. The exploration of ministers' work with suicide events gives us an insight into how the ministers view the phenomenon of suicide both as individuals, as faithful believers and as members of denominations. These three positions were not always the same and required some internal negotiation on the part of the ministers as the interview progressed. For instance we have noticed that suicide is often seen by ministers as unexplainable and surprising, as something that could happen to anyone; they suggest there is a thin line between being suicidal and not being suicidal. This is both the ministers' view and the ministers' view of how others view suicide. It offers us insight into their own theories of suicide but also their theories of how others view suicide. Ministers also offered the idea that a personal faith and a faithful community helps deter suicide and that a strong and active church presence in a community will help support people through the times of disconnectedness, during which they are most at risk. At the same time they believe that the Church has not always helped people in their distress, so sometimes adherence to a faith which is misguided either by self or by the Church itself, actually produces a disincentive to remaining alive. The Church itself promotes disconnectedness.

The suicide data gives us some knowledge of how the phenomenon is understood, by looking at the content of the theories produced, how they are produced and their relationship across the data sets.

Reflexive knowing

This occurs when researchers deliberately turn their attention to their own process of constructing a world. This requires self-reflection. Reflection is discussed throughout this book. Reflexive knowing implies intimate knowledge of the data. Triangulation (Ch. 2, p. 50) is recommended in order that the data can be given more rigour, breadth and complexity. Triangulation means using multiple methods and multiple means of analysis, including using more than one person by the use of more than one method of data collection or one method of analysis. An alternative used by the authors elsewhere is for the research team members who have not been involved in the interviewing to themselves interview the interviewers. A further type of triangulation, where there is a team of researchers, is for each to be interviewed by the principal researcher so that insights may be captured. Jaber Gubrium discussed this at a recent Gerontological Society meeting in Washington, USA.

Both these methods allow the reflexivity to be captured and retained in the final analysis.

Theological reflection

How do ministers and congregations think about suicide – what are their 'theories' of suicide?

During the focus group discussion there were very few specific and direct statements around why people attempt and sometimes complete suicide. The discussion concentrated on what could be done to support suicidal people and families who had been affected. However, the data shows an assumption within the congregational focus group discussion that suicide has a relationship to the spiritual and religious. That is, a lack of understanding, listening, friendship and sense of belonging increases the likelihood of suicidal behaviour. The focus group discussion came up with a number of ways of supporting people in danger of suicidal behaviour, and all of these revolved around the presence of support, friendship and comfort. It was felt that this was a setting where emotions could be expressed in a loving and accepting environment where there was no blame and where listening and, by implication, telling personal stories was encouraged and welcomed. We discuss these later.

This is also reflected in the ministers' responses. While it was agreed that some suicide was a direct result of mental illness, a distortion of the mind through illness that rendered the sufferer vulnerable, there was also a strong sense that suicide was precipitated by the individual's disconnection from community or social life. Somehow the person vulnerable to suicide had lost their place and space in the social fabric in which they lived. Their community had become unknown to them. The ministers expressed this in terms of disconnection, disillusion and brokenness. It was felt that people who found themselves in this situation tended to be more likely to attempt suicide.

Disconnection was expressed in terms of isolation, not fitting in with the main social groupings on offer, and feeling dislocated from what would be described as the 'normal' range of social life available in that area. The disconnection could be triggered by marital breakdown, lack of affection, or difficulty with relationships which might have had a long history, indeed might run across generations. Disconnection can be exacerbated by drinking alcohol or taking drugs; dis-inhibition often leads to aggression and increases disconnection. With the opportunity to act provided by access to the necessary means, taking one's life also becomes easier as one becomes more dis-inhibited.

Ministers also felt that in their experience the completed suicide act was explainable in terms of trying to find peace and stop hurting others.

They also felt that the Church did not give a strong lead and that the disconnection was linked to a lack of faith. No faith in anything other than oneself or a misintepretation of theology based on myth and prejudice made people very vulnerable.

To a great extent the respondents were articulating the theory of anomie developed by Durkheim (1951) nearly a century and a half ago, and the idea of hopelessness and estrangement discussed by Aldridge (1998). There was a certain frustration expressed by the ministers and the focus group around the apparent inability to tackle this disconnection, and a recognition of the dreadful consequences for families, friends and communities of failure to spot disconnectedness.

It was clear that the church community felt they had a role to play in addressing disconnectedness.

It is probably quite important to consider what the respondents felt the people who took their lives and those who tried were disconnected from. The idea of disconnection is gaining currency in discussions on the importance of spiritual well-being in health and social care. This pilot study is about

Highland. So what is it that could make Highland folk in particular feel disconnected?

Is Highland particularly vulnerable to disconnection?

A number of themes came out of this question put to the ministers. The focus group also indicated that there were particular characteristics of Highland that needed attention and were relevant to the discussion about suicide.

Changing times

The ministers noted that Highland was going through changing times. The growth of Inverness and the vulnerability of the Caithness communities are obvious examples. More specifically ministers saw Highland as moving to a tourist economy and at the same time a 'retirement culture'. The implications of this for the community makeup are disproportionate transient 'uncommitted' populations either on holiday or working in the seasonal holiday trades, and a diminishing youthful infrastructure, with much of the work opportunities within a tourist economy which specifically requires superficial and fleeting relationships.

Potentially very supportive

Ministers noted that small communities, which are characteristic of Highland villages, can be very supportive. People know each other and look out for each other. There are clearly demonstrations of genuine care for each other. Ministers pointed to attendance at funerals after a suicide.

The intimate culture and the beauty and peace of the Highlands is potentially a force for calm and spiritual restitution. However, the focus group noted that Highlanders tended to be reluctant to release emotions and that grief and expression of grief was 'a skill' that needed to be taught. Part of a supportive community is one that allows grief and its expression.

Highland has the potential to damage individuals

Related to the above theme is its converse. Ministers acknowledged that Highland communities can be very damaging to individuals. They mentioned disillusioned young people who return to Highland after further education elsewhere. These young people struggle to find appropriate work or meaningful roles. They are bombarded with information from global sources through advanced information technology which offers them opportunities and ways of life and thinking that are beyond their reach.

Ministers also noted the pervasive culture of drinking in Highland, which led to guilt over drinking too much and a vicious circle. Other guilts included sexual guilts, particularly among the homosexual community who felt diffident about expressing themselves. In Highland, privacy is much prized and highly valued. This means that some of the alternative expressions of individual needs and personalities are kept hidden to conform with the 'understood' cultural norm.

There was also reference in the interviews to the myth of the golden past which was expressed among Highland folk. This encouraged a romantic vision of how things had been. This romantic 'past times' often ignored the realities of harsh lifestyles. These myths however had real consequences in so far as they held back change and laid down inappropriate social norms.

The Highland character was also given description in some of the interviews. The idea of the ponderous highlander at ease on the hills far away from crowds was an image that came up, although there was little substance to back it up. Individuals and groups often operate on the basis of unsubstantiated opinion. Cultural assumptions, albeit out of date or mythical, can have real consequences in terms of their social pressure to conform.

In discussion with the focus group it was suggested that one of the features of Highlanders is that the role model of the physically very active loner is not a fashionable one. There is no role model on television for a forest worker or a farmer, and certainly no role model for young people to have spiritual lives. A successful highland male is portrayed in Highland as one who is engaged in physical work, whereas the role model on television is that of service, high tech 'smooth and clean' young men. The search for the meaning of maleness may be particularly difficult in a community where rather old-fashioned dominant values obtain.

Thanatos

Linked to this is a theme that we have called 'Thanatos' with reference to Sigmund Freud's concept around the death wish (1955) carried by all individuals and encouraged by particular configurations and circumstances. This was not a word used by the respondents but seemed appropriate to sum up references to 'darkness' that were difficult to describe but understood by the respondents. This included the beauty of the Highlands, which also carried with it some kind of dread. The dark Druid-type culture was also referred to. One minister maintained that people were strangers to each other. Another minister referred to the long dark winters, which attacked the soul. Disconnectedness seemed linked to darkness in the broadest sense.

Highland lacks or is missing basic modern attributes

Good, efficient transport and variety of employment was identified in particular here. In other parts of the country these are taken-for-granted aspects of modern life. In Highland they can be rare luxuries. This makes fluid movement between different social communities difficult and compromises the ability of the individual to exploit different environments as part of developing the self. Membership of a number of social groupings is a resource that is now becoming available widely in society in general. Individuals express themselves differently in different groups. If membership possibilities are limited to only one or two, perhaps family and school friends, this may deny the possibilities or full development of self. Multiple group membership helps individuals experiment with who they are and discover their core traits, and contributes to their spiritual development.

Finally in this theme of Highland culture there was a group of responses that wondered if Highland *was* in fact different to other places. People are people and there are drugs and drink in all communities. As with many other communities there is little for the young people to do, and as with many communities the past always is portrayed as better. It may then be the particular combination of factors that give Highland its particular characteristics.

What can be done to help?

As we have seen, the ministers and the focus group shared the view, fairly universally, that suicidal activities were the result of disconnection from society and meaning, and that suicidal behaviour was fundamentally a spiritual matter. Ministers and the focus group were asked what they thought were strategies for helping people overcome their wish to suicide or to support families and friends after a completed suicide. The themes show that the respondents saw suicide events as falling into different 'need' categories.

Help for families post-suicide

So often the suicide has been completed before the minister is involved. In discussing the individual case studies the ministers identified the importance of helping families and friends once a suicide had occurred. They identified the predominant feelings of guilt, bereavement, shock at the unexpected, and bewilderment. The need among the family and friends to address some of the why questions was overwhelming, but dealt with in very different ways. Ministers tried to respond to this variety. The importance of the funeral and the rituals associated with the funeral was highlighted. The funeral is an opportunity to clarify what happened and to confirm the unconditional love of God for all involved, by showing love and support within the church community.

The idea that suicide was seen as a sin by the Church was, in the opinion of all the ministers interviewed, inappropriate and a misrepresentation of the Church's position. While there was an acknowledgement that some theological positioning still holds this view, none of the ministers interviewed entertained it, neither did any of the focus group respondents. Indeed, a number said they would be shocked and outraged if they heard it said. The view of Norman Sartorius that suicide is a breakdown of trust between the individual and society was very much upheld. The focus of attention was on the social and spiritual responsibilities of the communities rather than any deficit or spiritual poverty of the individual.

One of the practical responses of the ministers was to listen to the unfolding of the suicide story and to recognize and support the emergence of natural coping mechanisms. They saw themselves and their church as offering light in the darkness and helping to 'hold' the unanswered questions about why. The minister and the church had the potential to offer stability in times of great turbulence.

The focus group came up with metaphors to describe the potential role for ministers/churches at this time. These included the lighthouse, distillery, cattle prod, referee or umpire, gatekeeper and megaphone. These roles were reflected in the actual descriptions of what ministers experienced. These are not easy roles and need support from the church community.

Help for individuals who are feeling suicidal

A second theme that came out of the 'strategies for helping' questions was how help could be given to suicidal individuals. This help can only be given if individuals in distress can be identified. The problem is, of course, that much of the internal grief that leads up to a suicide is hidden. However, the ministers and the focus group participants felt that there was a role for expressing unconditional love, mirroring that of Christ, and doing this through helping the individual to see what life does have to offer them and what they can offer life. They felt that showing the individual that they are not alone by 'being there' and listening were important supports. These supports were appropriate in either long-term situations or short-term acute preventative work.

Help with long-term preventative strategies

There were some strong beliefs that long-term spiritual support offering a framework for understanding and making sense of life in terms of spiritual paths was important. This could be facilitated by the church communities exemplifying unconditional love. In practical terms this could mean:

a   the setting up of awareness groups locally so that individuals who slide into spiritual trouble are identified and supported earlier.
b   changing the churches' response to suicide by offering regular prayer sessions for the congregation. Make suicide prevention a clearer part of regular church work. Locate suicide as a spiritual crisis.
c   providing opportunities for discussion and education in spiritual matters and purpose of life.
d   planning suicide education for senior pupils at school.
e   encouraging local projects which encapsulate some of the above ideas.
f   providing more information, particularly to schools, through the pulpit and to social groups.
g   building faith in communities.

Help with acute preventative work – emergency

This was also seen as an important part of preventative work. This required targeted visiting and implied some long-term preventative structures already in place. The awareness group would be able, for instance, to pick up emergencies and to provide targeted visiting if required. The focus group felt that group therapy might be helpful for those vulnerable. The purpose of these activities was to offer light in the darkness and support confusion through spiritual listening.

Collaboration with other professionals

Working in a multi-professional team seemed to appeal to all the respondents who with one exception felt that greater links with the healthcare services would be a good thing. The exception was that in some cases healthcare services are seen as culpable in the suicide through failure to act or support the suicide victim. Consequently, sometimes involvement of these same services with family grief was counterproductive. However, on the whole it was agreed that greater links would be a good thing and a support to the ministers and congregations.

What should the Church response be?

Care and Concern – practical support

The Church community should also be able to provide practical support. The funeral and the rituals associated with it are an act of practical comfort and concern. Visiting those bereaved and staying in touch with family and friends after a suicide was also seen as part of the required response.

The Church as somewhere good

This was about the Church providing an atmosphere, a mood, that encouraged people to see hope and reconciliation. The respondents expressed this in metaphor: light in the darkness, a place where confusion and incomprehension could be 'held';

the church community as a locus or repository for difficult or impossible feelings.

The idea of the need for a wailing place is associated with this mood of Church. It is within the Church that Practical Theology is manifest. Working with family and friends through their anger and grief and bereavement, and working with people in distress without making judgements, is the method by which the Church can find its own place in a community.

Training needs

The final theme that we will look at concerns the training needs and possibilities for the church community and its leaders. If there is agreement about the kind of church required as a response to suicidal behaviour and events, then there is even more agreement that there is a role for training as a mechanism for achieving this kind of 'church'.

The general feeling among the ministers was that there was little specific training for these kinds of situations. They expressed an undoubted need for it.

Equip the Church with relevant knowledge

The training needs were dominated by the feeling that no one knew enough about what led up to suicide or what the experience of attempted suicide or suicide loss was really about. There was also little consistent knowledge around mental illness and suicide, beyond common-sense understandings of the implications, for instance, of extreme depression.

Learn from the experience of others

The required knowledge could be gained by learning from the experience of others. All the ministers had had experience of suicide, sometimes very distressing experiences. They were able to identify these through the case studies, and they talked about these experiences in the interviews. However, they still felt that if they had had opportunities to talk to other ministers about their own experiences they would be better prepared for helping people during suicide events. The use of the case study for a training focus would be very helpful.

Working in teams with the health and social care professions

Although there seemed to be good relationships at an informal level between clergy and the health and social care professionals, largely promoted by local knowledge and small communities, there was little formal liaison reported among the respondents. There seemed to be some frustration about a lack of contact and a recognition of the need for stronger multi-professional liaison work. There was, however, little mechanism available to pursue that relationship.

One suggestion, repeated by several respondents, was to use the good offices of the chaplains, who bridge the world of the parish and the world of the hospital. The chaplains could offer a 'place' for multi-professional training.

This chapter has looked in some detail at the issues of

- the pre-research assumptions as they appear in the proposal thinking,
- five difficult questions that frame the research
- the method of semi-structured interviewing and its advantages and disadvantages for a pursuit of truth,
- the way in which the three types of knowledge explored in Chapter 2 manifest themselves in the study on suicide.

We now move on to look at a study that involved telephone interviewing and case-study observer participation and consider the issues around these methods for the pursuit of truth.

8

Participatory Research: Researching *with* Marginalized People

In our discussions around reflexivity in Chapter 2, we high-lighted, among other things, the importance of recognizing hidden power dynamics within the research process and the complexities of the relationship between the researcher and those who are being researched. Here we want to explore this dynamic further by examining a research approach which seeks to highlight and address some of the problematic issues surrounding the power dynamics of the research process. The approach we engage with here has come to be known as *participatory research*. Participatory research recognizes the importance of the starting position of the research enterprise and seeks to ensure that the perspective of the research subject is consistently held in constructive tension with that of the re-searcher and the research process (Kiernan 1999; Cocks and Cockram 1995; Rioux and Bach 1994). At heart this method of qualitative research assumes that the best people to research a given topic are those who have the most experience of it. Cornwall and Jewkes (1995) describe participatory research as research strategies which break

> the linear mould of conventional research . . . participatory research focuses on a process of sequential reflection and action, carried out with and *by* local people rather than *on* them. Local knowledge and perspectives are not only acknowledged but form the basis for research and planning.

Many of the methods used in participatory research are drawn from mainstream disciplines and conventional research itself involves varying degrees of participation. The key difference between participatory and conventional methodologies lies in the location of power in the research process.

Participatory research provides a framework in which people move from being the *objects* of research to *subjects* and *co-researchers*. This goal is achieved by ensuring that the individuals who traditionally have been the object of the research process are given an active role in designing and conducting the research. Participatory research has been utilized by a variety of different groups in a number of different contexts using various methods, but the bulk of the work has been done within education, with the primary method being action research (Alfricher *et al.* 1993; Burgess 1993).

In this chapter we will develop a way of doing participative research with a specific focus on the life experiences of one group of marginalized and often oppressed people: people with learning disabilities (see note at end of chapter, p. 253). The chapter will focus on a study carried out by John Swinton and Elaine Powrie (2004), which sought to explore the spiritual lives of people with learning disabilities using a participatory research methodology. Reflection on this project will provide a model for doing participatory research which is potentially transferable to working with other marginalized and disempowered groups of people.

The situation

What are learning disabilities and why should practical theologians be interested in them?

Put simply, by the term 'people with learning disabilities' we mean those human beings within society who are deemed by the majority to have significant intellectual and/or cognitive difficulties, limited communicational skills, restricted or no self-care skills, and who *may* have to have some kind of care and/or support throughout their lives. In terms of the research enterprise, the voices of people with learning disabilities have frequently been excluded from research approaches which assume them to be *objects* rather than the subjects of the research process. Recently, however, disability rights researchers have challenged this professional domination of research goals and are calling for disability research which is based on the experiences of people with disabilities and has a benefit to people with disabilities (for example, Barnes 1992; Oliver 1992; Ward and Flynn 1994; Zarb 1992). Taylor (1996) puts this strongly, stating that, 'the perspectives and experiences of people labelled mentally retarded [*sic*] must provide a starting point for all research and inquiries in the study of mental retardation'. From the perspective of participatory qualitative research, as per our introductory comments, it is assumed that those most able to inform understandings of what spirituality is, what it means, and the ways in which it functions in people's lives, are people with learning disabilities. Consequently, within the research project described below, participation by people with learning disabilities was sought during each step of the research process.

The spiritual lives of people with learning disabilities

Historically, people with learning disabilities have been the focus of a large amount of quantitative, medical, educational and rehabilitation research. This research has generally assumed people with learning disabilities to be the *objects* of the research process, and have centred on the 'problem' of learning disabilities and how best it could be minimized or prevented (Rioux and Bach 1994). Until recently, very little research has examined the goals and life experiences of people with learning disabilities (Ward and Flynn 1994). There is therefore a relative shortage of descriptive, firsthand information available to the disability community and service providers as they seek to work out effective forms of theological reflection, and political and ecclesial action, and effective policy and support services.

One dimension of the experience of people with learning disabilities that has been under-researched is the area of *spirituality* and the ways in which this dimension of their experience affects their lives and expectations in terms of life goals, care and support. In 2002 the Foundation for People with Learning Disabilities published its *Space to Listen* (Swinton 2002) a report based on a piece of qualitative research carried out in Scotland and England by Professor John Swinton. This feasibility study sought to provide an initial exploration into the significance of spirituality for the lives of people with learning disabilities. The report was based on a 10-year review of the literature on spirituality and people with learning disabilities, combined with a series of interviews with people with learning disabilities, carers and support workers. The key findings were as follows:

- Spirituality is a common human phenomenon that includes but is not defined by religion.
- There is evidence to suggest that spirituality plays a significant role in the lives of many people with learning disabilities.
- Carers and support workers are often unaware of the significance of this dimension and consequently fail to address it.
- Training is required to enable those supporting people with learning disabilities to recognize and deal effectively with this aspect of their experiences.
- People with learning disabilities need to be given accessible information and opportunities in order that they can make informed spiritual choices.
- Faith communities have the potential to offer support and friendship, but they need to be aware that certain exclusive forms of practice can serve to exclude and oppress people with learning disabilities.

This project indicated that there was a gap in care provision with regard to spirituality and spiritual care. It also suggested that there were significant issues relating to the marginalization and oppression of people with learning disabilities within the Church and society. The findings of this report indicated that there was a need for further exploration within this area in order to better understand the significance of the spiritual dimension of the lives of people with learning disabilities and to think through the appropriateness of current strategies of care and support.

To this end the Foundation for People with Learning Disabilities in partnership with the Shirley Foundation agreed to support a two-year nationwide participatory research study designed to explore the spiritual lives of people with learning disabilities and to examine the significance of this dimension of their experience for strategies of care and support. The study aimed to:

- Explore the meaning and significance of spirituality from the perspective of the experience of people with learning disabilities.
- Find out how carers perceived the spiritual dimension of people's lives, and assess whether or not they perceive this dimension to be a significant aspect of their caring task.
- Highlight concrete, practical strategies for the enabling of effective spiritual care within this area.

The method

Methodological assumptions

In the light of the negative history of research with people who have learning disabilities, it was decided that the project should seek to utilize a participatory research method. This approach has a particular methodology which it is worthwhile reflecting on at this point. Underpinning the approach of participatory research as it relates to disability, is a specific model and understanding of what disability is and the ways in which it is constructed by societies. This has come to be known as the *social model of disability*. The implications and assumptions of the social model of disability provide an important methodological dimension to participatory research.

The social model of disability has mainly been used to address the experience of people with physical impairments (Oliver 1990). It can however be extended to enable the analysis of the life situations and experiences of people with learning disabilities. The social model of disability suggests that many of the difficulties encountered by people with learning disabilities stem not from their lack of cognitive or intellectual ability, but from society's negative attitudes towards difference and the existence of a hypercognitive culture within which 'clarity of mind and economic productivity determine the value of a human life' (Post 1992). The social model assumes that within a society that had a different moral system that was not dependent on such things as intellect, reason, competitiveness, individuality and productivity, the concept of learning disability simply would not exist. In other words, the very term 'learning disability' indicates adherence to a particular moral code and system of valuing human beings which reflects the ideals of rationalism, individualism, liberalism and a capitalist economy. Within a society which uses the criteria of independence, productivity, intellectual prowess and social position to judge the value of human beings, people with psychological or intellectual disabilities will necessarily be excluded and downgraded as human beings of lesser worth and value. If this is so, it becomes clear that society is, at least partially, responsible for the disablement of impaired individuals. According to this model, it is not the physical or mental condition of the individual that makes them disabled. Rather it is society that, by placing barriers and developing systems of valuing which exclude, stigmatize or downgrade particular groups of people, transforms physical or mental impairments into disabilities. That is not to suggest that impairments are not important. Clearly if one has paraplegia or arthritis, this is not only a social construction. Likewise certain forms of learning disability such as Lesch-Nyhan syndrome, can cause a person to have a lower quality of life than they might want, quite apart from the type of society they experience their impairment in. It *is* however important to raise our consciousness of the crucial and often hidden role that society plays in disabling individuals with particular forms of impairment and difference. This model would suggest that an appropriate theological response to disability should begin not with charity, but rather with a careful analysis of the life experiences of people with disabilities and the type of society within which they live out their lives. The practices which emerge from such a reframe may be quite different from the expected norm.

Within the study described in this chapter, the methodological perspective of the social model of disability was utilized to enable the study critically to assess certain attitudes and values that surround the ways in which spirituality and spiritual care has come to be defined and the implications of this for the life experience of people with learning disabilities. For example, the wider literature informed us that the way in which society in general and religious communities in particular define 'spirituality' can implicitly exclude and marginalize people with learning disabilities. The assumption within certain religious traditions that spirituality is cognitively based and demands intellectual assent to certain verbal formulations excludes many people with learning disabilities, not because they are less spiritual, but because spirituality is defined in such a way as to exclude them. Based on a previous review of the literature (Swinton 2002), the study assumed the possibility that the ways in which society formulates and defines both spirituality and learning disability can serve, implicitly or explicitly, to exclude people with learning disabilities. The research was designed, as far as possible to recognize the possibility of such hidden power dynamics and to enable people with learning disabilities to retain their autonomy and power and to gain the opportunity of articulating their experiences clearly and openly with as little cultural bias as possible.

Methods and tools

Advisory Group

At the outset an inclusive advisory group was set up to ensure that the goals, and in particular the participatory objectives of the study were fulfilled. This group comprised:

- 2 people with learning disabilities
- 2 experts in qualitative research
- 1 care provider with an interest in the area of spirituality and theology
- 1 family carer
- 1 representative of the North East of Scotland Advisory Group on The Spiritual Needs of People with Learning Disabilities.

In line with the project's methodological perspective, it was seen to be vital that people with learning disabilities were not the *objects* of the research process, but were in fact active participant subjects throughout. The inclusion of people with learning disabilities in this group was a first step towards actualizing this aspect of the research process.

The group was focused in such a way as to ensure that the contributions that people were able to make could be made effectively and freely. A basic principle that underpinned the ethos of the group was that of *respect for difference*. The group was run as a collaborative team. The nature of a good team is that it brings together varied and different talents and expertise and works together to develop a constructive amalgamation based on the recognition of the significance of everyone's input. A good team does not seek after the lowest common denominator, but rather recognizes the creative possibilities of difference and strives to enable each member to participate and contribute the particular expertise that they may have. Within the advisory team each person was acknowledged as having their own areas of expertise, all of which were vital to the process, but not all of which were necessarily accessible to all participants. Meetings were structured in such a way that the information presented and the ideas and feedback that were collected were, as far as possible, accessible to those within the group who had learning disabilities. It was accepted that certain aspects of the project would be inaccessible to people with learning disabilities. In particular aspects of data collection and analysis were difficult and at points impossible to communicate in an accessible manner. However, this difficulty was not unique to group members who had a learning disability. Certain complex, technical aspects of the research process were equally difficult and inaccessible for others within the group who did not have specialist knowledge in qualitative research. In the end we concluded that the important thing was not so much that everyone could understand everything. Rather the most creative approach was to strive to create an atmosphere within which difficulties in understanding and differing opinions could be accepted constructively and in a non-threatening manner and dealt with positively in a way which did not exclude. In this way the power dynamics were minimized in a way which enabled the voices of the people with learning disabilities involved to be heard, respected and acted upon.

Sampling frame

A sample within participatory research does not aim to be representative. Its value lies in the inclusion of the participants within the data collection, analysis and dissemination, and the potential for the participants to use the findings in a meaningful way. Consequently we decided to use purposive sampling. Within purposive sampling, subjects are selected because of some trait or characteristic. Purposive sampling gains its power and informative potential from the way in which it selects particular cases which hold the potential to yield specific forms of information relevant to the project. Initially, we developed a nationwide network of organizations and individuals that were interested in the research topic. We co-ordinated visits to organizations, families, carers and individuals who expressed a wish to be involved in focus groups and interviews. Recruitment took place through a variety of routes: contacting self-advocacy groups throughout the UK, voluntary organizations throughout the UK, social services, carer support groups, religious groups, national organizations and leaders of communities from ethnic minorities. Table 7 outlines the primary research settings.

Table 7: Research Settings

Self-advocacy groups
Day centres
Care homes
Group homes
NHS Trust facilities
Family homes
Places of work

Data collection

Data was collected over a period of one year (2002). Data collection was conducted using a combination of methods, primary among them being:

- *in-depthinterviews*
- *focusgroups*
- *directobservation.*

The interview process

We carried out 19 individual interviews with people with learning disabilities:

- 6 individual interviews with people with learning disabilities
- 4 with people with high support needs
- 9 interviews with people with learning disabilities and their carers.

Individual interviews took place in a variety of settings including people's homes, day centres, religious communities, care homes, family homes and places of work. Interviews lasted from 20 minutes to an hour and a half, depending on people's concentration spans and willingness to engage in extended conversation. It was sometimes necessary to meet with individuals on more than one occasion in order that their perspective could be fully grasped, understood and properly communicated. The interview process comprised three stages:

1 Sharing the nature and purpose of the research in order to help people understand the issues which would be discussed.
2 Discussion and information sharing around issues of consent.
3 Conducting the interview.

One of the initial difficulties we encountered was how to communicate the meaning of the word 'spirituality'. If people were to be given a genuine opportunity to reflect on their spirituality we decided it would be necessary to create some basic conceptual parameters within which people could explore the areas that previous research had suggested constituted the 'spiritual dimension' (Swinton 2001). These parameters were always left open to be challenged and developed by the experiences and feelings of participants as this emerged in the interview process. To this end, an interview schedule was developed based on the perspective on spirituality expressed by people with learning disabilities who participated in the *Space to Listen* project mentioned previously (Swinton 2001). There spirituality was defined as: 'the quest for *meaning, purpose, self-transcending knowledge, meaningful relationships, love*

and *commitment*, as well as the sense of the Holy amongst us';
a definition which included but was not defined by religion.
The interview schedule consisted of the following questions:

1 *What is spirituality?* (a general question to see whether the
   term itself elicited a sense of meaning or resonance)
2 *What makes you feel good about yourself?* (value)
3 *What do you like best about your life?* (meaning)
4 *Are friends important to you? Why?* (connectedness/
   relationships)
5 *What do you want to do with your life?* (hope)
6 *Do you think there is a God?* (searching for the transcend-
   ent)
7 *Why do you think you are in the world?* (existential search
   for identity and purpose)

These questions opened up some fascinating areas of discussion and reflection. Question 1 enabled us to explore what
the word 'spirituality' actually meant for people, if in fact it
meant anything. The following questions enabled us to test
and deepen our understanding of the responses to Question 1.
For people who had no expressed idea of spirituality as a formal concept, the questions allowed the interviews to explore
those dimensions of human experience which have been recognized as spiritual and to examine what it meant for different
individuals.

Individual interviews with people with high communicational needs

One of the aims of this research study was to facilitate and
encourage participation from people with a learning disability regardless of their level of understanding and ability.
We aimed to allow people the opportunity to participate no
matter what their contribution might be. This was achieved
by using verbal and non-verbal modes of communication.
Pictures, symbols, coloured pens and paper were all available
during the interview and for the prior discussion within which

we obtained the person's consent to participate. Participants chose how they would like to conduct the interview and the ways in which they would like the interview recorded. In order to achieve maximum participation at times, an interpreter or moderator (someone who knows the participant well) was used. The interpreter directed questions and interpreted sounds and gestures in order that those participants with speech and language issues were able to respond and participate as fully as possible.

Participants were allowed to use whatever mode of communication was best for them. So, some communicated through signing, singing, drawing, writing or just looking at pictures. Sometimes the interviewer or interpreter drew the answers during our discussion. Participants were given the right to start or stop an interview at any time.

The significance of fragments

From the outset there was an obvious tension between the types of word/text-based qualitative research methods that were available and the sometimes limited communicational ability of those with whom we worked. While some people were very articulate, others communicated in ways other than words. This was one of the reasons for us utilizing a multi-method approach. However, participants' limited ability verbally to articulate ideas also raised another important perspective: *the importance of fragments*, that is, the suggestion that within a participatory research context with marginalized people who have limited verbal skills, the researcher *must* take seriously the importance of the fragments of truth that people offer. One of the more profound things we learned from the study overall was the challenge that people with learning disabilities offered to the way we all see the world. They challenged accepted understandings of such things as time, space, acceptance, friendship and indeed the meaning of spirituality itself (Swinton and Powrie 2004). Within the context of the research method, the participants deeply challenged the way that research should be done and precisely what researchers should take seriously as meaningful and valid data. Words, sentences, gestures, all took on varying degrees of significance as they were worked out and understood within the life experiences of the people with whom we worked. Very often direct observation was as important as reflection on transcribed texts.

Focus groups

We carried out ten focus groups – two with professional caregivers, five with people with learning disabilities and three with family carers and relatives. We held one or two sessions per group. These took place in a variety of settings, including self-advocacy groups, multi-ethnic user groups, day centres and residential units. Focus groups are useful for collecting 'rich data that are cumulative and elaborative; they can be stimulating for respondents, aiding recall and the format is flexible' (Fontana and Frey 2000, p. 652). The aim of these focus groups was to explore the meaning and significance of spirituality both personally and collectively within the group and to reflect on what this might mean for the spiritual care and support of people with learning disabilities. We were struck by the depth of the questions raised and worked through within the focus groups and the individual interviews. It was clear that people wanted to discuss such issues and that, given support, they were able to express and begin to work through some deep and complex existential issues. It was clear that within this group participants felt able to express feelings, emotions and desires and that they viewed this as a positive experience.

Direct observation

Partly because spirituality is not primarily a cognitive function, and partly because of the practical communicational issues highlighted previously, interviews were supplemented with direct observation. It is important to note that 'direct observation' is not the same as 'participant observation'. Trochim differentiates between the two in this way:

> *Direct* observation is distinguished from *participant* observation in a number of ways. First, a direct observer doesn't typically try to become a participant in the context. However, the direct observer does strive to be as unobtrusive as possible so as not to bias the observations. Second, direct observation suggests a more detached perspective. The researcher is watching rather than taking part. Third, direct observation tends to be more focused than participant observation. The researcher is observing certain sampled situations or people rather than trying to become immersed in the entire context. Finally, direct observation tends not to take as long as participant observation. (Trochim 2000)

Direct observation was very important for this study, particularly in relation to people with limited verbal skills. By observing people within their own context and reflecting on their words and actions, the researchers gleaned vital information that made their process of understanding much clearer and more authentic.

Ethical issues

We considered ethical issues to be of particular importance, bearing in mind the possibility of inadvertent abuse of a vulnerable population. We used the principles of *respect for persons, autonomy, confidentiality* and *freedom of choice* to underpin the research process (Rolph 2000; Department of Health 2001). Great care was taken to ensure that nothing was forced on the participants and that participation in the interview process was voluntary and solely at the discretion of the individual (WHO 1986). Participants were encouraged to choose how they would like to conduct the interview and how or if it would be recorded. Levels of consent were constantly monitored, assessed and checked with participants during the interviews.

Ethical guidelines were studied and applied from the Department of Health and the University of Essex: *Seeking Consent: Working with People with Learning Disabilities* (Department of Health 2001) and 'Guidelines on research ethics and working with people with learning disabilities' (Rolph 2000). The research has been an exercise that involves a joint search for meaning between researcher and participants. The research process was underpinned by the ethical principles of privacy, confidentiality and choice, where nothing was forced on the participants and levels of participation within the interviews was entirely voluntary and at their discretion (WHO 1986). This was constantly evaluated and checked with the participants during the interviews.

Consent

Consent had to be demonstrated both verbally and non-verbally by the participant in order to be part of an interview. Methods that they chose to use to communicate and record the interview were documented. Individuals and group members were informed that there were no right or wrong answers and that they could leave the interview at any time. An interpreter was advised that they could direct questions or interpret in order to develop a point without dominating the conversation. In order for true consent to be given, it must be discussed within specific conditions: a calm environment, adequate time, openness and honesty. Within the consent process it is important to explain clearly expectations and limitations within the research framework. Prior consultation about sensitive questions should always be given. Issues of understanding and retention have to be considered and we recognized the need for consent to be a continuous process. We have emailed participants and written to them personally when appropriate. We usually spent time with participants informally before interviewing them to allow them to assess the interviewer and decide if they wished to participate. The explanation of why we were conducting the research was given in as simple a manner as possible. Pictures depicting anonymity and safety of information were also used. The consent format proved comprehensive and acceptable to people with learning disabilities and organizational managers involved in the study.

Analysis

Using an approach based on aspects of the constant comparative method of Strauss and Corbin (1990, 1994), the analysis commenced after initial interviews were conducted and continued throughout the study. Interviews were recorded and transcribed and both the text and the recorded material were reflected on in depth. The researchers immersed themselves in the data, searching for themes and ways of understanding what people contributed. By reading the transcripts, listening to interviews/interactions, reflecting on interview details (researcher–participant relationship), reflecting on the meaning of drawings/posters and critical reflection on field notes, the interviewers were able to gain rich insights into the spiritual lives of people with learning disabilities and to articulate a number of significant themes. The analysis was constantly written and rewritten as the researchers engaged more fully with people's experience (Dey 1993; Glaser 1992).

Issues of validity

The research product was validated using the methods outlined in Chapter 4. Findings were discussed thoroughly with participants, and people with learning disabilities were closely involved with the development and presentation of the final research product and the various educational materials that emerged from the project.

Theological reflection

Through this process a number of key themes emerged which accurately represented the participants' perspective on the significance of spirituality for their lives. These themes provided rich insights into the spiritual lives of people with learning disabilities and raised perspectives and questions which have significant theological importance. For current purposes we will focus on the theological significance of two connected themes that emerged: *hospitality* and *friendship*. A focus on hospitality and friendship will enable us to illustrate the way in which this approach to qualitative research can unearth important theological questions and constructively challenge the accepted *modus operandi* of certain key practices of the Church.

Hospitality and friendship

It is clear that within the traditions which gain their shape from within the Christian tradition, hospitality is a moral imperative (Pohl 1999). As Pineda (1997, p. 29) puts it:

> The expectations that God's people are people who will welcome strangers and treat them justly runs throughout the Bible. This expectation is not based on any special immunity to the dangers unknown people might present – far from it. Rather, it emerges from knowing the hospitality God has shown to us.
>
> > When an alien resides with you in your land, you shall not oppress the alien. The alien who resides with you shall be to you as the citizen among you; you shall love the alien as yourself, for you were aliens in the land of Egypt; I am the Lord your God.
> > Leviticus 19:33–4 (p. 32)

While the juxtaposition of people with learning disabilities with 'strangers' and 'resident aliens' at first seems odd and possibly derogatory, as one reflects on their life experiences, it is clear that within a society which values cognition, intellectual prowess and social status above loving relationships, friendship and community, their status as citizens and indeed as fully human is always in question. Lisa Curtice (2001) argues that people with learning disabilities have been socially marginalized and their opportunities for employment and income have been seriously compromised. She highlights the ways in which people with learning disabilities are oppressed and marginalized within contemporary British/Scottish society.

> Only four per cent of adults with learning disabilities in Scotland are in employment. Despite care in the community, many still only count family members and staff paid to support them among their social networks (Felce *et al.* 1998). Often denied the status of adults, people with learning disabilities have been excluded from recognition as sexual beings (Brown 1994), as potential parents (Booth and Booth 1994a), as householders and tenants (Fitton and Wilson 1995) and as people able to make an active contribution to society. They have experienced abuse (Brown *et al.* 1995) and exclusion from basic services, such as health care (Espie *et al.* 1999). Whilst the number of people living in the community has increased because of the closure of long-stay institutions, much less progress has been made in enabling people to access mainstream services and to make friendships within the community.

To this list of oppressive experiences, Curtice adds spiritual deprivation and oppression. This oppression manifests itself in a number of ways:

- Communicational barriers that prevent carers and others from exploring the emotional and spiritual aspects of the lives of people with learning disabilities.
- Assumptions that spirituality and ideas about God require a high level of abstract thinking, leading to decisions as to what the 'necessary cognitive "threshold" for church membership' might be.
- A painful legacy within certain strands of theology that equate disability with sin, leading to blame, exclusion and alienation.

- Suspicion of the value base of religion.
- A general unwillingness to address spiritual issues, which is indicative of a wider failure to address emotional needs in people with learning disabilities.

Within such a context and bearing in mind the biblical imperative towards hospitality, it might be expected that religious communities would be ideally suited to provide support and welcome to this particular group of marginalized people. The current research project discovered some churches where people with learning disabilities were well integrated and their spiritual needs appropriately catered for. Diane's experience is a good example of this:

Interviewer:	You were saying before that you thought what was important in life was going to church?
Diane:	Yeah.
Interviewer:	Can you say what's good about those [church] organizations?
Diane:	They're good you know, good to make friends and then chat to them.
Interviewer:	You can make friends and chat and you enjoy that?
Diane:	I do.
Interviewer:	And do you think it's, that's a good place to do that?
Diane:	Yes, I do.
Interviewer:	Can you say why that's a good place?
Diane:	I do enjoy it more.
Interviewer:	Is that because of the people that go? What makes it really good?
Diane:	Good fun . . . friends.

It was clear that religious communities are often appreciated by people with learning disabilities and that they are capable of providing an important dimension to people's spiritual development, in terms of friendship development, enabling people to find a positive sense of identity and value, and in enabling people to develop a deep and meaningful faith. Nevertheless, as we listened to the experiences of people with learning disabilities, it became clear that churches could also be difficult and excluding places for people with learning disabilities. Two important problematic aspects of churches emerged:

1 Churches could be both exclusive and excluding
2 The form of friendship provided by some faith communities can be superficial, uncommitted and in a real sense unspiritual.

We will examine both of these observations in turn.

Religious communities can be exclusive and excluding

Religious communities can be deeply exclusive for people who are different. The exclusion of people with learning disabilities works itself out on two levels. At one level they are excluded by the particular ways in which the message of the community is communicated. Here the forms of teaching, liturgy, prayer and worship used by the community can simply be intellectually inaccessible for people who communicate and learn in different ways. One woman summed up this difficulty in her reflections on the spirituality of her son, George, who has profound and complex needs:

> I do think there's an issue of social access and intellectual access. Intellectual access mainly in the fact that now he's virtually 18 and he's an adult, but when we come to the sermons it usually lasts at least three quarters of an hour and it's meaningless to him so he'll sit and doodle on a wee notepad for all of that time, which I think is commendable that he's willing to sit for that length of time and doodle and beside us his mum and dad. So again I think *there's a lack of intellectual access* in general not just in our own church . . . how are people with learning disabilities going to learn

more about God and the Bible and Christian life if it's not taught at a level . . . if there's not an opportunity for them to access teaching that's really pitched at their spiritual level?

If people can't understand the Word, how can they accept it; if people can't understand who God is, how can they learn to love Him? Of the participants who participated in this study, none of their religious communities had consciously addressed this issue. In previous research it was noted that churches felt that there was no need to develop programmes or approaches to address this, as there were no people with learning disabilities who attended their churches (Swinton 2002). However, they had not considered that the reason for the absence of people with learning disabilities may be their current mode of community and teaching.

This intellectual exclusion was found to be compounded by various forms of social exclusion which relate in particular to the theme of friendship. In Chapter 1 we briefly explored the nature of Christian friendship. There we noticed that Jesus' friendships were for the marginalized, the excluded and those whom society rejected. This being so, one might expect the friendships offered by Christian communities to show a similar dynamic. Often this was not the case. The mother of a young man with severe communicational difficulties, who acted as an interpreter for him during the study told us of an experience that illustrates well the implicit social exclusion that people can experience within religious communities.

We have a lot of young people in our church, a very lively church, very contemporary church, but I never see any of the young people getting alongside George. None of them ever sit beside him in church, none of them have ever sat beside him in church, none of them have invited George round to their homes at any time and as a parent carer I sometimes find it difficult. I see them maybe all going off for lunch or whatever and George is going home with his mum and dad and I just think how he has perhaps missed out on social interaction in his teenage years. In fact maybe I could tell a little story. A couple of years back one of the teenage girls who was having her sixteenth birthday and after the church service all the young people were going back to her house for a birthday dinner and afternoon. You know we had sung happy birthday to her in the church and word was around obviously that you know the party was on and so on. But of course George wasn't invited and so as we drove off from the church we just felt saddened that once again it was just another example of exclusion and just how painful that was to us. Not knowing how George felt about that. We came home we had our usual Sunday lunch we often have guests on a Sunday; we didn't that day and I went through to his bedroom later on in the afternoon and he was cutting up bits of paper and I said to him, 'What's this you're doing George?' And he said 'I'm making up tickets for the party.'

This kind of subtle exclusion often goes unnoticed. George was not the victim of a deliberately unpleasant act. Had the young people known how George felt, they may have included him. The problem is that no one outside of the family did know and no-one took the time to get to know George, so the question was never asked. George's unspoken protest is an indictment on the unconscious and unintended thoughtlessness of this particular group of people. His look of sadness as his mother told us this story confirms the continuing sadness he feels even today.

Other research participants noticed a similar phenomenon of implicit and explicit exclusion in other contexts. One group of carers spoke about their experiences with a young man, Kieran, who has profound learning disabilities. After much debate the staff group decided to take Kieran to a local church. They viewed this from their perspective purely as a social event as they did not feel able to justify taking him on religious grounds. Nevertheless, they recognized this as an important dimension of Kieran's life and were keen to help him explore it. During the three months he attended the church, not one person spoke to him! Once, one person patted him on the head in passing but that was it! The staff wondered if people were scared of him or if they were embarrassed or uncertain about how to approach Kieran. Either way the experience was not a good one and after three months it was decided that there was little point in Kieran continuing to attend the church. As one member of staff put it: 'Kieran gets a more positive response in the local coffee shop!' Despite an expressed interest in Christianity, Kieran has not been involved in any form of church since then.

Churches have much potential, but before that potential can be actualized there are significant issues of education and consciousness raising which require to be addressed. If churches are going to become places where spiritual friendship can be developed and nurtured, these issues will have to be addressed effectively.

The form of friendship provided by some religious communities can be superficial, uncommitted and in a real sense unspiritual

The second point presents an equally serious challenge to the practices of the Church. It was clear that many people with learning disabilities benefited significantly from their encounters with religious communities, that some communities did attempt to be hospitable and that friendships did develop. However, the friendships that developed often tended to remain at a certain superficial level. Ina's experience illustrates this point well.

Interviewer: Where do you feel you belong?

Ina: Well I sort of feel I'm trying to help in the community, I'm participating.

Interviewer: You're trying to help within this community.

Ina: Em, [pause] well this area here, I'm trying to build up a friendship.

Interviewer:	You're saying you're trying to build up friendships, where about is that?
Ina:	At the church.
Interviewer:	At the church, and how are you getting on there?
Ina:	Ok.
Interviewer:	Is that by meeting people or by them inviting you into their homes or?
Ina:	By meeting people at the church and in the home.
Interviewer:	And how do you find that? Do you find that easy or difficult?
Ina:	Easy.
Interviewer:	Quite easy. So do you go to meetings during the week or do you go to people's houses or do you just see them at mass?
Ina:	Just see them at mass.

At one level Ina's quest for friendship and acceptance had been fruitful. Within the boundaries of the religious service of worship she seems to have found acceptance and, at a certain level, friendship. However, that acceptance and friendship appears to stop at the door of the chapel. She has never been invited into the homes of her religious friends, although she clearly desires this and sees it as a significant life-goal. Her friendships are limited to the spiritual boundaries of the religious service and the physical boundaries of the church building. This is not an uncommon pattern and was acknowledged as significant by other people with learning disabilities, parents and other carers and support workers from various religious traditions. One carer commented:

> I think that if you are someone living in a service it's so rare to be invited into anybody's home. You know when we sat round at staff training and looked at when last someone was invited into another person's house it is quite, quite rare.

Such limited practices of hospitality and friendship contrast starkly with the depth of friendship revealed in Jesus' practice of friendship. When Jesus states that 'Greater love has no one than this, that he lay down his life for his friends' (John 15:13) he reveals the theological depth of the relationship of friendship. As God lays down his life for God's friends so also those who are God's friends are called to lay down their lives for their friends, particularly those friends who are strangers in need of hospitality (Matthew 25). Limited friendship is not Christian friendship at all.

The challenge for churches then is not simply to integrate people with learning disabilities into their various and varied services of worship. Rather the real challenge is to be faithful to its calling to become a hospitable community-of-friends which offers committed and engaging friendships that reflect and embody the friendship, commitment and hospitality of Jesus. The task of the Church is *inter alia* to create forms of community which can become contexts within which meaningful friendships can be developed that will enable people with learning disabilities to participate in the whole of people's lives. Meeting-oriented friendship may have a role and a function, but if that is as deep as the relationship goes, there is a significant problem with the Church's practice of hospitality and friendship.

This brief theological reflection on the Christian practice of hospitality as it emerged from the qualitative research data indicates how the data of qualitative research can become engaged with the data of Christian theology and tradition in ways that throw up a significant challenge and corrective to the practices of churches and the implicit and explicit modes of practice that render them less than faithful.

Conclusion

In this chapter we have explored the idea of participatory research. Our focus on one particular group of marginalized and often voiceless people has shown the way that qualitative research can have a significant liberatory dimension which has the potential to give voice to the voiceless and offer important challenges to the practices and faithfulness of church communities. While our focus here has been on learning disabilities, the method and approach holds obvious potential for empowering other marginalized groups. This way of approaching qualitative research offers a vital and complementary perspective to the more researcher-oriented modes of research that have been presented in the earlier chapters of this book.

The research projects presented in the second part of the book have allowed us to see some of the ways that qualitative research can be grafted in to the practical-theological task in a way which retains the integrity of both disciplines and casts fresh light and revised thinking on situations. Used carefully and with discernment, qualitative research has a lot of potential for enhancing the practice of Practical Theology.

Note to p. 228. I use the term 'learning disabilities' in the British sense of the word to refer to a group of human beings who are deemed by the majority to have limited communication skills, restricted or no skills, significant intellectual and/or cognitive difficulties and who essentially will have to have some kind of full-time care throughout their lives. Other countries use terms such as mental handicap, mental retardation, etc.

Conclusion: Practical Theology as Action Research

When we first began to put this book together we titled it *Finding Truth in the World*. On reflection, this was obviously a grandiose statement which is theologically more than a little problematic. We don't find truth, Truth finds us! Nevertheless the idea of searching for truth remains an interesting one. Practical Theology seeks after modes of practice and understandings which are true and faithful. Qualitative research reminds us that the search for truth and faithfulness is a complicated process wherein we recognize the complexities of the world and work together to move towards a fuller understanding of the world in which we live. Where Practical Theology and qualitative research truly come together is in their recognition that the world is considerably more complex and interesting than the scientific model of truth would suggest. Practical Theology pushes us towards the acknowledgement of the importance of revelation as well as discovery; qualitative research draws our attention to the crucial fact that human experience is inherently interpretative and polyvalent. We live in fascinating worlds of meaning which rarely come to our notice until we are given the opportunity and provided with the necessary tools to reflect on the world. When we begin to reflect on that which is apparently mundane, we suddenly discover that the world is rich, beautiful and highly complex. Such reflection inevitably leads us to reflection on the way that we practise and why we practise the way that we do. The combination of these two disciplines provides a wonderful context for the development of fresh insights, challenging dialogue and revised and more faithful modes of practice. In this way qualitative research aids us in the process of renewing our minds (Romans 12:2) and seeing the world differently. However, it is never enough simply to *see* the world differently. The primary task of Practical Theology is not simply to see differently, but to enable that revised vision to create changes in the way that Christians and Christian communities perform the faith. Practical Theology is certainly a reflective discipline, but above all else, it is *a theology of action.*

Practical Theology as action research

One key point that needs to be carefully drawn out is the fact that Practical Theology is fundamentally *action* research. There are of course various schools of action research which have sprung up within the social sciences. However, we would like to suggest that Practical Theology presents as a quite specific form of action research with a particular understanding of the nature and purpose of action.

Action research in the social sciences

In the social sciences the term 'action research' relates to a family of research methods which find their primary focus in the utilization of the research process not simply as a way of gaining new knowledge, but also as a way of enabling new and transformative modes of action. The action researcher does not simply seek to observe and understand the world (although she certainly does this), she also seeks to change it. These two goals are carried out simultaneously in the process of participative research practices. The basic dynamic of action research is the dialectical movement from practice (action) to theory, to critical reflection on practice, to revised forms of practice developed in the light of this spiralling process. The data and the practice are constantly challenged, developed and revised as they interact critically and dialectically with one another. Action research always retains its focus on transformative action which is discovered and inspired by the research process. If we think back to the reflective model of Practical Theology presented at the end of Chapter 3, with its cyclical dynamic focusing on developing revised faithful practices, we can begin to see the connections between Practical Theology and action research. Both use a similar reflective process and both contain similar action-oriented and transformatively oriented dynamics and goals.

Practical Theology as action research

However, while there are similarities, there are also differences. Within the social-scientific model of action research the focus of action tends to be on generating solutions to particular problems. Practical Theology has a wider theological remit which involves challenging current practices in the hope that they will move closer towards faithfulness. This requires more than simply problem-solving. It involves consciousness-raising: a process of highlighting the fact that the way in which we often think the world is is in fact quite different from the way that it actually is when explored through a theological lens. So, for example, in Chapter 8 we looked at the spiritual lives of people with learning disabilities and discovered that the friendships that were offered by Christian communities were profoundly limited. In researching in this way we were not seeking to solve the problem of why people with learning disabilities found it difficult to find friends. Rather we were showing clearly that a central and profoundly spiritual relationship was being deeply misunderstood by Christian communities and that this misunderstanding was impacting upon the more vulnerable members of the community. It looked like these communities were acting faithfully, but in fact they needed to significantly change the forms of action that they were engaged in. Rather than seeking to solve problems, Practical Theology understood as a theology of action, through the process of complexification and cultural challenge, often ends up *creating* more and previously unrecognized 'problems'. In highlighting and articulating new problems in challenging ways, Practical Theology seeks to inspire and direct new modes of action/practice which will enable individuals and communities to function, not more effectively, but more faithfully.

Within the social sciences action research tends to focus on a cluster of approaches which are essentially participatory. That is, they seek to incorporate the research subjects as co-researchers. They are empowering methods which are designed to break down the traditional barriers and allow individuals and communities to take back control of every aspect of their lives including the research process. We previously explored one way in which the practical theologian can utilize such an approach. However, the practical theologian has an understanding of 'action' that offers a perspective which differs from the standard assumptions of action research. Heitink (1999, p. 126) suggests that action within the context of Practical Theology should be understood in this way: 'To act is to pursue a goal, to work toward an intentional and active realization of certain plans, by utilizing specific means in a given situation.' In other words, unlike the social sciences (MacIntyre 1981), there is an end or *telos* that transcends all particular forms of action. This *telos* constitutes the primary purpose and meaning of human life and the eschatological horizon of the practical-theological enterprise. For the practical theologian, action is not merely pragmatic or problem-solving, although it may contain elements of this. For the practical-theological action always has the goal of interacting with situations and challenging practices in order that individuals and communities can be enabled to remain faithful to God and to participate faithfully in God's continuing mission to the world (Chapter 1). Foret (in Heitink 1999, p. 130) puts this point well:

> Practical theology does not deal with human action in general, neither with the action of the believer nor the person who acts in the service of God, but specially with action that

has to do with the actualisation and the maintenance of the relationship between God and humanity, and humanity and God.

The mode of action that is engaged in by the practical theologian is therefore seen to be *mediative*, seeking to mediate between the practices of the Christian faith and the practices of the world. Action, within the horizon of the practical theologian, is never action for action's sake, but always action in the service of revelation and mediation of the gospel.

Converting the social sciences into the service of God

Such an understanding of action has important implications for the way in which Practical Theology views and understands the purpose of the social sciences. For the practical theologian, all qualitative methods are necessarily action-oriented. Even the most apparently observational method is used with an action orientation aimed at providing information that will inform the development of faithful and transformative practices. All of the aspects of qualitative research that we have explored in this book – ethnography, phenomenology, hermeneutics, in-depth interviews, reflexivity, and so forth – when utilized by the practical theologian become critical action-oriented tools as they are converted, sanctified and drafted into the service of God. When converted in this way, they become vital tools that are significant for the creation of meaningful and rigorous data that will enable the development of new and revised modes of action; modes of action that will enable faithful participation in the continuing mission of God. It is in this action-oriented dimension of the use of qualitative research methods that we most clearly see and understand what it means for qualitative methods to be *converted* in order that they can be used in the service of Practical Theology and ultimately God. In providing clarity within complex situations and by indicating new possibilities for transformative action and faithful practice, converted and sanctified qualitative research methods become powerful tools in the service of God and combine with practical theology to provide a vital perspective on the critical mediative task between Christian practices and the practices of the world.

Practical theology as worship

As we have seen, Practical Theology and qualitative research combine to offer us a way of exploring the richness and complexity of creation. They move us beyond naive and simplistic assumptions about the world and human beings and allow us to explore the inner and often hidden depths of human experience. Perceived in this way, we might describe this type of Practical Theology research as *worship*. It was Karl Barth who said that the ultimate aim of all theology is worship (2002). Barth points towards the importance of doing theology with a spirit of praise and wonder; approaching the task of discovering the things of God with a deep sense of awe. As we have seen in this book, theology does not relate only to the rational dimensions of human experience. At a fundamental level, theology is always oriented towards the worship and praise of God. As we convert qualitative research and graft it into the service of theological action, it enables us to enter into some of the depths and complexities of creation; as we listen critically but openly to the voice it brings to us, we are drawn into new understandings of and fresh perspectives on the divine drama. These new understandings should draw us into closer communion with God and inspire worship and praise at the intricacies and wonders of creation. It should not only help us to *understand*, it should also enable us to *love* God and *relate* more closely to God, ourselves and to one another (Matt. 22:37–40).

Conclusion

In this book we have not attempted to present a comprehensive overview of all forms of qualitative research. We recognize that there are aspects of qualitative research such as, for example, discourse analysis, feminist and critical methods, narrative approaches and a myriad of other valuable ways of doing qualitative research that we have not been able to address within the confines of this book. This omission should not, however, be perceived as a weakness. Our task has been to lay down some foundational understandings of how Practical Theology can utilize qualitative research in a way that retains the integrity of both disciplines and allows theology in general and Practical Theology in particular to remain faithful and confident in its identity and task. We have introduced the reader to some important principles within both disciplines and provided frameworks, methods and approaches that will allow practical theologians to expand and develop into other more specialized approaches to research. The solid foundation of knowledge and the reflections on its practical application presented here should provide a firm base for the development of practical-theological research which is rigorous, stimulating, diverse and faithful.

Taken as a whole this book has offered a vital insight into the relationship of Practical Theology to qualitative research and has presented an understanding and a way of approaching Practical Theology which is theologically coherent and practically vital. It is our hope that readers have found this book interesting, useful and challenging and that as they have worked through its implications, they have been enabled to think more clearly about this important area and in so doing, been inspired to practice more faithfully in terms both of their research and of their personal spiritual journey. That, at least, is our hope, our desire and our prayer.

References

Abbott, P., and Meerabeau, L. (eds) (1998) *The Sociology of the Caring Professions*, 2nd edn, London: UCL Press

Abbott, P., and Wallace, C. (eds) (1990) *The Sociology of the Caring Professions*, London: Falmer Press

Ackermann, D. M., and Bons-Storm, R. (eds) (1998) *Liberating Faith Practices: Feminist Practical Theology in Context*, Leuven: Peeters

Aldridge, David (1998) *Suicide: The Tragedy of Hopelessness*, London: Jessica Kingsley

Alfricher, A., Posch, P., and Somekh, B. (1993) *Teachers Investigate Their Work: An Introduction to the Methods of Action Research*, London: Routledge

Ali, C. A. (1999) *Survival and Liberation: Pastoral Theology in African American Context*, St Louis: Chalice Press

Arbuckle, Gerald (1991) *Grieving for Change: A Spirituality for Re-founding Gospel Communities*, New York: Continuum

Armistead, K. M. (1995) *God-Images in the Healing Process*, Minneapolis: Fortress Press

Atkinson, D. (1988) 'Research interviews with people with mental handicaps', *Mental Handicap Research* 1(1), 75–90

Austin, J. A. (1998) 'Why patients use alternative medicine: results of a national study', *Journal of the American Medical Association* 279(19), 1548–53

Aveyard, H. (2002) 'The requirement for informed consent prior to nursing care procedures', *Journal of Advanced Nursing* 38(5), 458–66

Aylott, J. (2002) 'Developments in learning disability nursing over the last 10 years', *British Journal of Nursing* 11(7), 498–500

Ballard, P. (1992) 'Can theology be practical?', *Contact* 109(3), 3

Barnes, C. (1992) 'Qualitative Research: valuable or irrelevant?', *Disability, Handicap and Society* 7(2), 115–24

Barth, Karl (1956) *Christ and Adam: Man and Humanity in Romans 5*, trans. T. A. Smail, New York: Macmillan

Barth, Karl (1961–2) 'Secular parables of the truth', in *Church Dogmatics* IV/3:1, Edinburgh: T & T Clark, par. 69, sec. 2

Barth, Karl (2002) *Prayer*, Louisville: Westminister John Knox Press

Becker, H. (1967) "Whose side are we on?", *Social Problems* 14, 239–47

Berger, P. L. (1963) *Invitation to Sociology: A Humanistic Perspective*, New York: Anchor Books

Berger, P. L., and Luckmann, T. (1979) *The Social Construction of Reality: A Treatise in the Sociology of Knowledge*, London: Penguin

Biklen, S. K., and Moseley, C. R. (1988) ' "Are you retarded?" "No I'm Catholic": Qualitative methods in the study of people with severe handicaps', *Journal of the Association for Persons with Severe Handicaps* 13(3), 155–62

Bogdan, R., and Taylor, S. J. (1998) *Introduction to Qualitative Research Methods: The Search for Meanings*, New York: John Wiley & Sons

Booth, S. (2002) 'A philosophical analysis of informed consent', *Nursing Standard* 16(39), 43–6

Booth, T., and Booth, W. (1994a) 'The use of depth interviewing with vulnerable subjects: Lessons from a research study of parents with learning difficulties', *Social Science and Medicine* 39(3), 415–24

Booth, T., and Booth, W. (1994b) *Parenting Under Pressure: Mothers and Fathers with Learning Disabilities*, Buckingham: Open University Press

Booth, T., and Booth, W. (1996) 'Sounds of silence: narrative research with inarticulate subjects', *Disability and Society* 11(1), 55–69

Boswell, B. B. (2001) 'Disability and spirituality: a reciprocal relationship with implications for the rehabilitation process', *Journal of Rehabilitation* 67(4), 20–5

Bowden, J. W. (1998) 'Recovery from alcoholism: a spiritual journey', *Issues in Mental Health Nursing* 19(4), 337–52

Breitbart, W., and Heller, K. (2003) 'Reframing hope: meaning-centered care for patients near the end of life', *Journal of Palliative Medicine* 6(6), 979–88

Brown, H. (1994) 'An ordinary sexual life?: A review of the normalization principle as it applies to the sexual options of people with learning disabilities', *Disability and Society* 9(2), 123–44

Brown, H., Stein, J., and Turk, V. (1995) 'The sexual abuse of adults with learning disabilities: report of a second two-year incidence survey', *Mental Handicap Research* 8(1), 3–24

Browning, D. S. (1983) *Practical Theology*, San Francisco: Harper & Row

Browning, D. S. (1991) *Practical Theology: Descriptive and Strategic Proposals*, Minneapolis: Fortress Press

Buber, M. (1958) *I and Thou*, trans. R. G. Smith, New York: Charles Scribner's Sons

Burgess, R. (ed.) (1993) *Educational Research and Evaluation: For Policy and Practice*, London: Falmer Press

Cambridge, P., and McCarthy, M. (2001) 'User focus groups and best value in services for people with learning disabilities', *Health and Social Care in the Community* 9(6), 476–89

Carlisle, S., and Hudson, H. (1997) 'The general practitioner and older people: strategies for more effective home visits?', *Health and Social Care in the Community* 5(5)

Carroll, S. (1993) 'Spirituality and purpose in life in alcoholism recovery', *Journal of Studies on Alcohol* 54(3), 297–301

Chopp, R. S., and Parker, D. F. (1990) *Liberation Theology and Pastoral Theology*, Decatur: Journal of Pastoral Care Publications

Cocks, E., and Cockram, J. (1995) 'The participatory research paradigm and intellectual disability', *Mental Handicap Research* 8(1), 25–37

Colin, R. (2002) *Real World Research: A Resource for Social Scientists and Practitioner-Researchers*, London: Blackwell

Cooper, H. (1998) *Synthesizing Research: A Guide for Literature Reviews*, 3rd edn, Thousand Oaks, CA: Sage

Corben, V. (1999) 'Misusing phenomenology in nursing research: identifying the issues', *Nurse Researcher* 6(3), 52–66

Cornwall, A., and Jewkes, R. (1995) 'What is participatory research?' *Social Science and Medicine* 41, 1667–76.

Couture, P., and Hunter, R. J. (1995) *Pastoral Care and Social Conflict*, Nashville: Abingdon Press

Curtice, L. (2001) 'The social and spiritual inclusion of people with learningdisabilities: a liberating challenge?' *Contact: The Interdisciplinary Journal of Pastoral Studies*, 17–22

Damaris, Rose (2001) 'Revisiting feminist research methodologies: a working paper', Ottawa: Status of Women Canada, 6 July 2001. Online: Status of Women, Publications: http://www.swc-cfc.gc.ca/pubs/revisiting/revisiting_1_e.html 6 July 2001

Davie, G. (1994) *Religion in Britain since 1945: Believing Without Belonging*, Oxford: Blackwell

Denzin, N. K. (1997) *Interpretive Ethnography: Ethnographic Practices for the 21st Century*, Thousand Oaks, CA: Sage

Denzin, N. K. (2002) *Interpretive Interactionism*, 2nd edn, London: Sage

Denzin, N. K., and Lincoln, Y. S. (1998) *Collecting and Interpreting Qualitative Materials*, Thousand Oaks, CA: Sage

Denzin, N. K., and Lincoln, Y. S. (2000) *Handbook of Qualitative Research*, 2nd edn, Thousand Oaks, CA: Sage

Department of Health (2001) *Seeking Consent: Working with People with Learning Disabilities*, London: Department of Health

Dey, I. (1993) *Qualitative Data Analysis: A User-Friendly Guide for Social Scientists*, New York: Routledge

Diekelman, N., Allen, D., and Tanner, C. (1989) 'The NLN criteria for the appraisal of baccalaureate programmes: a critical hermeneutical analysis', in N. Diekelman and D. Allen (eds), *The NLN Criteria for Appraisal of Baccalaureate Programmes: A Critical Hermeneutic Analysis*, New York: NLN Press

Douglas, J. D. (1967) *The Social Meanings of Suicide*, Princeton: Princeton University Press

Dowie, A. (2002) *Interpreting Culture in a Scottish Congregation*, New York: Peter Lang

Drane, J. (1991) *What is the New Age Saying to the Church?*, London: Marshall Pickering

Durkheim, E. (1951) *Suicide: A Study in Sociology*, trans. J. A. Spaulding and G. Simpson, New York: Free Press of Glenco

Dykstra, C., and Bass, D. (2002) 'A theological understanding of Christian practices', in M. Volf and D. C. Bass (eds), *Practicing Theology: Beliefs and Practices in Christian Life*, Grand Rapids: Eerdmans

Eaton, William W. (1986) *The Sociology of Mental Disorders*, New York: Praeger

Espie, C., Curtice, L., Morrison, J., Dunningham, M., Knill-Jones, R., and Long, L. (1999) *The Role of the NHS in Meeting the Health Needs of People With Learning Disabilities*, Report for the Scottish Executive Learning Disability Review

Farley, E. (1983) *Theologia: The Fragmentation and Unity of Theological Education*, Philadephia: Fortress Press

Felce, D., Grant, G., Todd, S., Ramcharan, P., Beyer, S., McGrath, M., Perry, J., Shearn, J., Kilsby, M., and Lowe, K. (1998) *Towards a Full Life: Researching Policy Innovation for People With Learning Disabilities*, Oxford: Butterworth-Heinemann

Fitton, P., and Wilson, J. (1995) 'A home of their own', in T. Philpot and L. Ward (eds), *Values and Visions: Changing Ideas in Services for People with Learning Difficulties*, Oxford: Butterworth-Heinemann

Flick, U.(1992) 'Triangulation revisited: strategy of validation or alternative?', *Journal for the Theory of Social Behaviour* 22(2), 175–97

Flick, U. (1998) *An Introduction to Qualitative Research*, Thousand Oaks and London: Sage

Fontana, A., and Frey, J. H. (2000) 'The interview: from structured questions to negotiated text', in N. K. Denzin and Y. S. Lincoln (eds), *Handbook of Qualitative Research*, 2nd edn, Thousand Oaks, CA: Sage, pp. 645–72

Forrester, D. B. (1990) *Theology and Practice*, London: Epworth Press

Forrester, D. B. (2000) *Truthful Action: Explorations in Practical Theology*, Edinburgh: T & T Clark

Fowler, J. E. (1981) *Stages of Faith: Psychology of Human Development and the Quest for Meaning*, San Francisco: Harper & Row

Fowler, J. E. (1995) 'The emerging new shape of practical theology', unpublished paper from the 1995 Conference of the International Academy of Practical Theology held in Berne

Fowler, J. W. (1987) *Faith Development and Pastoral Care*, Philadelphia: Fortress Press

Fowler, J. W. (1996) *Faithful Change: The Personal and Public Challenges of Postmodern Life*, Nashville: Abingdon Press

Francis, L. J., and Jones, L. J. (eds) (1996)*Psychological Perspectives on Christian Ministry: A Reader*, Leominster: Fowler Wright

Fraser, M., and Fraser, A. (2001) 'Are people with learning disabilities able to contribute to focus groups on health promotion?', *Journal of Advanced Nursing* 33(2), 225–33

Freud, Sigmund (1955) *Beyond the Pleasure Principle*, Standard edn, vol. 18, London: Hogarth Press

Frid, I., Ohlen, J., and Bergbom, I. (2000) 'On the use of narratives in nursing research', *Journal of Advanced Nursing* 32(3), 695–703

Fry, P. S. (2000) 'Religious involvement, spirituality and personal meaning for life: existential predictors of psychological wellbeing in community residing and institutional care elders', *Aging and Mental Health* 4(4), 375–87

Furnham, A. (2002) 'Exploring attitudes toward, and knowledge of, homeopathy and CAM through focus groups', *Complementary Therapies in Nursing and Midwifery* 8(1), 42–7

Gadamer, H. (1981) *Truth and Method*, London: Sheed & Ward

Gilbert, P. (1992) *Depression: The Evolution of Powerlessness*, Hillsdale, NJ: Lawrence Erlbaum Association

Giles, L. (1999) *Chaplaincy: The Church's Sector Ministries*, London: Cassell

Gill, R. (1975) *The Social Context of Theology*, Oxford: Mowbray

Gill, R. (1977) *Theology and Social Structure*, Oxford: Mowbray

Glaser, B. G. (1978) *Theoretical Sensitivity*, Mill Valley: Sociology Press

Glaser, B. G. (1992) *Basics of Grounded Theory Analysis: Emergence vs Forcing*, Mill Valley, CA: Sociology Press

Glaser, B. G. (1998) *Doing Grounded Theory: Issues and Discussions*, Mill Valley, CA: Sociology Press

Glaser, B. G. (ed.) (1994) *More Grounded Theory Methodology: A Reader*, Mill Valley, CA: Sociology Press

Glaser, B. G. (ed.) (1995) *Grounded Theory 1984–1994*, vol. 1, Mill Valley, CA: Sociology Press

Goodley, D. (1996) 'Tales of hidden lives: a critical examination of life hjstory research with people who have learning difficulties', *Disability and Society* 11(3), 333–48

Gorsuch, R. L. (2002) 'The pyramids of sciences and of humanities: implications for the search for religious truth', *American Behavioral Scientist* 45(12), 1822–38

Green, C., and Nicoll, L. (2001) 'Therapeutic caring: a learning disability experience', *Complementary Therapies in Nursing and Midwifery* 7, 180–7

Green, B. N., Johnson, C. D., and Adams, A. (2001) 'Writing narrative literature reviews for peer-reviewed journals: secrets of the trade', *Journal of Sports Chiropractic and Rehabilitation* 15(1), 5–19

Greenhalgh, T. (1997) 'How to read a paper: The Medline database', *British Medical Journal* 315, 180–3

Greenhalgh, T. (1997) 'How to read a paper: Getting your bearings (deciding what the paper is about)', *British Medical Journal* 315, 243–6

Greenhalgh, T. (1997) 'How to read a paper: Assessing the methodological quality of published papers', *British Medical Journal* 315, 305–8

Greenhalgh, T. (1997) *How to read a paper: The Basis of Evidence-Based Medicine*, London: BMJ.

Guba, E. (1990) *The Paradigm Dialogue*, Newbury Park, CA: Sage

Guba, E. G., and Lincoln, Y. S. (1994) 'Competing paradigms in qualitative research', in N. K. Denzin and Y. S. Lincoln (eds), *Handbook of Qualitative Research*, Thousand Oaks, CA: Sage, pp. 105–17

Hardie, H. F. R. (1968) *Aristotle's Ethical Theory*, Oxford: Clarendon

Hart, C. (1998) *Doing a Literature Review: Releasing the Social Science Research Imagination*, London: Sage

Hay, D. (1990) *Religious Experience Today: Studying the Facts*, London: Cassell

Heelas, P., Woodhead, L., Seel, B., Tustin, K., and Szerszynoiki, B. (2005) *The Spiritual Revolution: Why Religion is Giving Way to Spirituality*, Oxford: Blackwell

Heitink, G. (1999) *Practical Theology: History, Theory, Action Domains: Manual for Practical Theology*, Grand Rapids: Eerdmans

Hekman, S. (1986) *Hermeneutics and the Sociology of Knowledge*, Cambridge: Polity Press

Hiltner, S. (1954) *Preface to Pastoral Theology*, New York and Nashville: Abingdon Press

Homiletics Online (23/6/05) http://www.homileticsonline.com/subscriber/interviews/hauerwas.asp

Howie, J. G. R. (1989) *Research in General Practice*, 2nd edn, London: Chapman & Hall

Hudson, H., and Bennet, G. (1996) 'Action research: a vehicle for change in general practice', in P. Pearson and J. Spencer (eds), *Promoting Teamwork in Primary Care: A Research Based Approach*, London: Edward Arnold

Humphreys, M., Hill, L., and Valentine, S. (1990) 'A psychotherapy group for young adults with mental handicaps: Problems Encountered', *Mental Handicap* 18, 125–7

Hurley, S. L. (1989) *Natural Reasons: Personality and Polity*, New York: Oxford University Press

Husserl, E. (1963) *Ideas: A General Introduction to Pure Phenomenology*, New York: Collier Books

Iler, W., Obershain, D., and Camac, M. (2001) 'The impact of daily visits from chaplains on patients with chronic obstructive pulmonary disease COPD: a pilot study', *Chaplaincy Today* 17(1), 5–11

Jamieson, A. (2002) *A Churchless Faith: Faith Journeys beyond the Churches*, London: SPCK

John of the Cross, St (1959) *Dark Night of the Soul*, ed. and trans. E. A. Peers, New York: Image Books

Johnstone, E., Freeman, C. P., and Zealley, A. (1998) *Companion to Psychiatric Studies*, 6th edn, Edinburgh: Churchill Livingstone

Karp, D. (1996) *Speaking of Sadness: Depression, Disconnection, and the Meanings of Illness*, New York: Oxford University Press

Kiernan, C. (1999) 'Participation in research by people with learning disability: origins and issues', *British Journal of Learning Disabilities* 27(2), 48–51

King, S. R., Hampton, W. R., Bernstein, B., and Schictor, A. (1996) 'College students views on suicide', *College Health* 44(5), 283–7

Kleinman, A. (1980) *Patients and Healers in the Context of Culture: An Exploration of the Borderland between Anthropology, Medicine and Psychiatry*, Berkeley, CA: University of California Press

Knox, M., and Hickson, F. (2001) 'The meanings of close friendship: the views of four people with intellectual disabilities', *Journal of Applied Research in Intellectual Disabilities* 14(3), 276–91

Koch, T. (1996) 'Implementation of a hermeneutic inquiry in nursing: philosophy, rigour and representation', *Journal of Advanced Nursing* 24(1), 174–84

Koch, T. (1998) 'Story telling: is it really research?', *Journal of Advanced Nursing* 28(6), 118–19

Koch, T. (1999) 'An interpretive research process: revisiting phenomenological and hermeneutical approaches', *Nurse Researcher* 6(3), 20–34

Koenig, H., McCullough, M., and Larson, D. (2001) *Handbook of Religion and Health*, Oxford: Oxford University Press

Krueger, R. A. (1994) *Focus Groups: A Practical Guide for Applied Research*, 2nd edn, Thousand Oaks, CA: Sage

Kuhn, T. S. (1962) *The Structure of Scientific Revolutions*, 1st edn, Chicago: University of Chicago Press

Kuhn, T. S. (1970) *The Structure of Scientific Revolutions*, rev. edn, Chicago: University of Chicago Press

Kunst, J. L. (1992) 'Towards a psychologically liberating pastoral theology', *Pastoral Psychology* 40(3), 163

Larson, D. B., Sawyers, J. P., and McCullough, M. (1997) *Scientific Research on Spirituality and Health: A Consensus Report*, Rockville, MD: National Institute for Healthcare Research

Legood, G. (1999) *Chaplaincy: the Church's Sector Ministries*, London: Cassell.

Lincoln, Y. S., and Guba, E. G. (1985) *Naturalistic Enquiry*, London: Sage

Lincoln, Y. S., and Guba, E. G. (2000) 'Paradigmatic Controversies, Contradictions, and Emerging Confluences', in N. K. Denzin and Y. S. Lincoln (eds), *Handbook of Qualitative Research*, 2nd edn, Thousand Oaks, CA: Sage, pp. 163–88

Litosseliti, L. (2003) *Using Focus Groups in Research*, London: Continuum

Long, T., and Johnson, M. (2000) 'Rigour, reliability and validity in qualitative research', *Clinical Effectiveness in Nursing* 4, 30–7

Macmurray, J. (1961) *Persons in Relation*, London: Faber & Faber

MacIntyre, A. (1981) *After Virtue: A Study in Moral Theory*, London: Duckworth

McDougall, P. (2000) 'In-depth interviewing: the key issues of reliability and validity', *Community Practitioner* 73(8), 722–4

McFadden, S. H. (2000) 'Religion and meaning in later life', in G. T. Reker and K. Chamberlain (eds), *Exploring Existential Meaning: Optimizing Human Development across the Life Span*, Thousand Oaks, CA: Sage, pp. 171–84

McGoveran, P. (1990) 'The personal development programme: group psychotherapy for people with mental handicaps', *Mental Handicap* 18, 163–5

McLeod, J. (2001) *Qualitative Research in Counselling and Psychotherapy*, London: Sage

Mason, J. (1996) *Qualitative Researching*, London: Sage

Mental Health Foundation, Statistics on Mental Health: http://www.mentalhealth.org.uk/page.cfm?pagecode=PMMHST (accessed 27 July 2005)

Milbank, J. (1990) *Theology and Social Theory: Beyond Secular Reason*, Oxford: Blackwell

Miles, R. (1999) *The Pastor as Moral Guide*, Minneapolis: Fortress Press

Miller-McLemore, B. J., and Gill-Austern, B. L. (eds) (1999) *Feminist and Womanist Pastoral Theology*, Nashville: Abingdon Press

Milne, R., and Bull, R. (2001) 'Interviewing witnesses with learning disabilities for legal purposes', *British Journal of Learning Disabilities* 29(3), 93–7

Mitchell, D. (1999) 'How do whole time health care chaplains in Scotland understand and practice spiritual care?', *Scottish Journal of Healthcare Chaplaincy*, 2(2)

Morse, J. (ed.) (1994) *Critical Issues in Qualitative Research Methods*, Newbury Park, CA: Sage

Morse, J., Kuzel, A. J., and Swanson, J. M. (eds) (2001) *The Nature of Qualitative Research*, Thousand Oaks, CA: Sage

Morton, A. and Francis, J. (eds) (2000) *The Sorrows of Young Men: Exploring their Increasing Risk of Suicide*, Edinburgh: Centre for Theology and Public Issues, University of Edinburgh

Moustakas, C. (1994) *Phenomenological Research Methods*, London: Sage

Mowat, H., Stark, C., Swinton, J., and Mowat, D. (2006) *Religion and Suicide: An Exloratory Study of the Role of the Church in Deaths by Suicide in Highland*, Mowat Research Publications

Murphy, M. K., Black, N. A., Lamping, D. L., McKee, C. M., Sanderson, C. F. B., Askham, J., and Marteau, T. (1998) 'Consensus development methods, and their use in clinical guidelines development', *Health Technology Assessment* 2(3) i–iv, 1–88

Murphy, N., and Kallenberg, B. J. (eds) (2003) *Virtues and Practices in the Christian Tradition*, Notre Dame, IN: University of Notre Dame Press

Murray, Kris, A. 'Process, emergence, and recursivity', http://www.svcc.edu/academics/classes/gadamer/gng.htm (accessed 30 Nov. 2005)

Murray, S. A., Kendall, M., Boyd, K., Worth, A., and Benton, T. F. (2004) 'Exploring the spiritual needs of people dying of lung cancer or heart failure: a prospective qualitative interview study of patients and their carers', *Palliative Medicine* 18, 39–45

Narayanasamy, A., and Owens, J. (2001) 'A critical incident study of nurses' responses to the spiritual needs of their patients', *Journal of Advanced Nursing* 33(4), 446–55

Newbigin, L. (1989) *The Gospel in a Pluralist Society*, London/Grand Rapids: SPCK/Eerdmans

Northway, R. (2000) 'Disability, nursing research and the importance of reflexivity', *Journal of Advanced Nursing* 32(2), 391–7

Oliver, M. (1990) *The Politics of Disablement*, London: Macmillan
Oliver, M. (1992) 'Changing the social relations of research production?', *Disability, Handicap and Society* 7(2), 101–14
Orchard, H. (2000) *Hospital Chaplaincy: Modern and Dependable?*, Sheffield: Sheffield Academic Press

Pattison, S. (1989) 'Some straws for the bricks: a basic introduction to theological reflection', *Contact* 99(2), 2–9
Pattison, S. (1994) *Pastoral Care and Liberation*, New York: Cambridge University Press
Pattison, S., and Woodward, J. (2000) *The Blackwell Reader in Pastoral and Practical Theology*, London: Blackwell
Patton, J. (1993) *Pastoral Care in Context: An Introduction to Pastoral Care*, Louisville: Westminster John Knox Press
Pineda, Ana Maria (1997) 'Hospitality', in D. C. Bass (ed.), *Practicing our Faith*, San Francisco: Jossey Bass
Pohl, C. D. (1999) *Making Room: Recovering Hospitality as a Christian Tradition*, Grand Rapids: Eerdmans
Polanyi, M. (1958) *Personal Knowledge: Towards a Post-Critical Philosophy*, Gifford Lectures, University of Aberdeen, 1951–2, London: Routledge & Kegan Paul; Chicago: University of Chicago Press
Poling, J. N., and Mudge, L. S. (eds) (1987) *Formation and Reflection: The Promise of Practical Theology*, Philadelphia: Fortress Press. Online at http://www.religion-online.org/showbook.asp?title=586
Popper, K. R. (1998) *The Logic of Scientific Discovery*, London: Routledge
Porter, L., and Ouvry, C. (2001) 'Interpreting the communication of people with profound and multiple learning difficulties', *British Journal of Learning Disabilities* 29(1), 12–16
Post, S. (1992) *The Moral Challenge of Alzheimer's Disease*, Baltimore: Johns Hopkins University Press
Post, S., Puchalski, C. M., and Larson, D. B. (2000) 'Physicians and patient spirituality: professional boundaries, competency, and ethics', *Annals of Internal Medicine* 132(7), 578–83
Prudo, R., Harris, T. and Brown, G. W., 'Psychiatric disorder in a rural and an urban population; 3. Social integration and the morphology of affective disorder', *Psychological Medicine* 1984 May, 14(2): 327–45

QSR NVivo (2002) http://www.qsrinternational.com

Ramcharan, P., and Grant, G. (2001) 'Views and experiences of people with intellectual disabilities and their families: the user perspective', *Journal of Applied Research in Intellectual Disabilities* 14, 348–63

Reedier, F. (1988) 'Hermeneutics', in B. Sartor (ed.), *Paths of Knowledge: Innovative Research Methods for Nursing*, New York: National League for Nursing Press

Rioux, M., and Bach, M. (eds) (1994) *Disability is Not Measles: New Research Paradigms in Disability*, Toronto, Canada: Roeher Institute

Ritchie, J., and Lewis, J. (eds) (2003) *Qualitative Research Practice: A Guide for Social Science Students and Researchers*, London: Sage

Robson, C. (1993) *Real World Research: A Resource for Social Scientists and Practitioner-Researchers*, London: Blackwell

Robson, C. (2002) *Real World Research*, 2nd edn, Oxford: Blackwell

Rolph, S. (2000) *Legal and Ethical Issues in Interviewing People with Learning Difficulties*, http://www.esds.ac.uk/aandp/create/guidelines-learningdifficulty.asp

Rose, D. (2001) 'Revisiting feminist research methodologies: a working paper', Urbanisation, Culture et Société, Institut national de la recherche scientifique. http://www.swc-cfc.gc.ca/pubs/revisiting/revisiting_1_e.html

Ryan, S. (1996) 'Living with rheumatoid arthritis: a phenomenological exploration', *Nursing Standard* 10(41), 45–8

Samaritans, Information Sheet: Depression and Suicide: http://www.samaritans.org/know/informationsheets/depression/depression_sheet.shtm

Sandelowski, M. (1986) 'The problem of rigour in qualitative research', *Advances in Nursing Science* 8(3), 27–37

Scottish Church Census (2002) http://www.scottishchristian.com/features/0305census01.shtml

Scottish Executive (2001) *Cancer in Scotland: Action for Change*, Edinburgh: Scottish Executive

Scottish Executive (2002) *Spiritual Care in NHS Scotland: Health Department Letter 76*, Edinburgh: Scottish Executive

Scottish Executive (2003) *A New Public Involvement Structure for NHS Scotland Patient Focus Public Involvement*, Edinburgh: Scottish Executive

Scottish Journal of Healthcare Chaplaincy, 'Chaplains focused on the new chaplaincy guidelines': http://www.sach.org.uk/journal0602.htm (accessed 30 Nov. 2005)

Shuman, J. J., and Meador, K. (2003) *Heal Thyself: Spirituality, Medicine and the Distortion of Christianity*, New York: Oxford University Press

Silverman, D. (2000) *Doing Qualitative Research: A Practical Handbook*, London: Sage

Sim, J. (1998) 'Collecting and analyzing qualitative data: issues raised by the focus group', *Journal of Advanced Nursing* 28(2), 345–52

Skene, R. A. (1991) 'Towards a measure of psychotherapy in mental handicap', *The British Journal of Mental Subnormality* 37(2), 101–9

Smith, B . (1990) in R. J. Hunter (ed.), *Dictionary of Pastoral Care and Counselling*, Nashville: Abingdon Press

Smith, B. (1996) 'The problem drinker's lived experience of suffering: a hermeneutic–phenomenological study', unpublished MSc in Nursing thesis, University of Aberdeen

Smith, B. A. (1998) 'The problem drinker's lived experience of suffering: an exploration using hermeneutic phenomenology', *Journal of Advanced Nursing* 27(1), 213–22

Smucker, C. (1996) 'A phenomenological description of the experience of spiritual distress', *Nursing Diagnosis* 7(2), 81ff.

Stack, S. (1983) 'The effect of religious commitment on suicide: a cross-national analysis', *Journal of Health and Social Behavior* 24(4), 362–74

Stark, C., Hopkins, P., Gibbs, D., Rapsonm T., Belbin, A., and Hay, A. (2004) 'Trends in suicide in Scotland 1981–1999: age, method and geography', *BMC Public Health* 4(1), 49

Stein, D., Witztum, E., and Brom, D. (1992) 'The association between adolescents' attitudes toward suicide and their psychosocial background and suicidal tendencies', *Adolescence* 27(108), 949–59

Stephenson, C., and Beech, I. (1998) 'Playing the power game for qualitative researchers: the possibility of a post modern approach', *Journal of Advanced Nursing* 27(4), 790–7

Stiles, M. K. (1994) 'The shining stranger: application of the phenomenological method in the investigation of the nurse–family spiritual relationship', *Cancer Nursing* 17(1), 19–26

Strauss, A. (1987) *Qualitative Analysis for Social Scientists*, London: Cambridge University Press

Strauss, A., and Corbin, J. (1990) *Basics of Qualitative Research: Grounded Theory Procedures and Techniques*, Newbury Park, CA: Sage

Strauss, A., and Corbin, J. (1994) 'Grounded theory methodology', in N. K. Denzin and Y. S. Lincoln (eds), *Handbook of Qualitative Research*, Thousand Oaks, CA: Sage, pp. 273–85

Swinton, J. (1999) *Building a Church for Strangers: Theology, Church and Learning Disability*, Contact Monograph, Edinburgh: Contact Pastoral Trust

Swinton, J. (2000a) *The Spiritual Dimension of Pastoral Care: Practical Theology in a Multidisciplinary Context*, ed. with D. Willows, London: Jessica Kingsley

Swinton, J. (2000b) *Resurrecting the Person: Friendship and the Care of People with Severe Mental Health Problems*, Nashville: Abingdon Press

Swinton, J. (2000c) *From Bedlam to Shalom: Towards a Practical Theology of Human Nature, Interpersonal Relationships and Mental Health Care*, New York: Lang

Swinton, J. (2001) *Spirituality and Mental Health Care: Rediscovering a 'Forgotten Dimension'*, London: Jessica Kingsley

Swinton, J. (2002) *A Space to Listen: Meeting the Spiritual Needs of People with Learning Disabilities*, London: Mental Health Foundation

Swinton, J. (2006) *Raging with Compassion: Pastoral Responses to the Problem of Evil*, Grand Rapids: Eerdmans

Swinton, J., and Narayanasamy, A. (2002) Response to: 'A critical view of spirituality and spiritual assessment' by P. Draper and W. McSherry (*Journal of Advanced Nursing* 39(1), 1–2), *Journal of Advanced Nursing* 40(2), 158–60

Swinton, J., and Powrie, E. (2004) *Why Are We Here: Understanding the Spiritual Lives of People with Learning Disabilities*, London: Foundation for People With Learning Disabilities

Taylor, S. J. (1996) 'Disability studies and mental retardation', *Disability Studies Quarterly* 16(3), 4–6

Thomson, J. (1990) 'Hermeneutic inquiry', in L. Moody (ed.), *Advancing Nursing Through Research*, vol. 2, Newbury Park: Sage

Tillich, P. (1951) *Systematic Theology*, vol. 1, London: SCM Press

Tongprateep, T. (2000) 'The essential elements of spirituality among rural Thai elders', *Journal of Advanced Nursing* 31(1), 197–203

Tracy, D. (1975) *Blessed Rage of Order*, New York: Seabury

Trochim, W. M. (2000) *The Research Methods Knowledge Base*, 2nd edn, Cincinnati: Atomic Dog

Van der Van, J. A. (1993) *Practical Theology: An Empirical Approach*, Kampen: Kok Pharos

Van der Van, J. A. (1998), *Education for Reflective Ministry*, Louvain: Peeters

Van der Zalm, J. E. (2000) 'Hermeneutic–phenomenology: providing living knowledge for nursing practice', *Journal of Advanced Nursing* 31(1), 211–18

Van Deusen-Hunsinger, D. D. (1995) *Theology and Pastoral Counseling: A New Interdisciplinary Approach*, Grand Rapids: Eerdmans

Van Manen, M. (1990) *Researching Lived Experience: Human Science for an Action Sensitive Pedagogy*, New York: State University of New York Press

Ward, L., and Flynn, M. (1994) 'What matters most: disability, research and empowerment', in M. H. Rioux and M. Bach (eds), *Disability is not Measles: New Research Paradigms in Disability*, Ontario: L'Institut Roeher, pp. 29–48

Webber, Robert (2002) *The Younger Evangelicals: Facing the Challenges of the New World*, Grand Rapids: Baker

White, E., and Barnitt, R. (2000) 'Empowered or discouraged? A study of people with learning disabilities and their experience of engaging in intimate relationships', *British Journal of Occupational Therapy* 63(6), 270–6

Willig, C. (2001) *Qualitative Research in Psychology: A Practical Guide to Theory and Method*, Buckingham: Open University Press

Willows, D., and Swinton, J. (2000) *The Spiritual Dimension of Pastoral Care: Practical Theology in a Multidisciplinary Context*, London: Jessica Kingsley

Wimberly, A. S. (1994) *Soul Stories: African American Christian Education*, Nashville: Abingdon Press

Wong, J. G., Clare, I. C., Holland, A. J., Watson, P. C., and Gunn, M. (2000) 'The capacity of people with a 'mental disability' to make a health care decision', *Psychological Medicine* 30(2), 295–306

Wong, P. T. P. (1998) 'Spirituality, meaning, and successful aging', in P. T. P. Wong and P. Fry (eds), *The Human Quest for Meaning: A Handbook of Psychological Research and Clinical Application*, Mahwah, NJ: Lawrence Erlbaum Associates, pp. 359–94

Woodward, J. (1998) *A Study of the Role of the Acute Health Care Chaplain in England*, London: Open University Press

World Health Organisation (1986) 'Lifestyles and health', *Social Science and Medicine* 22(2), 117–24

Wright, L. S., Frost, C. J., and Wisecarver, S. J. (1993) 'Church attendance, meaningfulness of religion on, and depressive symptomatology among adolescents', *Journal of Youth and Adolescence* 22(5), 559–68

Wright, M. C. (1959) *The Sociological Imagination*, New York: Oxford University Press

Yaconelli, M. (2001) *Messy Spirituality: Christianity for the Rest of Us*, London: Hodder & Stoughton

Zarb, G. (1992) 'On the road to Damascus: first steps towards changing the relations of disability research production', *Disability, Handicap and Society* 7(2), 125–38

Index of Names and Subjects